Penny Marshall

PENNY MARSHALL

An Unauthorized Biography

LAWRENCE CROWN

RENAISSANCE BOOKS
Los Angeles

Library of Congress Catalog Card Number: 99-63527
ISBN: 1-58063-074-X

10 9 8 7 6 5 4 3 2 1

Design by Susan Shankin

Published by Renaissance Books
Distributed by St. Martin's Press
Manufactured in the United States of America
First Edition

"I was born with a frown."

PENNY MARSHALL, 1988

CONTENTS

Acknowledgments

My thanks to Frank Sanello, veteran show-business journalist and celebrity biographer; and Kurt Peer, author of *TV Tie-Ins: A Bibliography of American TV Tie-In Paperbacks*.

My thanks also to Ned Comstock, efficient and helpful library assistant at the University of Southern California's Cinema-TV Library, and to Robert Hoey, dedicated compiler of a comprehensive *Laverne & Shirley* episode guide.

And a special thanks to the many journalists and critics who have interviewed and reviewed Penny Marshall over the years. My method has been to analyze and deconstruct their work.

Without you, this book would not exist.

INTRODUCTION

Family. community. Did Penny Marshall, Hollywood A-list feature-film director, crack through the glass veiling with art and craftsmanship, or was it just simple networking and traditional film- and TV-industry nepotism as usual, combined with a crowd-pleasing proclivity for sentimentality and shtick?

You might think that TV series like *Happy Days* (1974–84) and *Laverne & Shirley* (1976–83), and movies like *Big* (1988), *Renaissance Man* (1994), and *The Preacher's Wife* (1996) offer only simple pleasures and innocent fun and that they wouldn't raise serious issues about the prerequisites for success and the nature of failure, about the company-town structure of Hollywood and the mentality of the media, or about how the business of show business gets done.

But they do.

Who are you? I wonder: A nostalgic Boomer who grew up with the TV theme song "We'll do it our way . . ." and *schlemiel, shlemazel?* A Gen-X student of irony, raised on the "camp classics" of 1970s TV? Perhaps a rising Generation Next woman of the media, avid for role models in the Hollywood entertainment business still dominated by the Old Boys, who hopes Penny is the Ida Lupino of her generation?

Whether you're a scholar of women's studies or a fan of TV talk show host Rosie O'Donnell, whether you loved *Laverne & Shirley* as a child or wonder about the sensibility of the woman who made *Big* (1988), *Awakenings* (1990), *A League of Their Own* (1992), and other big-screen movies, or even if the dese 'n' dose Bronx accent just makes you smile, you're the reason I wrote this book.

Generally, film critics have reflexively dismissed many of the feature films Penny's directed as middlebrow and middle-of-the-road at best. But to many others, Penny Marshall—who is pro-woman, pro-choice, pro-gay-and-lesbian and other minority rights, and a social and Democratic Party activist—is a heroic figure of the first rank, working the System from within. A mere 9 percent of Hollywood's working directors today are women (up from only 5 percent in 1988).

Penny Marshall is a unique figure, on an almost unprecedented journey, and how she has come so far on her path raises important questions. Perhaps examining her journey from Garry's little sister, to the most popular TV comic since Lucille Ball, to the first woman to direct a hundred-million-dollar-grossing film would be instructive—as instructive for me as for you.

Nonetheless, I approached this project with some qualms, because of my doubts about the pop biographer's art. For one thing, it's too reductive, particularly when it comes to writing about a living, feeling, human being. For another, I'm not comfortable applying the censorious, self-righteous standards of the current marketplace, even to celebrities, who after all, many would argue, deserve it because they seek out the spotlight. But could you live up to the tisk-tisk standards of the tabloids? Because I couldn't, and I doubt that the *tabloidistas* themselves could, I try not to be hypocritical in my public judgments.

But as I've seen writing about celebrities practiced, the problem is not treachery and anonymous tattletale telling so much as it is co-optation, even in these post-Princess Di times. More and more, what you read and see about a celebrity is what that celebrity's spin doctors want you to know.

Is there a fair way to tell a celebrity's story—from a vantage point higher than the gutter, but also somewhat more distanced than the view afforded from inside the celebrity's (or the celebrity publicist's) pocket? I'm convinced there is; that is, by returning to basics—to traditional journalistic principles. To do this means avoiding those uninformed sources whose shadowy hissings are at the very least self-serving, even when they're not outright wrong. This means including only those unidentified voices who meet the traditional standard (that is, confirmation by two independently verifiable sources), which means depending primarily on those forthright persons who will speak publicly and for attribution.

Because Hollywood is a company town, with relatively few outlets and opportunities to practice the movie- and TV-making crafts, going on the record with negative comments means putting a livelihood at risk. Who would do it, particularly when the tabloids stand ready to pay for the same tidbits, allowing their sources to remain in the shadows?

When it comes to writing about a public figure, whether a celebrity or a politician, adhering to traditional journalistic standards primarily means depending on the plentiful nuggets to be found in a diligent search of the public record. After all, a person like Penny Marshall, who's been in the spotlight now for more than a quarter of a century, has accumulated a vast trail of comments and oft-told stories. And she's been observed in print by a wide variety of professionals. Over the years, a dialogue, and a dialectic, has developed.

(In Hollywood, managing publicity in various, more or less unseemly ways is a high, and highly paid, art. In recent years, publicists have begun to routinely require approval of the writer assigned to interview an A-list star or quote approval over the finished article. Sadly, to get the interview in a savagely competitive marketplace, editors often comply. Nonetheless, what's true on the Internet is true even in today's corporate Hollywood: in some sense information wants to be free.)

Of this vast public record we can ask informed questions and tease out conclusions: Is the celebrity's public persona consistent over time? Or is the celebrity locked into that persona, in the same way that 1970s blondes such as Farrah Fawcett and Suzanne Somers are condemned to an identity defined by their hair?

In recent years, critics, whose thumbs-up or four-stars are tailor-made for print and television advertisements, have become ever more crucial to studio marketing plans. With fifty million dollars and more partly riding on this positive critical reaction, how does the celebrity react to negative criticism and independent commentary, and particularly to repeatedly criticized themes? And what happens when the private life is out of sync with the public persona? Is the celebrity forthright or disingenuous about personal setbacks and failings?

So here you will find the TV shows, the films, the life, and an interpretation of both. And the dish—the on-set arguments, the accusations of nepotism, the traumatic divorce, the drug use? It's all here, too. In proper perspective, I hope.

Some distances can't be measured in miles. Gather round the Motorola and remember back to the days before there was a Nick at Nite or a TV Land; before E! was online and every home throughout the land could receive one hundred channels of cable TV. Remember back even farther, back before this new golden media age of ours, when the three great national networks vied for dominance over all of television in the United States.

Once upon a time, just after the Second World War, when television was no more than a laboratory curiosity, near the Grand Concourse in the fabled Bronx, in an unfashionable section of the New York melting pot, to a struggling show-business family a little girl was born.

Consider the journey of Carole Penny Marscharelli, born in the Bronx, New York, on October 15, 1942. It's not just a continent, for example, that stands between a lower-middle-class girlhood in the Bronx and Hollywood celebrity that only comes from being atop the Nielsen ratings and starring in America's number-one TV show. Consider the even greater psychic distance in becoming a ditzy television sitcom queen with the whole country laughing at your silly hijinks, your deadpan morose manner, and your funny accent, while the critics vacillate between sneering at the mindless fun and grudgingly acknowledging you as, just maybe, the new Queen of Comedy—the new Lucille Ball. Then you become the first woman to direct a hundred-million-dollar-grossing Hollywood movie, guiding world-famous actors like Robert De Niro and Tom Hanks as they hit their marks on the sound stage.

Can this be the same Penny Marshall who once seemed perfectly type-cast as Mrs. Rob Reiner—the real-life, stay-at-home wife of Meathead, his character on *All in the Family* (1971–78)? The same woman who for years after said repeatedly, and wistfully, that her only real goal ever had been to hang out with funny, talented people—the kind her older brother and her second husband just naturally gathered around themselves? The basic biographical facts are simple enough:

Grew up in New York, in the Old Neighborhood centered around broad Mosholu Parkway, a boulevard bordered by maple trees and lined with multistory apartment houses, the second-grandest street in the entire borough of the Bronx at this time.

Headed west after high school to major in psychology at the University of New Mexico. Dropped out in her junior year to marry a fellow student.

Daughter Tracy born in 1964. Divorced in 1966. Worked as a secretary. Taught dance. Choreographed for the local musical theater group. Acted in local musical theater.

Moved to Los Angeles in 1967 where big brother Garry was already established as a TV comedy writer, writing jokes and funny bits for Rat Pack comic Joey Bishop, who briefly had his own late-night television talk show, as well as for TV greats Lucille Ball and Danny Thomas.

Temped at office jobs, took acting classes, struggled.

Got bit parts and the occasional commercial (including one for shampoo with Farrah Fawcett, who was cast as the Girl with the Beautiful Hair, while Penny was the Girl with the Stringy Hair).

Then big brother Garry, having become a TV producer, cast her in *The Odd Couple* (1972–75), in which she played Jack Klugman's secretary Myrna Turner.

Married Rob Reiner in 1971. In 1974, won a prominent role in the short-lived *Paul Sand in Friends and Lovers* TV series (1974–75), in which she costarred with Jack Gilford and Steve Landesberg.

And then big brother cast her again—in *Happy Days,* on which she reluctantly guest-starred as "Laverne DeFazio" in 1976.

A mere three months later she was in her own ABC-TV network show, touted almost from the beginning as the new Lucy, and began living the Hollywood dream. In her case, this eventually included divorce, the cancellation of her series after the better part of a decade on top, and a post-divorce drug use period in the 1980s during which she hung out and partied with the likes of Jack Nicholson, John Belushi, and the rest of the original *Saturday Night Live* crowd.

But did Carole Penny Marshall make it oncamera in the first place just because she was Garry's little sister? Without a doubt. However, it is hard to believe that family connections alone could have kept her in the spotlight all these years.

As she herself said in 1988, in the afterglow of the opening weekend for *Big,* her first box-office hit, "I'm sure people thought I got parts because my brother was being nice, and at first I probably thought the same thing. . . . 'But my brother finally told me—'I'm not giving you a job 'cause I'm nice, I'm not *that* nice.'"

And a few years later, Garry, who as a child had been allergic to "more than 128 foods," addressed the issue himself in a comical first-person reminiscence in *McCalls* magazine: "During my years in television, critics said I was making nepotism an art form. But I thought I was simply protecting myself: My sisters [Penny and Ronny] knew all my allergies and could tell me what foods to stay away from at the studio commissary."

And why was it "Laverne," of all people—and not, say, Barbra Streisand who directed *Yentl* (1983), Jodie Foster who directed *Little Man Tate* (1991), or Diane Keaton who directed *Unstrung Heroes* (1995), or Amy Heckerling who directed *Clueless* (1995)—who became the first woman, as well as the first actress, to direct a hundred-million-dollar-grossing movie?

Hollywood has always been a town where nepotism and the Old Boys' Network have played a prominent part.

To this day, you can find the Old Boys breakfasting at the Four Seasons, lunching at Le Dôme and taking tea (or sipping cocktails) at the Polo Lounge in Beverly Hills. There they are, at the same tables, day after day, deal-making, back-slapping, gossiping about each other between cell phone calls, proving the old adage that Hollywood is simply high school with money.

(And Hollywood—the Hollywood of insiders—is as small as a high school, too. That's why *Variety* and *The Hollywood Reporter,* the daily show-business trade papers, are so important despite their relatively small circulations. Even combined, they're read by at most the equivalent of several urban high schools full of people per day—their joint readership totals only several thousand people, but it's the right few thousand people—making them Hollywood High's school papers.)

But even more specifically than the one over-arching Old Boys' Network of insiders, Hollywood is a networking town, a small enclave of inter-related and overlapping networks, a town of mafias, where everyone actually inside the Biz does know everyone else.

There's the Oklahoma Mafia, the Northwestern (i.e., Chicago) Mafia, the Carnegie Tech (i.e., Pittsburgh) Mafia, the Ivy League Sitcom-Writers Mafia (Harvard itself has staffed easily half of prime time TV's sitcoms), even the Old Girls Network (but just in the past decade or so). And of course, there are those colorful, down-to-earth, savvy guys 'n' gals from the Old Neighborhood back east; that is, the Bronx and Brooklyn Mafia. This is the network of actors, producers, writers, and directors who share in common an outer borough accent, an affectionate nostalgia for good deli food and Nathan's hot dogs, row houses and extended families, kids playing stickball, and neighbors gossiping together on the stoop.

Networks and mafias are not as sinister as they sound. On the Internet, for example, what are user groups if not cyber-mafias of like-minded individuals, electronically obsessing together over topics like gun control, the love lives of specific movie stars, or ethnic recipes? Men and women everywhere gravitate toward their like, acting out of an old tribal instinct—the basis for fraternities and sororities, for clubs and affinity groups of all types. Why should the Dream Factory be any different?

One of the most successful Hollywood networks, ironically enough (considering that their shows often were derided by the critics), is the gang of TV writer/producers and actors from the late 1960s, the 1970s, and the early 1980s. Many of these talented individuals went on to huge success in feature films, including the writer/producer team of Lowell Ganz and Babaloo Mandel, who each got their start on the various Garry Marshall TV shows, and actor/directors such as Ron Howard, Henry Winkler, Rob Reiner, Tom Hanks, Danny DeVito, and, of course, Penny.

Just how did that happen? Garry Marshall, a natural-born *paterfamilias* gave many of his sitcom actors their first opportunity to direct, for one thing.

And for another, the one-time TV actors were in the right place at the right time—a decade before their first successes, a chasm of distrust and disdain still separated Hollywood's movie and TV worlds. Old-line movie executives feared the new small-screen medium and despised its pop-culture celebrities. Then, as the post-war baby-boom generation grew old enough to buy movie tickets, TV stars like Clint Eastwood and Steve McQueen broke through to stardom in feature films, and TV executives began to take over the major film studios. Seemingly overnight, the TV-trained sensibilities of sit-com actors turned directors became eagerly sought after.

And, lastly, these people wield the power because they've stuck together—working for each other, helping each other, advising and sticking up for each other. More than the story of one family then, this is a story of family—not simply the one you're born into, but the one that you create.

Chapter One

THE BRONX AND BEYOND

LIKE MANY OTHER little girls born in the 1940s in an Italian-Jewish neighborhood of an outer borough of New York City, whose star-struck parents made their living working in the arts, Carole Penny Marscharelli was named after a movie star—in her case, Carole Lombard. Lombard was a radiant blonde and a gifted comedienne who blazed across the 1930s and early 1940s silver screen in almost seventy films, including such classics as *Twentieth Century* (1934), *My Man Godfrey* (1936), and *Mr. & Mrs. Smith* (1941).

With her sizzle and sass, and her endearing vulnerability, Carole Lombard in many ways anticipated Marilyn Monroe by two decades. She was twice married to actors, first to William Powell and then to Clark Gable, and died young in a plane crash during a World War II war bond drive.

Her namesake was born into show business, but the show business little Carole Marscharelli's parents knew and worked in was as different from the show business of Hollywood as the Bronx is from Beverly Hills.

Oftentimes, the elite of Hollywood live behind protective barriers—not just the high walls and security cameras surrounding their estates in Brentwood, Bel

Air, or Beverly Hills, but behind the walls their managers, agents, and publicity advisors construct to protect them from unwanted, or unauthorized, attention.

In this era of the celebrity stalker and the paparazzo with the telephoto lens, such protections are, for the most part, quite understandable. Nonetheless, celebrities who expect long careers in the Dream Factory town of Hollywood do have workaday tasks to attend, and those include doing publicity each time a project is released—whether it's a movie, a TV show, a book, or even a multimillion-dollar commercial campaign. In the entertainment trade, where marketing and publicity expenses for a typical Hollywood theatrical release reach into the tens of millions of dollars, it's called getting free media, and those who balk at it may find their careers in jeopardy.

Whether it was for *Laverne & Shirley* or *Big* or *Renaissance Man* or *The Preacher's Wife,* Penny Marshall has done her publicity bit. She has always demonstrated a shrewd understanding of how the business operates. And nothing if not a trouper, she's submitted to interviewers' questions again and again over the years (a tedious chore that no doubt adds to the weariness that her interviewers so often notice), so that the story of Carole Penny's early years has by now become an oft-told tale.

Penny's father was making industrial films when she was born on October 15, 1942. Tony Marshall, who lived into his nineties, also worked as an advertising art director and eventually held various producer and consultant positions on his son and daughter's TV shows.

Penny's ambitious mother, Marjorie Ward Marshall, was a popular dance teacher who taught scores of neighborhood children in a studio set up in the basement of their Bronx apartment house. This was where Penny and her brother Garry, nine years her senior, who was sickly and asthmatic as a child, were first introduced to the rhythms and the rigors of show business.

"I hated it," Penny recalled years later during the first explosion of her TV success, remembering those early teen years when she was part of her mother's sixteen-member dance group, the Marshallettes, "but she used to threaten me. My mom used to say that if I didn't want to dance, I'd have to spend all day Saturday cleaning up the house or doing the grocery shopping."

Her mother was dedicated to the discipline of the dance and she thought the youngest of her three children should be too. However, years after Penny first moved out of her parents' house, and even long after she was a grownup, Marjorie's youngest child still resented it.

"It was like, 'So-and-so could do it, why can't you be more like so-and-so?'" Penny recalled more than three decades later: "I think when the thumb came out of my mouth, the cigarette went in.

"My mother did drag us around to tap dance for all the soldiers. Fort Dix, Fort Hamilton . . . anywhere. Insane asylums. Every telethon, we were there," she said in another interview that took place decades after the traumatic fact.

Decades later her brother also still remembered the childhood sibling rivalry for his busy parents' attentions: "I . . . was sick a lot, so I would throw up. Ronny would pucker up her chubby cheeks and hold her breath. Penny would attempt dangerous stunts such as walking along the window ledge of our building. My mother referred to Penny as 'the world's worst child.'"

"I had a very high I.Q.," Penny reminisced about her childhood, "but my mother had to get me out of honors classes, because I didn't like them. I didn't want to be with the achievers. I was obsessed with being regular."

Being regular, being just one of the kids, is a theme that Penny has returned to again and again throughout her life. The Old Neighborhood of her youth was an urban, immigrant melting pot that in the 1940s and 1950s was dubbed the "cradle of stars" because of the many show-business and artistic luminaries raised there. Being regular meant being ambitious and pursuing excellence.

In the summers, like many other urban children, she was sent away to the country to summer camp. Although she was Italian-Catholic, she was from an

Italian-Jewish neigborhood so little Carole Penny always went to a Jewish camp in the Catskills. "My mother wanted me to meet and marry a Jewish fellow," she said, "because she was convinced that Jewish men make the best husbands."

"I was a tomboy myself," Marshall told entertainment journalist Stephen Farber, during a joint interview in 1992 with her daughter, Tracy Reiner, while both were promoting *A League of Their Own,* the women's baseball movie directed by Marshall in which Reiner had a featured part. (Tracy had been in *Big,* too, but most of her small part ended up on the cutting-room floor.) "My mother would always say, 'Let the boys win. They don't like it if you are better than they are,'" Penny recalled.

Of her father Tony, who became a producer on her big brother's most successful shows, Penny said years later, after her mother had died and her father had reached the age of ninety: "He had the personality of a lamppost."

Throughout the years of publicly reciting their own legends, while doing publicity for their various TV and film projects, both Penny and Garry Marshall have painted a romanticized, but far from idealized, portrait of the Old Neighborhood. They describe it as a place where the boys and girls of Walton High School in the Bronx either were part of popular-kid cliques, like the Magnets, a girl gang, or—like too-smart, tomboy Penny—they were shunned.

"I was the 'bad seed' or the 'world's worst,'" Penny said of herself, the bitterness still apparent decades later. Her brother, also recalling that far-away, long-ago time, called her "too bright for the territory. . . . There was nothing much for her to do."

Like many sensitive teens who come from competitive families, Penny always seemed eager to strike out on her own and begin a new life. "My father sent me west," she said during the heady early years of her *Laverne & Shirley* fame in the late 1970s. "He says it was because I loved horses, but I think he had this dream that I'd lose my accent."

At the University of New Mexico, she met and married Michael Henry, a college athlete who was part Hopi Indian. When their only child, Tracy, was born, Penny, a twenty-one-year-old mother, dropped out and took a secretarial job to support the family while her husband stayed in school. After two years of this kind of life and the drudgery it entailed, the marriage ended in divorce in 1965.

"It was Peyton Place time," Penny said later of the period when she was a young divorced woman alone in New Mexico with a small child, surviving by doing secretarial work, local theater, and choreography. "I practically had a scarlet 'A' on my forehead in Albuquerque as a divorced mother . . .

"Most of the mothers . . . wouldn't let their sons date me because I was a divorced woman with a kid. I didn't know what to do. I had no future in New Mexico, and if I went back to New York, my family would have treated me like a child."

Penny, like many young women of the era, opted for a new start. When living in New Mexico finally became intolerable in 1967, she called for help from her brother in Hollywood, where the locals were renowned for a tolerance that was all-embracing, and the local morals were, well . . . looser.

"The women in Hollywood were all neurotic," she said. "They had all been married for a minute somewhere. I didn't feel like an outcast."

For a young mother whose big brother had headed west himself at the tender age of twenty-four and achieved a measure of show-business success as a comedy writer on *The Joey Bishop Show* (1967–69), what could be more natural than to move to Los Angeles with her baby daughter and try her hand at acting?

When she appeared in Los Angeles, baby daughter in tow, Penny was just a "name on a birthday card," said Garry Marshall. He'd been away, first in college and then in the Army, when she was growing up. Nonetheless, he did the right thing by his little sister—just as he did for his other sister, Ronny, who ended up in various production positions on his shows, when she came to town after her divorce. "I asked [Penny] what she had in mind, and she said, 'I don't know; I'm not good at anything.' One day, though, she told me that she'd done the part of Ado Annie in a New Mexico production of *Oklahoma* and her eyes almost lit up. She's not a very enthusiastic person, so you have to watch for little signs. . . . Anyway, I got Sheldon Leonard to use her in a tiny dramatic part [Leonard was an actor, probably best known as Harry the Horse in the movie *Guys and Dolls* (1955), turned successful television producer whose series included *The Danny Thomas Show* (1953-71) and *The Dick Van Dyke Show* (1961-66)].

"She was awful, and she was ready to retire there and then. But I decided to try her as Jack Klugman's secretary in an *Odd Couple* [1970-75] segment."

"When I came out to Hollywood . . . he was the one who took me under his wing," Penny said, in one variation of a litany of thanksgiving to her brother she would repeat throughout her career. "Without him, I wouldn't have a life or a career." Eventually, when he gave her work on his TV series, he insisted, "I wouldn't give you a part if I didn't think you could do it. I'm not risking my career for you." He said, "You get a temp job, acting classes, and unemployment. That's how it works."

"I've been accused of running my shows like a camp, but that's what I did," said Garry Marshall, the man who gave out buttons to his cast and crew that read *Life Is More Important Than Show Business*. "We set a tone. . . . They understood that family was important."

There's no way to tell Penny Marshall's story without telling her big brother's as well. Garry Marshall was a sickly child, suffering through allergies and repeated bouts of pneumonia and asthma, but with an irrepressible *joie de vivre* nonetheless. He played the drums, studied journalism, and his quick-witted sense of humor made everybody laugh. You can see the young-adult Garry playing the drums in the background of Monty "Let's Make A Deal" Hall's number at the end of the "A Different Drummer" episode of TV's

The Odd Couple, as well as, a few years later, in the big calypso dance number that concludes the "Suds to Stardom" installment of *Laverne & Shirley*.

As a writer, he went from bylines to punchlines, supplying jokes to newspaper columnists and stand-up comedians. Soon he was writing jokes for Jack Paar's New York-based *Tonight Show* and for Rat Pack comic Joey Bishop. (Phil Foster, who had been in TV since its infancy and who would later play "Papa Frank DeFazio" on *Laverne & Shirley*, was the one who recommended Garry as a joke writer when Bishop got his own TV show on the West Coast.)

After Bishop brought Garry out to Hollywood to write for his new, but short-lived, nighttime talk/variety program (on which Bishop's sidekick was Regis Philbin), Marshall also wrote for such small-screen icons as Lucille Ball, Danny Thomas, Dick Van Dyke . . . and Carl Reiner, whose son would one day marry Garry's little sister.

Within a single decade, by the end of the 1970s, Garry Marshall went from merely a hired jokemeister to one of TV's most prolific producers. At the height of his television-sitcom productivity, he turned an incredible, almost impossible, TV hat trick, placing four weekly series in the Nielsen ratings' top five most-watched series. They were *Laverne & Shirley, Happy Days,* and *Mork & Mindy* (1978–82), in the first three spots, with *Angie* (1979–80), another Marshall creation, at number five.

Today, Garry is a film director whose feature credits include *The Flamingo Kid* (1984) and *Pretty Woman* (1990), a romantic comedy starring Richard Gere and Julia Roberts that grossed more than $178 million at the domestic box office.

Garry's tenth film, in production in early 1999, was *Runaway Bride*, a romantic comedy about a woman who has left a string of would-be bridegrooms at the altar and the reporter assigned to write about her. The film reunited Gere and Roberts for the first time since *Pretty Woman*. Meanwhile, never one to be professionally idle, Garry had a recurring role from 1994–98 on the sitcom *Murphy Brown*, playing Candice Bergen's slick, manipulative boss.

After years of ratings success combined with the indifference of critics, Garry's string of TV hits has won him a measure of respect—not only for the craftsmanship of the teleplays and the ensemble casts, but for the wholesome family values, once considered hopelessly old-fashioned and middlebrow, he invariably espoused. Inside Hollywood, he's beloved—a father figure whose brood includes not only his blood relations, Penny and her six-years-older sister Ronny Hallin, but such actor/directors (and cultural icons) as Henry Winkler and Tom Hanks, to whom he gave their starts.

In Los Angeles in the late 1960s and early 1970s, Penny was a secretary by day and an acting student by night, and soon was getting commercials and turning up in bit parts on Marlo Thomas's *That Girl* and other situation comedies, mostly those for which her brother wrote.

One night in the late 1960s she went with friends to Barney's Beanery, a venerable West Hollywood bar/restaurant, that was then, as it still is now, a hangout for young actors and others in show business to get out for a few drinks and a game or two of eight-ball. It was a chance to maybe do a little flirting, a little bragging and, of course, to commiserate about the indignities of auditioning and struggling to get a foot inside the door of the business. There she met a cerebral and ambitious young actor named Rob Reiner.

Back in the late 1960s, Rob was a young man with whom Penny had a lot in common: they both had a famous close relative (in his case, a dad, in show business). They both were insecure and ambitious, and each was funny and tended toward depression. As performers they were character actors; no one would mistake them for leading players. And, just as if it had been fate, they'd both come from the same part of the Bronx.

After dating a few months, they moved in together. In 1970, young Reiner signed on to play the character of Michael Stivik in a new CBS-TV network sitcom called *All in the Family* that, upon its premiere in January 1971, shot to the top ranks of the ratings, where it could be found every week until a certain series about two Milwaukee brewery girls debuted a few years later.

By April 10, 1971, when Penny married Rob Reiner in the back yard of his parents' house in Beverly Hills during his hiatus from shooting *All in the Family,* Penny herself had progressed from guesting on sitcoms to a recurring role as Myrna Turner, Oscar Madison's secretary on *The Odd Couple,* Garry's first hit TV series.

Though her critical notices as nasal-twanged, well-meaning, hang-dog Myrna were almost uniformly positive, after a few seasons Penny opted for the role of traditional wife. She spent her days nurturing—and feeding—the show-business gang of writers and comedians, rising actors and Beverly Hills High School graduates—who hung out at the couple's relatively modest two-bedroom North Hollywood house, which they shared with Penny's daughter Tracy, who took her new stepfather's last name.

"I'd . . . feed everybody," Marshall recalled two decades later. She has said that it was then, while spending time nurturing her husband's friends, by and large the sort of creative, driven people who rise to the top in professional show business, that she first developed her work ethic from their example. These were people like the writer/producer James L. Brooks (who produced *The Simpsons* for TV and on film directed *Terms of Endearment* [1983], among others), actors Richard Dreyfuss, Albert Brooks, Ted Bessell, and others.

That work ethic was put to a severe test in the mid-1970s, when, after a guest stint as one of two working-class Milwaukee girls on her brother's hit ABC sitcom, *Happy Days,* she suddenly found herself headlining a television show of her own.

Marshall's rise from decorative supporting player to incandescent TV star was the quintessential, headlong, overnight ascent, and that fame exacted a high price on her. Even in the first two seasons (1976, 1976–77) of *Laverne & Shirley*, the gossipy whispers, which sometimes broke into print, described a troubled marriage. As a tabloid-like article of the mid-1970s had it: "She has been seen with other guys or gone off with others at parties. Only recently she shocked a lot of people at a TV taping session. Rob was not there and according to those who saw Penny, she cuddled up to Chris De Rose of *The San Pedro Beach Bums.* She made herself comfy on Chris's lap— and as fans watched in amazement the two hugged, squeezed each other, and shared kisses on the cheek."

The San Pedro Beach Bums was a short-lived sitcom in the fall of 1977, and Chris De Rose, a.k.a. "Chris DeRose"—a young actor from the Old Neighborhood—who was born in Brooklyn and raised in a New Jersey orphanage, was one of its stars. He also guest-starred in such series as *Baretta, Kojak, The Rockford Files,* and *CHiPs,* and in the 1980s was a regular on the soap opera *General Hospital.* Eventually, he became a well-known animal activist, even going to jail once for his anti-vivisectionist beliefs.

By 1983, after nearly eight years as Laverne in the hit weekly primetime sitcom (including a season when *Laverne & Shirley* was the number-one show on American TV), her marriage to Rob Reiner had ended and her mother was succumbing to Alzheimer's disease. No doubt partly in response to the drugs-and-clubs-are-hip ethos of those times, and partly to relieve the stress in her personal life, Penny by then was out partying with Carrie Fisher, Paul Simon, Robin Williams, and the rest of the fast-lane *Saturday Night Live* performers and writers of the time, who were reportedly deep into cocaine and other drugs. (John Belushi, a member of that crowd, died of a drug overdose in 1982.) She also was dating singer/songwriter Art Garfunkel, who guest-starred on one episode of *Laverne & Shirley,* and actor David Dukes.

"In 1980, Carrie and I took acid for the first time," she admitted years later. "I didn't like it."

Her pal of the time was Carrie Fisher, probably best known as Princess Leia in the *Star Wars* trilogy. Fisher guest-starred on one of the final episodes of *Laverne & Shirley* in 1983 and shares with Penny the same October 15 birthday. (Other luminaries who share their natal day: the poet Virgil, the philosopher Friedrich Nietzsche, the boxer John L. Sullivan, the historian Arthur Schlesinger, the auto executive Lee Iacocca, and the writers P. G. Wodehouse and Mario Puzo.) Penny and Carrie's annual party, given every year since the mid-1970s, has become a Hollywood fixture.

"I was wild," Penny said, speaking about her lifestyle during that period. "I wasn't doing all of the drugs Belushi did—I wasn't into needles. But yes, I smoked pot. Near the end he went his own way. I still saw him. But I didn't approve of what he was doing."

What was it like around Penny in those first years of the 1980s, with her marriage over, her mother dying, and the constant turmoil on the set of *Laverne & Shirley* boiling over, which lead to the final break with costar Cindy Williams?

Penny, as she still does to this day, built a nest for herself, a refuge in her Hollywood Hills house. She launched an extensive refurbishing and redesign campaign. One of the workers, who encountered Penny maybe fifteen or twenty times during the approximately six months he spent working there on a restoration of her eleven-thousand-foot-house, remembers there were two rules:

One, "never start working before noon, the assumption being that she was out late every night, partying with Carrie Fisher and Jack Nicholson. . . . The rumor was she was heavily into cocaine back then." (Penny herself never confirmed that particular rumor publicly, as she did the stories about smoking pot and taking LSD.)

When one of the workers accidentally violated Rule One, and came unannounced into her bedroom early in the morning hours, "We could hear the shrieking clear on the other side of the house," the source recalled.

Rule Two was "never mention the name of her ex-husband anywhere in the house."

Daughter Tracy lived with her back then, and their refrigerator was stocked with the best take-out food to be found anywhere in Los Angeles, the source remembers, adding that Penny looked "exactly like she did on TV—not pretty, toothy, but not homely" either.

"There was a sense of melancholia about her," presumably because, in the wake of her divorce, "she was lonely."

She was "sweet," according to this recollection, "paid her bills on time" and was "just as charming as she was on *Laverne & Shirley*."

By all accounts, it was that work ethic, learned as a young girl in the Bronx, as practiced around the Reiner house when she and Rob were married, then honed on the weekly series set that pulled her through, even as others in that toot-Hollywood milieu were overdosing or detoxing at prestige substance abuse clinics. Perhaps in addition to her show-business career, Penny owes her very life to her brother Garry, who not only had cast her as TV's Laverne, but gave her the tools to carry on even after the inevitable cancellation of the long-lasting series.

The human impulse to get high, to relieve the stress of overwork—to say nothing of the pressure of the TV spotlight—is an understandable one. However, does that mean condoning illegal and dangerous substances like cocaine?

No, but it does require us, at least, to consider the white-hot times: In the 1970s, for example, *Playboy* magazine was decrying the hysteria about the "alleged" dangers of coke. And in the early 1980s, at least in certain Hollywood celebrity circles, the white powder was offered openly, even presented at times like just another hors d'oeuvre, on elegant silver platters, to guests at elegant dinner parties.

High Concept: Don Simpson and the Hollywood Culture of Excess, the recent biography of the producer, who, with his partner Jerry Bruckheimer, was responsible for such "high-concept" pictures as *Flashdance* (1983), *Beverly Hills*

Cop (1984), and *Top Gun* (1986), paints a vivid portrait of the drug culture of the period. Simpson, who died in 1996 of an overdose, was for many years *the* symbol of show-business excess. His exploits and appetites were well known, but tolerated, inside the business community.

His publicist remembers a 1983 birthday dinner for film director Paul Schrader, thrown by Simpson at a Beverly Hills restaurant, at which Penny was present: "Drugs were in evidence, if only by the conspicuous periodic absence of the diners: Schrader and Simpson would suddenly dash off to the men's room together," according to the *High Concept* account.

Chapter Two

ON TV

PENNY MARSHALL'S FIRST brush with fame came long before she ever set foot in Hollywood.

Perhaps the first famous person she ever met eventually became her father-in-law. When Penny was growing up, in one of those truth-is-stranger-than-fiction coincidences, her Bronx neighbor was Carl Reiner (b. 1922), who lived in the more elegant precincts along the Grand Concourse. Even then Reiner was a local celebrity and well known to viewers of the new medium of television as a writer/performer on Sid Caesar's groundbreaking series *Your Show of Shows* (1950–54). Once, when she was still a shy child, Penny ran into him and asked him for his autograph.

By then, however, Penny had already been bitten by the acting bug. The Marshallettes, her mother's dance troupe, were on TV's *Ted Mack's Original Amateur Hour* when Penny was a young hoofer and they won first prize. When she was fourteen in 1956, she tap danced with a group on *The Jackie Gleason Show* on CBS-TV.

In her post-divorce, single-mother phase in 1960s New Mexico, she did a two-season stint in a stage production of *Oklahoma!* as Ado Annie Carnes, the part played by Gloria Grahame in the 1955 Fred Zinneman-directed movie. Then, in Hollywood, Penny made her network acting debut during the 1967–68 season of *The Danny Thomas Hour*, for which her brother wrote, playing a receptionist in an episode called "My Friend Tony." The installment starred Jack Klugman, with whom she would later costar (playing a secretary), in *The Odd Couple*.

On the big screen she made the tiniest of appearances—often in non-speaking parts—in such drive-in fare as *The Savage Seven* (1968), in which she played "Tina," a girl in a motorcycle gang.

She also turned up in her brother's failed pilots and short-lived unsuccessful series. In 1972, for example, Penny was billed simply as the Bank Teller in *Evil Roy Slade*, a two-hour TV movie created from two different versions of the failed pilot for a Western comedy, written and produced by Garry Marshall and Jerry Belson, and directed by Jerry Paris. The telefilm is notable for its cast, however, a veritable *Who's Who* of television comedians from the period, including Mickey Rooney, Milton Berle, and Dom DeLuise, as well as Henry Gibson (*Laugh-In's* dirty old man), Edie Adams (Ernie Kovacs' blonde-bombshell comedienne wife), Pat Morita (who later would play a recurring role on *Happy Days*), John Ritter (of *Three's Company*), Dick Shawn (probably best known for his "Springtime for Hitler" turn in the 1967 movie *The Producers*), and John Astin (of TV's *The Addams Family*) in the title role.

A year before her fateful guest-starring appearance on *Happy Days*, Penny was in *Wives*, a proposed half-hour CBS-TV sitcom written and created by her brother, who also produced it with their father. In it she played Connie, one of the five wives who, if the show had been picked up by ABC, would have gathered each week to play cards and solve their problems with their (always unseen) husbands. Pat Morita also turned up in this pilot, playing the Waiter. Of the actresses who played the wives (in addition to Penny, they were: Phyllis Elizabeth Davis, Janie Sell, Candice Azzara, and Jacque Lynn Colton), only Penny went on to achieve the kind of iconic fame that makes an actor's face, voice, and mannerisms synonymous with a role and, sometimes, even with an era.

The Odd Couple

Before she was hired by her brother to play Myrna Turner, Oscar Madison's long-suffering secretary, on the TV version of Neil Simon's *The Odd Couple,* Penny Marshall auditioned for—and nearly got—the part of Archie Bunker's daughter on *All in the Family.*

Though she became one of the finalists during the auditioning process, in the end Norman Lear and the show's other producers decided she wasn't right—too old and not cutie-pie enough—to play the role of Meathead's wife. Even though she was already playing the part in real life, the plum assignment went to Sally Struthers.

According to her character's official bio, Myrna Turner is "Oscar Madison's nasal-voiced secretary at the New York paper for which he writes a sports column. Although Oscar would be completely lost in a mess of papers and unwanted leftovers without her able assistance, he rarely shows her much appreciation. But Myrna doesn't seem to mind. Shy by nature, she assumes it is her lot in life to be taken advantage of by more vociferous people.

"Myrna is known for her whiny Bronx accent and her monotone laugh, which is reminiscent of Felix Unger's (Tony Randall) sinus-clearing honking. She deeply cares for her boss and tries to get him to take better care of himself. . . . She finds a more sympathetic admirer in Oscar's roommate Felix, who encourages her to break out of her shell so that she could truly shine as the beautiful person she is deep down inside."

For shy, insecure, Bronx-born, nasal-voiced Penny, who cared deeply but quietly as well, Myrna was hardly a stretch. Writer/producer Garry Marshall was in the ideal position to create a character for his little sister so right that it seemed as if she'd been born for the part. She shined in it, catching the favorable notice of critics for the first time in her career, who called her "good support" (*Variety*) for the series' stars.

Myrna was part of *The Odd Couple's* comic relief, a pinch hitter who'd come in for one or two scenes per episode to deliver a funny line or two, or do a fun piece of business with a prop—a cartoon horse's head, for example, in the episode in which Oscar is mortified when he finds himself on the game show *Let's Make a Deal*, or a voodoo doll in the episode in which Felix has insomnia.

Her bell-bottom jeans and platform shoes, her colorful patched-cloth handbag with the fringe along the bottom, her long straight hair parted just off the middle or braided into pigtails and even her pale lipstick are a veritable compendium of late 1960s–early 1970s youth fashion.

Still, Penny was as insecure as Myrna about her looks and her talent and her legitimacy as a costar on the show, and she said repeatedly at the time that Klugman and Randall, the two stars of the program, teased her mercilessly about her family connections to their show.

"There were times Jack Klugman would literally have to pick me up and move me to my mark, because I was too petrified to walk," she said later, during the first season of her *Laverne & Shirley* success. "In those days, if I moved on stage, it was only to back into a wall."

When the inevitable reunion TV movie for *The Odd Couple* series aired in September 1993, Penny, who by then could gain no conceivable career advantage by participating, agreed to reprise her Myrna Turner role in a cameo. Once again the critics, who generally didn't like the bland, derivative TV movie, singled her out for praise, saying, typically, that she came to the telefilm's rescue.

Laverne & Shirley

To the utter amazement of all concerned, *Laverne & Shirley* landed atop the Nielsen TV ratings in its very first broadcast as a midseason replacement in January 1976.

As Garry Marshall explained at the time to *Daily Variety*'s savvy veteran television columnist Dave Kaufman, even the show itself was a *Happy* accident.

In 1974, his sister Penny had been convinced to take a one-episode *Happy Days* guest-starring role, along with Cindy Williams, a pert film actress until then best known for her role as dimply cute cheerleader Laurie Bolander in George Lucas's 1973 breakthrough picture, *American Graffiti*.

American Graffiti, a teen movie set in the late 1950s, starred an expert ensemble cast of the young and soon-to-be famous, including Richard Dreyfuss, Harrison Ford, Paul LeMat, MacKenzie Phillips, Suzanne Somers, and, as Laurie's clean-cut, straight-arrow boyfriend . . . Ron Howard.

"I got Cindy and Penny to see a *Happy Days* script which was not planned as a spinoff," Garry Marshall said a few scant months after the fact. "I told Penny, 'Your father [a producer on *Happy Days*] wants you to do this as a favor,' and she did it."

Neither Penny nor Cindy, it turned out, had wanted to do the guest-star turn on the Paramount Television show, and both had to be cajoled into it. Penny was eventually given her choice of which of the two girls she wanted to play, and Cindy agreed only after a personal appeal from Henry Winkler, who on *Happy Days* played everyone's favorite duck-tailed, leather-jacketed, juvenile-delinquent-with-a-heart-of-gold, Arthur "the Fonz" Fonzerelli. Winkler was Cindy's friend, and someone whom she had once casually dated.

Penny and Cindy (b. 1947) had first met nearly a half decade before, on the set of a memorably mistitled movie, *The Christian Licorice Store,* the story of a tennis champ (Beau Bridges) who succumbs to Hollywood's decadent, corrupting, and commercializing influences. The movie, the feature-film debut of James Frawley, a director at the time best known for helming most of the episodes of *The Monkees* TV series, was aimed squarely at the youth market. Though the film was made in the late 1960s, it wasn't released until 1971—a testament to its lack of commercial possibilities.

The film's twentysomething screenwriter, Floyd Mutrux, was quoted in the press handouts that accompanied its premiere as saying that he'd thought of the title first, then imagined the picture's opening and the ending (a hilly panorama and a car crash, respectively). "I figured . . . I have this great title, a good opening, a powerful ending," he said, according to a trade review from the early 1970s. "What I need is a film to go in between."

According to the reviewers, exactly what he didn't do was deliver the movie's middle. Instead, the movie was what the critics described as a mish-mash—part Los Angeles travelogue and part what we now would call a music video, with portentous, elliptical dialogue—was "too personal in its reliance on visual imagery and obtusely symbolic song lyrics more than on expository dialog" (*Variety*). The result was "one of those movies with little plot, a good deal of visual scope and a simple, relaxing mood" (*Show* magazine).

In this tale of "pretty young people in front of pretty scenery," the future Laverne and Shirley were bit players so unimportant that their uncredited parts ended up carpeting the cutting room floor.

The year before *Laverne & Shirley* debuted, the two young actresses, both out of work at the time, were hired by Francis Ford Coppola's company as TV writers working in tandem on the development of a proposed Bicentennial spoof of American history. Though the show never made it to air, it was most likely then that Penny's brother first began to think of them as a team.

On the *Happy Days* TV set at last, Cindy Williams and Penny Marshall improvised much of their bit. They created their characters—sweet Shirley and blunt Laverne, two working-class girls from the local brewery out on a blind date with Richie and the Fonz—out of an alchemy of the writers' lines, Garry Marshall's actual boyhood memory of a fight between two girls in a restaurant he witnessed during a date in the 1950s, and the two young actresses' own actual personalities.

Happy Days episode forty-nine, "A Date with Fonzie," directed by Jerry Paris, introduces the two brewery bottling-plant girls. It begins—where else?—in Arnold's diner on Valentine's Day, and Richie Cunningham (Ron Howard) has just broken up with his girlfriend of four months. So of course friend Fonzie (Henry Winkler) takes immediate action to get Richie's flagging confidence back, dragging his sincere but naive pal out to the best pick-up joint in town, which just happens to be—*Exactimundo!*—the local supermarket.

Richie tries his best, but all he manages to do is annoy one female shopper and provide unwitting cover for another, who proceeds to do some shoplifting, so Fonzie—*Aie!*—has to resort to drastic measures. He calls two of his "chicks" to go out on a double date that Saturday night!

"There they are," says Fonzie back in the Cunningham house, showing Richie their pictures in a big, black yearbook. "Laverne DeFazio and Shirley Feeney." He cups his hands out, jiggling, as if appraising a pair of invisible breasts. "Whoa-oh!"

When Richie asks what if they say no, Fonzie strikes a pose: "They don' know th' word no," he exclaims, picking up the phone and dialing. The date is made.

And so ends the episode's first act. After the commercial break, we find ourselves back in Arnold's at eight o'clock on Saturday night.

Laverne and Shirley enter to the strains of *Love Me Tender, Love Me Do . . .* on the jukebox, and Laverne yells out, "Hey! Fahn-zee!"

They join Richie and the Fonz in a booth. "Pleased t'meetchya," says Shirley shyly when she meets Richie, her date for the evening. Without another word, she curls right up to him and buries her head against his neck.

Ralph (Donny Most) and Potsie (Anson Williams)—Richie's pals and Fonzie's pawns—are in the adjoining booth, gawking wordlessly at the two girls. Laverne shoots them a look and snaps, "How'dja like yer eyes closed—fer good?"

Fonzie proposes they all go back to Richie's house where Richie lives with his parents and his sister and where Fonzie has a guest apartment. Before long, Laverne goes off for some necking with Fonzie, leaving Richie uncomfortably alone with Shirley, who blithely observes . . .

"She's a bimbo, but she is my best friend."

As awkward, nervous Richie fumbles in his attempt to get romantic with Shirley, Richie's parents (Tom Bosley, Marion Ross) and sister (Erin Morton) come home.

"I'll drive myself home," Shirley tells Richie briskly, after his bemused and scandalized family has been ushered upstairs. "Laverne can hitch."

And with a final off-screen kiss, Laverne and Shirley's first television appearance comes to an end. In the end credits of "A Date with Fonzie," Cindy comes first as Guest Star, but Penny is listed as *Special* Guest Star. It was a harbinger of things to come.

Then, as now, primetime television with its incessant, voracious need for product, was nothing if not an opportunistic medium.

Inevitably, a TV series evolved from the ambiance of *American Graffiti* (1973), a wistful recreation of idyllic high-school nights of car hops and cruising, of teen angst, and pre-Beatles rock 'n' roll in the early 1960s ("Where were you in '62?" the movie's publicity campaign asked), just before American innocence was exploded by the war in Vietnam. *Happy Days* itself started off inauspiciously enough, deriving specifically from an episode of the ABC-TV network anthology series *Love, American Style* titled "Love and the Happy Day," first broadcast in February 1972. The segment was about the day the Cunningham family bought its first TV set. Ron Howard played Richie, Anson Williams was Potsie, and Marion Ross played

Mom. However, Dad and sister Joanie were played by other actors (Harold Gould and Susan Neher).

Graffiti's success, with Howard playing essentially a big-screen version of Richie, came just a year later, and ABC's executives promptly ordered up the spin-off series.

Happy Days was set in an idealized, sanitized version of the President Dwight D. Eisenhower 1950s—a safe, compliant time when youth rebellion meant beret-wearing, goateed beatniks reading incomprehensible, pretentious, angst-ridden poetry to melodramatic bongo-drum accompaniment in smoky subterranean coffee bars. It was an era—at least as it's now fondly remembered—without any suggestive clothing or even crime, when families ate dinner together and the kids always had lots of fun things to do.

Happy Days was not a spin-off of *Graffiti* in a direct, linear sense. In fact, it didn't even come from the same producing and distributing studio (*Graffiti* was from Universal, *Days* from Paramount). However, both movie and series did feature piping-voiced Ron Howard, already a TV veteran who'd grown up playing Opie on *The Andy Griffith Show* (1960–68), in his familiar male-ingenue role.

Penny's brother Garry was the creator of *Happy Days,* writing its pilot episode which aired in January 1974, with none other than brother-in-law/ actor Rob Reiner and his writing partner Phil Mishkin. The Marshalls' father, Tony, was one of the show's producers.

In the mid-1970s at ABC, then the struggling, perennially cellar-dwelling third TV network, the top executives were trying to carve a distinct identity with primetime programs aimed squarely at females and young viewers. And, for the first time, they were selling advertisers demographics rather than actual ratings. It's still a truism of the television business, as valid today as it was at the dawn of the medium: TV doesn't sell shows to audiences; rather, it sells audiences to advertisers.

Ratings are a measure of overall audience; that is, of the total number of eyeballs watching. Demographics, now a commonplace of the industry, was a brand-new ploy back in the early 1970s and was greeted with great skepticism by advertisers and show people. The simple idea behind the demographics strategy was that some TV viewing audiences were better than others. Teens with discretionary dollars were preferable to pensioners on fixed incomes because they had more pocket money to spend.

At least that was the argument of the first demographers. Today, with aging baby boomers making up a disproportionate share of the potential TV audience, that argument has been turned on its head in some quarters. This is particularly true at CBS, which traditionally has appealed to an older audience than the other two original broadcast networks.

Demographers in the 1970s argued that advertisers should pay premiums for shows that appealed to these better audiences, even if they were lower in the ratings than the competition's greater mass audience. As the years passed, and cable and VCRs shattered that original audience mass, this argument, which ABC first advanced to hoots of derision from Hollywood and Madison Avenue alike, which likened it to selling sizzle rather than the steak, has come to be the accepted TV dogma.

Now, advertisers routinely pay the demographic tariff to reach desirable audiences, who today are most widely considered to be youngish people, particularly men, eighteen to forty-nine years old.

The top ABC executives of the 1970s, Fred Silverman (the only man ever to head the programming divisions of ABC, CBS, and NBC) and Michael Eisner (who went on to head Paramount Pictures and is currently the head of the Walt Disney Company), liked the *Happy Days* episode in which brash working-class brewery girls Laverne and Shirley go out on a double date with Richie and the Fonz. They wanted to see more.

As part of their strategy to attract more women viewers, ABC already had Penny under a holding contract. As noted earlier, she had had a recurring role in *Wives,* a failed pilot produced by Garry that ABC had seriously considered airing the season before. So the network executives were only too happy to consider the inexpensive eight-to-ten minute show presentation that Garry Marshall, with prolific producers Tom Miller and Ed Milkis, put together for them. The brief presentation took the place of the traditional pilot, a sample episode of the prospective series mounted at a cost sometimes even back then reaching the mid-six figures. If Marshall had insisted on doing a pilot first, thereby forcing the network to potentially invest hundreds of thousands of dollars to find out if the two girls from *Happy Days* worked on their own, there might never have been a *Laverne & Shirley*.

"The last time I tried a presentation," Marshall quipped to *Daily Variety* in early 1976, "was on *Me and the Chimp*, but this one came out a lot better."

Explaining the failure of that short-lived 1972 series in which Ted Bessell, who later became Penny Marshall's production partner and already was well known as Marlo Thomas's on-camera boyfriend on *That Girl,* was paired with a chimpanzee named Buttons, Garry Marshall opined drolly that he'd cast the wrong chimp.

A lot better, indeed. *Laverne & Shirley,* one of sixteen midseason replacements that the three networks threw on the air in January 1976 (others included *The Bionic Woman* and *Donny and Marie*), debuted at 8:30 P.M. on January 27, 1976, a Tuesday, at the top. It was the first premiering TV series ever to start at number one and, almost miraculously . . .

It stayed there.

Its audience—nearly fifty million people!—was phenomenal, and particularly so by the fragmented-audience, narrow-casting standards of the present day.

Years later in 1996, Garry Marshall recalled for the *New York Daily News,* the morning those anxiously awaited debut ratings came in: "We couldn't find it [in the ratings list] . . . because we were looking down in the twenties." In other words, the show had shattered even its own producers' wildest expectations.

By mid-year, with the traditional TV season over, ABC, that perennial loser in the annual three-network race, was within a hairbreadth of dethroning CBS. Acclaimed as the Tiffany Network, the diamond standard in television, CBS had been number one almost from the dawn of the medium. The reason that distraught, disbelieving, or just bemused critics were forced to acknowledge was simple:

Schlemiel, shlemazel . . .

That bit of business that begins every episode of the show—Laverne and Shirley, arm in arm, skipping down the street, singing out the infectious bit of doggerel, *Schlemiel, Shlemazel, Hassenpfeffer Incorporated,* that segues into their theme song, "Making Our Dreams Come True" (". . . *and we'll do it our way, yes our way . . .*")—was actually a childhood rhyme, sung by jump-roping kids in the Marshalls' Bronx neighborhood.

The first two words are Yiddish, which is the mother tongue of the East European immigrants who, in the first half of the twentieth century, settled in and around New York and were a major presence in the Bronx. It has also become the *lingua franca* of professional show business as well, where everyone has an eye for a *schmuck* or a *goniff* or a pretty young thing with a *schaine punim.* The language, derived from both German and Hebrew, is widely recognized for its facility in expressing truths about human nature and human relationships, a quality which is abundantly demonstrated in these linked definitions:

shlemazel (noun): Unlucky oaf. The sort of person who has soup spilled upon her by somebody else.

schlemiel (noun): Clumsy oaf; klutz. The sort of person who, when at a fancy restaurant, invariably spills her soup.

"They shot [the presentation] on Friday night, edited on Saturday, the ABC brass saw it in New York on Sunday and we were told we were going on the air on Monday," said Penny Marshall a scant half-year later in May 1976. "Then we did a couple of *Happy Days* to make it seem like a spin-off."

In the first of those follow-up *Happy Days* appearances—episode fifty-seven, "Football Frolics," in which Richie, Ralph, and Potsie decide on a night of "volume babysitting" to raise enough money to buy Bears-game football tickets—Laverne and Shirley show up in the second act, and again the same basic elements are showcased.

When they enter, both wearing coats and carrying purses, Shirley, the decorous one, has a proper fur lining on her coat collar and is wearing black gloves. Once again, they're on their way to a double date. First though, they're dropping off a little boy named Booker they agreed to babysit. They can't watch him after all, Shirley explains prissily, because Laverne has arranged for this double date. "No sense of responsibility," Shirley tisks. "She wanted to leave [Booker] in a locker in the bus terminal."

The second follow-up episode, number fifty-eight, "Fonzie the Superstar," adds another soon-to-be familiar element—Laverne and Shirley doing physical *shtick*.

When the Fonz, in a buckskin-fringed jumpsuit, sings "Heartbreak Hotel" for a crowd of screaming teenage girls at Arnold's, his do-wop-wopping back-up singers are none other than Laverne and Shirley. But first, at rehearsal, they have the now traditional row about the quality of their respective vocal abilities.

Later, but before Fonzie finally comes out for his big number, they are back-up for Arnold (Pat Morita) who sings—in the key of Asia Minor, he says—a bit of "By the Light of the Silvery Moon," with Laverne and Shirley counterpointing, "Not a fork, but a spoon . . ."

Richie introduces them as the Arnoldettes, a name that must have, however faintly, resonated with the former precision-tapping Marshallettes of Penny's childhood. And when they're finally doing their back-up dance routine behind the Fonz at the end of the act, Penny is confident and stylish—clearly, these are moves she's known since she was a child—while across Cindy's face passes a severe look of concentration and she keeps glancing over and down, as if she's watching Penny's feet.

Looking back almost a quarter century later, how does one explain the phenomenal success of a modest little sitcom about two struggling working girls in Milwaukee in the 1950s?

The show was generally well-crafted along traditional vaudeville lines, with hoary comic routines given ironic little twists and often interspersed with played-for-laughs dance numbers, as in, for example, the "Shotgun Wedding," the second half of a two-parter that begins as a *Happy Days* episode. In that installment, Laverne and Shirley have a square-dancing hoedown showdown with the daughters of a Swedish farmer who's holding Richie and Fonzie at shotgun point.

Joking about Swedish accents and cross-pollinating the two 1950s-era sitcom hits became standard operating procedure. In the 1979 "Fonzie's Funeral" two-parter on *Happy Days*, the mourners at the Heavenly Rest Funeral Home include not only Laverne, who wails that the Fonz was the only guy who'd ever "hickied his initials" on her neck, and Shirley, who forcibly prevents Laverne from taking Fonzie's boots as a souvenir, but also include *Laverne & Shirley* regulars Lenny, Squiggy, and Carmine.

As late as her 1998 *Nash Bridges* guest-starring spot on Don Johnson's cop series, Penny was still doing inside jokes about Swedish accents: her detective character's ex-husband is a Swede, she explains to Nash's sidekick [played by Cheech Marin], who, it turns out, also has a Swedish spouse. In the middle of the TV detective show, they do a little routine about Swedish foods and foibles.

Laverne & Shirley was pleasantly energetic, if not terribly consequential—thought the critics of the time—and it appealed to the same rising sense of nostalgia that propelled *Happy Days* to solid, if not spectacular, ratings success.

It helped that the series was a spin-off, it gave the show that familiar quality that American TV viewers of the time found so comforting. After all, *The Mary Tyler Moore Show* (1970–77) had led to *Rhoda* (1974–78) and *Phyllis*

(1975–77), and *All in the Family* (1971–83) had begotten *Maude* (1972–76) and *The Jeffersons* (1975–85).

No sooner had the Nielsen TV viewing/rating families given *Laverne & Shirley* the double thumbs-up than plans were made to spin off from it. Under consideration were both a Fonzie spin-off, in which the Fonz would become father to a younger version of himself, and a Lenny (Michael McKean) and Squiggy (David L. Lander) spin-off, in which the two brewery truck drivers pals of the series leads would join the Army. Neither made it beyond the wishful-thinking stage.

By the 1970s, Americans generally were exhausted by current events and looking for escape, and escapist fare, at home on TV. The bloody Vietnam War had divided the generations and ended in defeat. Watergate, which had ended in fiasco and the forced resignation President Richard Nixon, followed. The baby boomers, that huge demographic cohort born after the Second World War, who were in their teens and twenties in the 1960s and early 1970s, had exploded in outrageousness, youthful excess, and serious political protest. All in all, they shattered their parents' fondest dreams and contradicted their dearest beliefs.

By the mid-1970s, the decade of the 1950s—before the baby boomers erupted, before the drugs and the war, and before American self-confidence was so shaken—became a treasured memory, burnished in hindsight by both the kids and their parents. Edgier TV shows like *All in the Family*, producer Norman Lear's daring experiment in topicality which premiered in 1971, and *Maude*, a spin-off of *Family* in 1972, addressed the most contentious issues of the day from abortion to gay rights. The shows received great critical acclaim and multiple industry awards. In contrast, *Laverne & Shirley*, Emmy-less, led the way back to the future, anticipating TV's current, multichannel nostalgia wave.

By comparison, during the run of his hit TV show (*All in the Family*), Rob Reiner twice won an Emmy as Best Supporting Actor. Penny and Cindy remained awardless, although the Hollywood Radio and Television Society did name them as its Women of the Year in 1977, a public-relations honor that was more a recognition of their ratings popularity than anything else.

Laverne & Shirley was also shrewd counter-progamming to the prevailing, engaged, and issues-oriented zeitgeist on TV. As Garry Marshall, its creator, put it to journalist Rip Rense years later: "In the '70s everybody wanted feminist leads—let's have wonderful women on TV with brains and beauty! I said, I don't think so. I think most women would rather have somebody like them, who is struggling, trying to make ends meet, and the only thing they've got going for them is friendship. And that's why I did *Laverne & Shirley*!"

Garry Marshall's protestations aside, many of the show's most ardent fans at the end of the twentieth century continue to believe that Laverne and Shirley are important, in fact, precisely because they were feminist role models—independent, albeit unglamorous. As one fan, who took to the Internet in the 1990s with an academically oriented defense of the show, put it: "Laverne and Shirley were working class women. That was one of the show's major assertions and appeals. . . . *L & S* was not a working class traditional family [like *All in the Family*]. [Laverne and Shirley] were a working class family of two women."

In the mid-1970s the show-business trade papers, which then catered almost exclusively to the insider *cognoscenti*, were important critical bellwethers in a way that—in our present era of human-interest tabloidization and entertainment television—they no longer are. Their initial reaction to *Laverne & Shirley* was important, because the trades in the 1970s set the tone, and right from the beginning both the *Hollywood Reporter* and *Variety* demonstrated an ambivalence about the antics of Laverne DeFazio and Shirley Feeney that was downright schizophrenic.

On the one hand, the papers admitted that whatever it was the two brewery girls were doing worked, garnering spectacularly high ratings and popularity (nearly half of all Americans watching television at that time viewed the premiere episode), and in show business delivering was—and still is—the most important attribute of all. On the other hand, it was all just so damned mindless and low-brow.

In the debut episode, called "The Society Party," written by Bob Brunner (who also had a cameo as the foreman at the brewery) and directed by Garry Marshall, the brewery owner's pretentious nephew, Ted Shotz, invites the girls to a formal dress party at his grandmother's mansion. He wants to prove that he can relate to the little people, he says, and soon Laverne and Shirley are oohing over their invitation.

Because Laverne already has a date with Fonzie that night, young squire Shotz magnanimously says she can bring him too. And because, of course, the two blue-collar brewery girls don't have appropriate formal wear, they ask two friends from the plant for help getting the two dresses (size five for Shirley and size ten for Laverne). This simple favor introduces the sublimely clueless Leonard "Lenny" Kosnowski (Michael McKean) and Andrew "Squiggy" Squiggman (David L. Lander).

Despite Laverne's dubiousness, Lenny and Squiggy come through in their own inimitable way, showing up that night—at the very last minute, of course. Arriving at the girls' basement apartment at 730 Hampton Street with two beautiful gowns, Squiggy explains that the dresses are from his uncle's wax museum.

In the opening of the installment's second act, Laverne and Shirley appear at the party. One particularly stuck-up couple, the Stewarts, announce unctuously that Laverne and Shirley's dresses are in fact stolen from their daughters and they threaten to call the police.

Just as the party seems about to dissolve into chaos, the Fonz takes charge and makes a typically straightforward and commonsensical plea:

He promises that Laverne and Shirley will return the dresses, which he assures the others, including uppity Mrs. Stewart, naturally they didn't know were stolen. However, before long, Mrs. Stewart and Laverne get into a hassle. Thereafter, the two girls remove the purloined dresses and are now clad in only their slips. In a triumph of pluck over snobbery, while Fonzie gives them a double thumbs up, Laverne and Shirley march out of the society gathering.

Later, back at the apartment, another long-running element of the series is showcased: Shirley's optimism and Laverne's pessimism.

"All and all it wasn't such a bad evening," Shirley opines hopefully.

"Learn something from it, your hopes are too high," Laverne tartly replies.

To which Shirley responds: "Tisk-tisk-tisk. You are a gloomy Gus." And Shirley retorts, "I never said I was a saint, Shirl."

At the episode's end, Shirley gives a brief, but heartfelt speech about holding on to her dreams—during which Laverne, Lucille Ball-like, twists up her face, bugs out her eyes, and mugs.

Said *Daily Variety,* (January 27, 1976) reviewing the premiere: The "high-decibel duo [is a] . . . zippy idea which might just catch on."

The episode was a "diversion," the *Variety* reviewer continued, "directed at good speed by Garry Marshall so that the wrinkles in Bob Brunner's whiskered script don't show."

Said the *Hollywood Reporter* (January 27, 1976) of *Laverne & Shirley,* which the network had wisely scheduled on Tuesdays at 8:30 P.M., right after *Happy Days,* "Although it has the potential to make it on its own, it is presently straining too hard for laughs." Of course, when it comes to *shtick*-based humor, the idea of straining too hard misses the point: it's the laughs that count, not how you get them.

In the new show's second episode, Marshall (Penny), Marshall (Garry), Marshall (Tony, their father), and company poured it on, even joking for the second week in a row about the disparity in dress sizes between Cindy (size five) and Penny (size ten).

The second episode, "The Bachelor Party," was written by Lowell Ganz and Mark Rothman (the series' co-creators with Garry Marshall) and was the first of many *Laverne & Shirley* entries directed by Jerry Paris. In this episode, Carmine "the Big Ragu" Ragusa (Eddie Mekka), Shirley's boyfriend, makes his first appearance. He jogs and shadowboxes his way into the Pizza Bowl, the combination pizza joint and bowling alley owned by Laverne's father. Outside the establishment, fly both a U.S. and an Italian flag. Poppa Frank DeFazio (Phil Foster) begins his own marathon run in the series, beginning with this episode.

The episode's story is simple to the point of being practically non-existent, just an excuse for assorted bits of business. It seems Laverne's father is out of town for the weekend, leaving Shirley in charge at the Pizza Bowl. When Fonzie (wisely, again brought in from *Happy Days* to guest-star) shows up offering fifty dollars if Laverne will let him and his buddies throw Milo an after-hours bachelor party, Shirley predicts a smutty disaster. However, Laverne sees it as a golden opportunity to prove to her father that she's just as good as any son.

Ever since Lucy gave birth on TV on the same day as Lucille Ball gave birth in real life in the early 1950s, the best situation comedies have incorporated and transmuted their actors' real lives and real personalities into bits of plot and characterization on the show. In a speech that must have resonated with Penny, Laverne fervently declares to Shirley that she wants to be able to hand her father the money and tell him: "I made this for you. Your daughter, not your son. The one you used to call dopey."

Of course, the gang (including Milo, Lenny, Squiggy, and Carmine, with satirist/character actor Harry Shearer in a cameo) gets rowdy when the girl who's meant to jump out of the cake doesn't show up. And even though Laverne's only too willing to substitute, it's only censorious but tiny, size-five Shirley who can fit into the skimpy costume the girl in the cake left behind.

When Shirley, most reluctantly, does pop up, gallant Carmine comes to her aid, wrapping her in a red-checkered tablecloth, while Fonzie comes to

Laverne's aid, convincing the disappointed bachelor-party revelers not to destroy her father's restaurant.

"A disgusting experience," Shirley concludes with a shiver. But it's all worth it, because when Poppa Frank finally does show up at the end of the episode, he calls Laverne "Muffin"—not "Dopey"—and declares himself "glad I gotta daughter." Nevertheless, a moment later, from outside the open window of Laverne and Shirley's basement apartment, he's yelling at her to draw the curtains and calling her—what else?—Dopey again.

Once again, the unlikely series ended the week at the top of the ratings.

To explain *Laverne & Shirley*, Los Angeles–based *Daily Variety*'s older, Manhattan-based sister publication, weekly *Variety,* coined the term "proletarian comedy" to describe the new sitcom. (*Variety* had been coining its own "slanguage," such as "helmers," "ankle" projects, and the like, since the vaudeville era.) Taking note of "The Society Party" episode's smashing premiere rating, and pointing to the working-stiff humor of *The Honeymooners* in the 1950s, as well as CBS's critically acclaimed *All in the Family,* the Bible of show business proclaimed (February 4, 1976) that "the handwriting is clearly on the wall and it spells prole-tv."

Laverne & Shirley was the ratings sensation of 1976, watched weekly by almost half of the entire viewing audience and powered *Happy Days,* which had been at best a moderate success on its own, into the top ten.

On January 10, 1978, two years after the show's debut, 27,410,000 households tuned into *Laverne & Shirley*—"more people than had tuned to any situation comedy in TV history," according to a September 30, 1976, article in *Daily Variety. Laverne & Shirley* stayed on the air for seven-and-a-half seasons. In the overall rankings for the first four years, it finished in either first or second place.

By the start of its first full season, in September of 1976, the critics—especially the influential show-business trade papers—thought they had figured the show's popularity out:

"The slapstick comes off okay," said *Variety*, "but it's the appeal of the two women that really makes the show.

"Williams brings a snappiness to [Shirley] and it works well enough. But it's [Penny] Marshall's near-pathos, or wistfulness, that makes Laverne something outside the sitcom world."

Yet neither the show nor Penny ever became a critical favorite or, perhaps more importantly, was considered hip—either at the time or in the wave of reevaluation that has elevated *The Brady Bunch* (1969–74) and *Bewitched* (1964–72) to the status of beloved cultural icons.

Even while *Laverne & Shirley* was on the air, it was Lenny and Squiggy who became the pop cult figures and drew the most raves from fans. And even now at the end of the twentieth century, in our era of cable-ready nostalgia for kitsch TV, it's not Penny but Cindy Williams for whom retro-minded critics grow misty.

Consider this: When asked to evaluate his favorites among the low-brow offerings of the small screen, one TV-raised newspaper art critic, accustomed to reviewing the high arts of museums and the academy, proclaimed unequivocally:

"Conventional wisdom be damned. Cindy Williams was the real comic genius in *Laverne & Shirley*, not Penny Marshall. . . . Marshall mugged, Williams was sly."

Laverne & Shirley was a three-camera film (as opposed to videotape) shoot, costing, in the mid-1970s, about $250,000 per episode. The advantages of film versus tape have been debated endlessly, but back in the 1970s, film had a richer look, while videotape looked flat and overly bright. Tape was cheaper, but film, with the three cameras covering different angles for each bit of business, and particularly for the complex sight gags and the kind of physical *shtick* that was *Laverne & Shirley's* specialty, was easier to edit, to cut rhythmically and for maximum impact.

Each weekly episode was filmed on a sound stage at the Paramount Studios in Hollywood before a live audience, on a Tuesday. The sessions could easily last from early evening until the post-midnight hours. The actual filming was like putting a new two-act stage play before a small audience, only this play was interrupted by camera set-ups and repeated takes. Filming was the culmination of an often frantic process that recycled weekly during the shooting season. It began with Wednesday through Friday rehearsals and camera blocking for the new script (figuring out where each camera belongs at each moment, and whether it's taking a long shot, a medium or two-shot, or is in close-up).

Based on these first rehearsals, the weekends, which were supposed to be the time when the actors learned their script lines, often were a period of furious rewriting by the writers and producers. Mondays were devoted to final camera blocking and more rehearsals and, for the actors, memorization of the dialogue and bits of business that might have changed drastically since the last time they'd looked at the script. Tuesdays, which started in the early mornings for the technical crew, meant yet more rehearsal. Then, in the late afternoon, a dress rehearsal took place before an initial studio audience. A second audience, around three hundred people (invited guests and tourists alike) trooped in around the dinner hour. A comic—often Garry Marshall himself—warmed them up with jokes, then introduced the young cast, and then . . .

Show time!

From the start, the critics may have found the *Laverne & Shirley* story lines to be inconsequential. By contrast with the Norman Lear sitcoms of the day like *Maude* and *All in the Family*, it was far too cute, too unreal, too optimistic, and of course almost completely irrelevant to the issues of the time. However, almost from the start all was not sweetness and light behind the cameras at the top-rated television series.

On screen, Cindy Williams was pert, ever-idealistic, ever-apprehensive Shirley Feeney. However, in real life, she was a high-strung, bone-thin twenty-nine-year-old film actress with an ulcer. Well received by the critics in both George Lucas's *American Graffiti* and Francis Ford Coppola's *The Conversation* (1974), she'd been turning down TV offers for years.

Williams was beset by doubts about the medium of TV and what a series might do to her sparkling film career. She was also very concerned about the *Laverne & Shirley* writers and producers' fairness as well. She was surrounded not just by the usual professional family, but quite specifically by the Marshall family: Penny, brother Garry, sister Ronny Hallin, and their father Tony, who had all worked together on *Happy Days*. To Cindy, they must have seemed everywhere on the set—and she felt besieged.

Even Penny's young daughter Tracy was on the *Laverne & Shirley* set from time to time, acting in a few episodes. Michael McKean and David L. Lander (Lenny and Squiggy) had been performing the dopey duo together since their college days as drama students at Carnegie Tech, and were Marshall people as well. They'd been signed by Garry Marshall, who'd seen their impromptu performance at a party given by Penny and Rob Reiner was friends with the duo and had even been Lander's roommate for a time during his bachelor days.

Cindy Williams was born Cynthia Williams on August 22, 1947, in Van Nuys, California, and raised by blue-collar parents. Her mother was a waitress; her father an electrician and an electronics gadgeteer, whose ideas never quite translated into financial success. She grew up first in Irving, Texas, a suburb of Dallas, and then in Van Nuys and the other western suburbs of the San Fernando Valley, where she was surrounded by kids from wealthier, better-connected families.

Because they lived in Encino and Van Nuys, bedroom communities for the TV networks and the Hollywood studios, a half-hour or so away by automobile commute, her fellow school kids sometimes boasted a show-business-celebrity parent in the family. From high school on, until Cindy dropped out of the Los Angeles City College theater department in her third year, she acted in school plays, including productions of *After the Fall, Our Town,* and *The Diary of Anne Frank.*

Cindy's first break came when she was making the rounds as a struggling actress and a hot young Hollywood writer/producer interviewed her. Once she had Garry Marshall's backing, Cindy, like Penny, started breaking through in show business. She got both her first manager and agent on recommendations from Garry, as well as her first guest-starring role—on *Room 222,* the early 1970s TV sitcom created by James Brooks, another Marshall friend.

Williams' other early TV appearances included the short-lived TV version of Neil Simon's *Barefoot in the Park* and episodes of *Love, American Style,* both of which Garry Marshall produced for ABC-TV.

Like Penny, Cindy turned up early in her career on TV commercials, including spots for both Pampers and Foster Grants. Like many A-list stars and directors, including Jack Nicholson and Francis Ford Coppola, she got her big-screen start in Roger Corman's B-picture factory, with small, low-paid roles in quickie movies like *Gas-s-s* (1970) and *Beware! The Blob* (1972).

Coincidentally, another actor in that version of *The Blob* was Richard Stahl, playing a character named Edward Fazio. Stahl later turned up in the debut episode of *Laverne & Shirley,* playing the snooty Marshall Stewart, who comes face to face with Laverne DeFazio. He also guest-starred in "The Right to Light" episode of *Laverne & Shirley,* as the officious Milwaukee Gas & Electric clerk with a passion for his punch-card-spewing, late 1970s vintage computer.

In the 1990s Cindy has appeared on television about once a year, usually guest-starring in a single episode of a series. In 1997 she had a big-screen role in *Meet Wally Sparks,* starring Rodney Dangerfield. On TV, she's guest-starred in such series as *Touched by an Angel, Night Stand, Lois & Clark: The New*

Adventures of Superman, and the short-lived *Hope and Gloria* (in an episode that also featured Eddie "Carmine Ragusa" Mekka). She's guest-voiced on the PBS kid's show *The Magic School Bus,* and has appeared in such TV movies as *The Stepford Husbands, Escape from Terror: The Teresa Stamper Story,* and *Perry Mason: The Case of the Poisoned Pen.* She also appeared on a television commercial for Jenny Craig, the weight loss company.

Clearly, the Marshalls looked out for each other. However, Cindy Williams was not part of their family, or at least she must not have felt that way during *Laverne & Shirley.* For their parts the Marshalls must have thought she was less than grateful for those early guesting and other breaks.

One sign of how excruciatingly difficult the relations would be between the two leads on the hottest show on TV was the difficulty they had deciding on on-screen billing for the series. Would Penny be billed first, or would Cindy? Or would they be billed equally? If so, who would get the coveted position on the left side of the screen, presumably the first name that viewers reading the titles would see? That one was settled in a fashion that would have done Solomon, the ancient Hebrew king known for his wisdom in settling disputes, proud. Both names came on screen at exactly the same time. Penny got the coveted left side, but Cindy's name was up higher on the right, which ostensibly balanced them out.

Still, less than two months into the fall season of 1976—the show's first full season on the air—Cindy Williams walked off Stage Twenty on the Paramount studio lot. The hit production immediately ground to an unscheduled halt.

The problem? Penny Marshall was getting all the attention—and all the funny lines. "I had signed to do this terrific character," Williams complained several months later to *TV Guide* (June 18, 1977), "but the show was thrown together so quickly that the terrific part got washed away. 'Come on, fellas,' I said, 'let's get back on the track.' But they never did. The thing was that

Laverne, the cynic, was easier to write for than Shirley, the idealist. That's when I really started to get unhappy."

According to an anonymous comedian who guest-starred on the show sometime during its first two seasons, "The thing was like a circus. I was handed a script and read it. I looked over at Cindy, it didn't make sense. I asked her 'What the hell's going on?' . . . Everything is played around Penny Marshall. Cindy and all the rest of the cast just stand around most of the time like part of the wallpaper. Cindy's a darling girl but most of the time she was nearly in tears."

Both top-ten Garry Marshall TV series were filmed on the Paramount lot, on adjoining sound stages. "The cast of *Happy Days* used to put glasses up to the sound stage wall to hear Penny and Cindy beating up on the writing staff next door," Garry recalled decades later in an online interview with his daughter Lori, a journalist.

"What happened was that all the writers knew Penny," Williams recalled to *TV Guide* in August 1982, the summer before the show's last season, when relations between her and the producers were once again at the breaking point. "They knew she could do physical humor. They didn't know me. They thought I was the one who did the sweet stuff. I was disappointed, and I kept telling them I was . . . and they didn't hear me. So one day, with my knees knocking, and shaking all over, I slithered off the lot and came home. Honestly, I thought they might arrest me. When a woman stands up for herself they call her a bitch, and worse. And there's no getting around it: I went through hell and so did everyone else."

The Williams walkout in late 1976 lasted two days. She demanded—and got—a change in the writing staff. As a result, the program's head writers, originally from *Happy Days,* were let go. After a three-week halt during which new, presumably more Shirley-friendly scripters came in and the producers regrouped, production resumed.

It seemed to be *shtick* and hijinks as usual, and before Christmas, Cindy and Penny were harmonizing again . . . this time on an oldies album titled *Laverne & Shirley Sing.*

They had top-notch back-up singers and the cuts included such girl-group standards as "Da Do Ron Ron" and "Chapel of Love," as well as "Graduation Day," "Sixteen Reasons," and "I'm Walking."

It was a novelty album, a holiday-season stocking stuffer for their many fans, and it made them part of the long and less-than-golden tradition of TV celebrities, from Barbara Eden to William Shatner, who had been seduced by the recording studio. In fact, *Happy Days'* stalwarts Anson Williams, Donny Most, and Scott Baio all were lured into recording their own songs at one time or another.

One of the more charitable critics of the time offered by way of a compliment that the *Laverne & Shirley* album was "more than adequate."

Even under the best of circumstances, without the bruising clash of egos and the explosions of temperament, shooting a weekly television series is extremely demanding and stressful work. Scores of livelihoods and hundreds of thousands of dollars are at stake. The spotlight of ratings success only turns the heat up on the pressure cooker that's the environment of any TV series set.

Laverne & Shirley—its young stars catapulted to the proverbial overnight success, their actorly egos on edge, the producers shuttling from TV series to TV series, new writers- and directors-for-hire coming and going with head-pounding speed—was by no means the exception.

"We were high in the ratings," said Michael McKean in an April 1978 *TV Guide* profile, "but no one felt secure and the people in charge were panicking. We were getting yelled at. Then it became messiah time. Every day they would bring some guy around and say, 'This is the messiah. He is going to save the show.' Next day, new messiah."

"We were shocked by success," Thomas L. Miller, one of the show's executive producers, said at the same time to *TV Guide*. "It was a difficult year all around—one none of us wants to go through again."

The on-set conflicts, acknowledged publicly from both sides of the camera, on what had become the number-one show on TV didn't escape the notice of the tabloids. The *Star* reported that Penny Marshall and Cindy Williams had gone from earning $8,000 per episode when the show debuted to $25,000 per episode after it reached number one in the ratings.

Cool though they may have been toward each other and about other matters involving their perks on the series, the two actresses soon united to demand $50,000 each per episode, according to the same tabloid, or more than $1 million dollars for an entire new twenty-two-episode season of new installments.

And though that figure may have seemed excessive or outlandish to many (though it pales beside the million-dollar-per-episode benchmarks of the present day), before long each actress was making a salary of $75,000 per episode!

Laverne & Shirley opened its third season with a story set in New York City, in Laverne's Old Neighborhood, during an Italian festival. It featured Phil Foster in a plot about the reconciliation between Papa Frank DeFazio (Foster) and his Italian mama (Peggy Stanton) from whom he's been estranged.

Interestingly, the installment resonates in many ways with Penny's real life and the Marshalls' family history. First, there's the obvious one: it's set in the Old Neighborhood—and for the occasion the narrow streets on the back lot of Paramount had been dressed to look like something out of *The Godfather*. Second, we learn that Papa Frank has Americanized his name, changing to Frank from Fabrizio, just as the Marshalls had once Americanized their own Italian surname from Marscharelli. Last, the plot requires Laverne, on Papa Frank's behalf, to climb the greasy pole of success, in a feast-day contest, to earn her formidable grandmother's respect for her father by winning a trip to Italy. However silly the pole-climbing *shtick* is, it does hit on a serious issue.

Papa Frank is a "grown man . . . afraid of his own mother," who calls him "stupid." In the episode, Papa Frank is just as dismayed at being called stupid, as Laverne has been when he had criticized her as "dopey." Penny faced a similar situation with her own real-life mother, who had considered her the "world's worst."

But because this is a Marshall TV comedy, everything, no matter how serious, pays off in a joke, the sillier the better. Therefore, when Laverne asks Papa Frank if he meant it when he called her stupid, he replies sweetly: "Only the time you ate the dog food."

That this would echo with Penny's actual life is not surprising. "In my family, if we ever had a problem," Penny told *Woman's Day* in July 1992, "we'd put it in a comedy. When Rob and I were breaking [up], I went to talk to my brother . . . [at] a place in Encino [California] where the waiters entertain you. Here I am in tears and a guy with a parrot on his arm sings, 'Hi, would you like the waffle?' I'm part of a sketch. . . . [We] said, 'We'll use this someday.'"

Two more elements in the Old Neighborhood episode are of special interest: First, though Penny's marriage to Rob Reiner by this time may have been on the proverbial rocks, she's never looked better on camera than she does in this third-season opener. This held true whether she was wearing an off-the-shoulder red blouse, worn with a plastic red belt and rolled-up jeans that flattered her figure, or in Madras plaid shorts that showed off her dancer's legs. Second, in the episode's final scene, there's the obligatory DeFazio family reconciliation with everyone in tears and hugging. When Shirley comes into the room, she begins to cry too and the DeFazios open their arms to her, wordlessly admitting her into the family circle.

Is it possible for anyone in the know to watch this sequence without wondering about Cindy Williams, who so transparently felt left out of the Marshall family circle, and her real feelings at this moment?

But back then all this was subtext at best. Critics of the time had generally given up bewailing the show's lack of wider social relevance, conceding there's "no use arguing with success" (*Variety*) and claiming that the hit show wasn't even narrative storytelling: "It's slapstick. There's no textuality, nothing to analyze."

The show was certainly a throwback to *I Love Lucy,* the most popular comedy in the 1950s, during the Golden Age of American television. The Laverne-Shirley duo reminded reviewer after reviewer of Lucy and Ethel: one wide-eyed, brash, and fearless; the other timid and proper, forever getting dragged into scatterbrained schemes. It was a comparison that Penny's brother encouraged. "No one else on TV is doing early Lucy," Garry noted of his sister's talent to the *Unicorn Times* in May 1978. "The other ladies on sitcoms are classy; they're smart and they dress well. But Laverne's the kind of gal who could knock the stuffings out of Mary Richards and Rhoda, and for good measure, wipe the floor with Phyllis."

Perhaps no episode illustrates that comparison so well as "Suds to Stardom," in which both of the show's comic duos—Laverne and Shirley and Lenny and Squiggy—audition for the annual Shotz Brewery Showcase talent show. The episode, written by Buzz Kohan and directed by James Burrows (who went on to fame and multiple Emmys as the house director for *Cheers*), illustrates Penny and Cindy's wacky physicality in a Carmen Miranda–like calypso dance number.

The highlight of the episode is yet another high point for fans of the entire comedy series: Lenny and Squiggy, in matching black-sequined rock-star jackets singing "Star-Crossed," a delirious satire of 1950s-era teen-angst pop songs.

That song, with Lenny strumming accompaniment on his guitar, is surely a precursor of *This Is Spinal Tap*, the hilarious 1984 big-screen rock "mockumentary" that Michael McKean co-wrote with Christopher Guest. McKean also costarred in *Tap* as guitarist "David St. Hubbins." The cult favorite, generally regarded as the funniest Hollywood movie ever made about the pop-music business, was the first feature film directed by Rob Reiner.

Though the improvement in Cindy's dancing ability from the initial episodes of the first half season is apparent in "Suds to Stardom," it's Penny's prancing that makes the second act calypso number special. Cindy is able to hold her own as a dancer by this episode, the fourteenth, having learned the routine, but a careful viewer won't for a second forget that it's an actress, not a dancer, who's on screen, just going through moves, however skillfully. In other words, when she's dancing Cindy seems more like Cindy and less like Shirley. However, Penny is somewhere well beyond simply performing the routine well. Elbows akimbo, eyes bugged out, she stays in character throughout the entire musical routine, in the same way that Lucille Ball, also a trained dancer, did in her on-camera efforts, when, for example, Lucy was trying out as a dancer for Desi Arnaz's Ricky. In "Suds to Stardom" that's Laverne, not Penny, out there dancing!

Garry Marshall appears briefly in this installment, in the wordless part of the mournful-looking drummer in suit and tie. He is part of the group backing up Laverne and Shirley. His *Odd Couple*-producing partner Jerry Belson also has a cameo in the episode as Mr. Wardcraft.

Given the opportunity, though, Garry did not cite this as his favorite episode of either of his 1950s-era hit TV shows. With a commendable generosity, he told his daughter in their Internet online interview that his favorite was the installment of *Happy Days* that introduced Laverne and Shirley. "My sister Penny had been out of work," he said in the 1990s, "and that episode not only gave her a job for a week, but led to *Laverne & Shirley*, which ran for eight years. Whenever a family member of mine gets a job, it always makes me happy."

On the surface, Penny and Rob Reiner had much in common—they were struggling actors who, seemingly overnight, and without too much struggling, became TV stars after getting their starts because of their famous relatives. Rob's first movie role was in 1967's *Enter Laughing*, directed by his father, Carl Reiner. But Rob's father was already famous everywhere, a prominent member of the first generation of TV celebrities, when Rob was born; Penny's brother achieved an inside-the-industry fame as a relatively young man.

Rob's family moved away from the Bronx, first to the suburban good life in New Rochelle, in Westchester, New York, then on to the even better life among the pools and palm trees of Beverly Hills, California. It was there, on the West Coast, that he grew up around the famous and accomplished people with whom his father worked—people like Sid Caesar, Mel Brooks, Neil Simon, Woody Allen, Norman Lear, and Dick Van Dyke. As a Beverly Hills High School student, Rob grew up with people who would become famous in their own right—talented and ambitious young people like Richard Dreyfuss and Albert Brooks. As a teenager, Rob co-founded an improv comedy group. As a twentysomething young man he wrote for the *Smothers Brothers Show* (1965–66), where his writing partner was another struggling young comic named Steve Martin.

Once Penny and Rob were married, their home became a salon, in the same way as had Estelle and Carl Reiner's home, where young and rising Holly-wood talents gathered. Penny and Rob's North Hollywood house, particularly in the pre-*Laverne & Shirley* days, was where writers, actors, directors, and comics from such improv and stand-up stalwarts as the Committee and the Credibility Gap came to hang out and, courtesy of Penny, eat a home-cooked meal.

Throughout it all, Penny redecorated and remodeled, even setting up an in-home nursery for the child with Rob Reiner that she would never have. She listened and she learned, but above all, despite the husband and the house, the success and the circle of friends, she continued to worry.

"I'm constantly asking Rob if he likes me, if I'm nice, if I'm happy. At parties I ask him if I'm having a good time," she said even then, right at the very height of her celebrity, bewailing her inability to enjoy her own success. "It's all such nutsiness. Here I am with a happy marriage, a great kid, a new house . . . a TV show that's a hit, Cindy and I are in great demand on TV—and I'm sitting in a corner wailing! I'm happy, I really am. And I'm grateful. But I worry."

In October 1978, Penny and Rob Reiner—each in a hit series, each one of the most famous people in all of America—made their joint TV-movie debut, acting together in the two-hour ABC movie called *More Than Friends*.

She played Maddy Pearlman, an actress pursuing Hollywood success; he was Alan Corkus, a Bronx English teacher, sports fanatic and, most importantly, a would-be novelist. Maddy and Alan grew up "in the shadow of an elevated train trestle in the Bronx . . . [becoming] special pals who shoo-be-dooed their way out of the '50s," is how a network publicity release of the time put it, "and into all the laughter and tears of falling in love. Life was easy for Alan and Maddy until college, when the facts of life advanced the young couple one step further—from bosom buddies to uncommitted lovers."

This romantic comedy was loosely based on Marshall and Reiner's own relationship, which was an important selling point for the movie in *TV Guide* and other TV listings of the time. It was shot partly on location in the Bronx of Rob and Penny's youth and in other New York Old Neighborhood locations, and the story was about the strains on a relationship caused by the pursuit of artistic and Hollywood success.

The movie is told in flashback and voiceover narration as the fictional book Alan has been writing based on his relationship with Maddy. It begins in the Bronx, on high-school prom night in 1958. The TV movie—and Alan's novel—follows Maddy and Alan for the next thirteen years—through girl-next-door friendship, teenaged first love, and the tempestuous ups and downs of the flamboyant, raised-consciousness 1960s.

Eventually, Maddy, the aspiring actress, gets her own TV series—but she can't find happiness without her old beau from the old neighborhood.

"Penny and I have always been curious about doing an acting 'duet,'" Reiner was quoted as saying in a network press release touting the movie's 1978 debut. "I have to admit, though, that it's very difficult. You expend an enormous amount of energy thinking about the other person's feelings and you must be very careful that you don't let that concern detract from your own performance. If you have an artistic disagreement, you can't call your costar a shallow, self-centered so-and-so as you storm off the set, because eight hours later, at the end of the day, guess who's coming to dinner."

Though quotes attributed to individuals in press releases, in reality, often are written by press agents and other anonymous spin doctors, given the imminent end of Penny and Rob's relationship, Reiner's unusually acerbic, almost bitter, remark does have the ring of truth.

This would not be the last time that Reiner mined his relationship with Penny for dramatic and comedic material. *When Harry Met Sally . . . ,* the well-received 1989 comedy starring Meg Ryan and Billy Crystal that he directed, was widely believed to be based on his experiences after the breakup of his marriage with Penny. *The Story of Us,* a film Reiner directed in early 1999, takes up the story of a couple, married for fifteen years, trying to deal with the pressures of a long-term relationship. It stars Bruce Willis, Michelle Pfeiffer, Paul Reiser (*Mad About You*), and Rita Wilson (*Volunteers* [1985] and *Sleepless in Seattle* [1993]), the actress probably best known for her real-life role as Tom Hanks' wife.

The high price paid for ending relationships and making new ones is clearly something that's been much on Rob Reiner's mind. For example, in

1988, years after his divorce, he observed to this author that if a divorced man who starts dating again behaves honorably, he's sure to be humiliated.

Penny and Rob's *More Than Friends* was co-written and co-produced by Reiner and Phil Mishkin, his writing partner on the *Happy Days* pilot episode. It was smartly directed by James Burrows, who later became the network sit-com premiere director, guiding, among many others, most of the episodes of the long-running NBC hit *Cheers*.

In the cast of *More Than Friends* were such other TV sitcom stalwarts as Dabney Coleman, playing a married man who has a fling with Maddy, and Michael McKean as a rock star. This late 1970s version of *Friends* did well in the ratings for ABC. It captured a thirty share of the audience, meaning that three out of every ten people watching television at the hour it was broadcast tuned in to *More Than Friends*.

Most of the critics, though, were less than thrilled. What was clearly intended to be a small-screen *Annie Hall* (1977)—a bittersweet romantic comedy about two people in love and out—was generally judged an artistic misfire. "An unfortunate dose of the cutes," the *Hollywood Reporter* huffed. "Too many hyphenates in back of the camera and not enough humanity in front of it."

Daily Variety called the telefeature a "slow-moving, charmless teleplay." However, both show-business trade papers, while criticizing Reiner's contribution as writer and actor, complimented Marshall on the range of her acting skills. To reviewers used to the familiar *shtick* of Laverne, Maddy came as a pleasant surprise. As *Daily Variety* put it, "Marshall, with luminous eyes shining, suggests she could play more intriguing roles with touching results."

Could she? For Penny that glowing accolade turned out to be a glimpse of the path not taken.

A year later, in 1979, at the very height of her TV popularity, Penny Marshall's marriage to Rob Reiner began to crack apart, almost as if Rob and Penny were succumbing in real life to the same strains *More Than Friends* had limned for Alan and Maddy. And for a time, on the tumultuous set of *Laverne & Shirley,* where Cindy had been counting her lines and taking a stopwatch to her on-screen time to make certain parity was upheld, a truce was called in the Penny-Cindy war.

"Cindy was there," Marshall said a few years later in August 1982 to *TV Guide.* "The rest of my life was in turmoil. Some days I would have massive anxiety attacks. Cindy would guide me through the script. . . . There were days when I could not be funny, and yet she was. Cindy and I had been through so much together that she understood."

Penny and Rob's divorce became official in 1981. Gossips had whispered suggestively, trying to unravel a tangle of reasons, all more or less fodder for the tabloids. In the end all the reasons could be grouped together under one overarching explanation: the pressures of fame. And two scant years later her mother, Marjorie, succumbed to Alzheimer's disease, a degenerative mental disease characterized by premature senility and mental degeneration.

"Maybe it's good," she joked at the time about her mother's failing faculties with bitter black humor, her brother remembered years later, "she won't know who I am and will like me better."

In the 1970s, the escalating program syndication business, in which hit network series were re-sold to individual stations around the country for additional airings off-network, became the financial engine that drove the television business.

The growth of off-network syndication was an unintended consequence of Federal Communications Commission regulations meant to curtail the power of what was then the three-network monopoly. Those regulations returned a half hour of programming in the early evenings, which had been previously programmed by the three networks, to individual stations and prohibited the networks from owning and syndicating their own shows. The hope had been that the TV stations would develop their own community-oriented programs for the primetime access period. Instead, in an example of how legislation often results in the creation of the Law of Unintended Consequences, that primetime access period was filled with cheap-to-produce game shows like *Jeopardy* and *Wheel of Fortune,* and former network weekly hit series, usually comedies, that had accumulated enough episodes to be stripped—that is, aired every week night at seven or seven-thirty. Shows from *Lucy* to *Seinfeld* could live on, generating income perpetually in off-network syndication.

By mid-1979, *Laverne & Shirley* was sold into syndication for a per-episode price that broke the previous record held by *Happy Days,* which had gone into syndication two years before. Before *Happy Days,* the average syndicated comedy made less than $20,000 per episode; Fonz and the gang had set the bar at $35,000. *Laverne & Shirley* was sold for a stunning $54,000 per episode to one TV station in New York.

That pot of gold—the $50,000 plus per episode, multiplied by the scores and scores of stations around the country that were airing the show in syndication—was the irresistible incentive for keeping *Laverne & Shirley* in production. The goal was to accumulate new episodes as long as possible and meet every demand of its youngish and still restless cast, no matter how outrageous.

To keep a long-lasting sitcom fresh from year to year, invariably new elements must be added periodically. In its fourth season (1977–78) *Laverne & Shirley* was moved out of the 1950s and into the early 1960s. In its sixth season (1979–80), the setting changed from Milwaukee to California. But by the seventh season (1980–81), the old "guileless nonsense . . . what makes the show so enduring and endearing," was no longer charming everyone. And while the *Hollywood Reporter* (October 15, 1981) thought the new Hollywood locale and the opportunity to do breaking-into-show-biz-themed stories had given the series a "new lease on life," to *Daily Variety* (October 15, 1981) the show appeared to be "beginning to show its age."

The seventh season wasn't to be its last, but the end was near for the most famous comedy team on TV since *I Love Lucy*.

The 1982–83 season of *Laverne & Shirley* was one of its most-watched ever, averaging in its first half a 20.2 rating and 30-percent share. This surprised most observers because one of its two titular stars had only appeared in a total of just two episodes that season.

Thirty years earlier, when Lucille Ball became pregnant, her pregnancy was written into the story arc of her show, and Lucille gave birth by cesarean section in real life on the same day as Lucy did on the show. It was the single biggest ratings triumph in the history of television up until that time.

By contrast, when Cindy Williams became pregnant, it signaled the end of the long-running *Laverne & Shirley* TV series. In November 1982, newly married to Bill Hudson of the Hudson Brothers musical comedy group, she gave birth to their first child, a daughter. But earlier on, in August, she had walked off the set again . . . this time for good. On her way out, she filed a $20 million lawsuit against the show's producers. She charged that the Marshalls had reneged on a verbal agreement to accommodate her pregnancy by writing it into the show. She also claimed that the same producers had reneged on a further agreement to change her work schedule and pay her agreed-upon per-episode fee even if she missed filming days because of her pregnancy.

"I did not ask for more money," Williams said at the time to *TV Guide*, "all I asked for was my hours in writing. They refused. They then charged that I wasn't able to do the job because I was pregnant. . . . I take great offense that they say I can't work because I am pregnant. What they really want to do is to ace me out of the show, and finally give it all to Penny."

No pregnancy agreement had existed, the producers countered, stating that part of the problem was simply that the pregnant Williams was unable to do her on-camera job. Perhaps most important of all, though, the surprisingly buoyant ratings seemed to give the producers no incentive to woo Cindy back. So they simply wrote her out of the series, having her character wed an Army medic and join him on overseas duty.

What was the Shirl'-less *Laverne & Shirley* like for its final twenty episodes in 1982–83? Much the same as it had been. Penny's many friends pitched in—both *Playboy's* Hugh Hefner and actor/writer Carrie Fisher were guest stars on one show, and Anjelica Huston had a walk-through cameo in another.

Carrie, Laraine Newman from *Saturday Night Live*, and others did side-kick turns with Penny that, earlier, certainly would have been played by Cindy. So it was Carrie—not Cindy—who tried out to be a *Playboy* Bunny in one installment with Laverne; and it was Laraine—not Cindy—in a two-part entry who ended up in a death-row jail cell with Laverne. Otherwise, the stories and on-camera bits remained the same.

One noticeable change was that Laverne got a makeover. She became a bit more glamorous-looking, her blonde hair now teased and sprayed into a bouffant-like Beverly Hills 'do—and she was given a fashion-photographer boyfriend—even as her Old Neighborhood accent perceptibly thickened.

"You are a natural," her boyfriend tells her adoringly in one of the California episodes, "the camera does not lie."

Other installments of *Laverne & Shirley* made sly references to the real Penny, for example by giving Laverne a taste for Pepsi with milk and having her develop an ulcer. In yet another segment, Laverne is distressed that Shirley has deserted her without saying a proper goodbye. Without Shirley to play off of, the sitcom's writers had to stretch, sometimes well beyond the breaking point of credibility.

But the physical, *I Love Lucy*-like *shtick* remained the same: in "The Fashion Show" entry, for example, Laverne sneaks into her new boyfriend's all-important fashion photography show and ends up strutting down the runway in a gigantic gondola hat with which she knocks out the boyfriend's client. Just as when Lucy's antics haunted Ricky Ricardo's career.

Laverne & Shirley, still high enough in the ratings to win its time period, was now in reality just *The Laverne Show.* Penny might have finally gotten it all, but the cost, which included her marriage, had been high. At the end of that season, the show was finally trending down, and when it went off the air on May 10, 1983, it was with a last episode that turned, ironically, on the issue of nepotism. In it, Papa Frank, threatened with the loss of his restaurant, runs for public office, opposing a crooked councilman whose family has been enriched because of nepotism.

Though they'd been named Women of the Year by the Hollywood Radio and Television Society, neither lead actress in *Laverne & Shirley*, which was the most popular show on television in the second half of the 1970s, ever received peer-group recognition in the form of an Emmy or any other such prestigious award. To this day the show is rarely, if ever, included, along with *I Love Lucy, The Mary Tyler Moore Show, All in the Family, M*A*S*H, Cosby*, and *Seinfeld*, in any listing of the medium's best comedies.

Time seems to have healed the rift between Penny and Cindy, who in 1988 even showed up for the *Big* premiere, a crucial moment in Penny's burgeoning career as a film director.

A dozen years after the show's demise, when the *Laverne & Shirley* cast reassembled for the inevitable TV reunion in 1995, Penny Marshall said: "I wish we'd had more confidence in ourselves so we could have enjoyed all the success that was happening rather than be afraid . . . because the industry didn't think it was much of a show. I guess we got scared, so that's why we sometimes fought writing and stuff like that."

Despite the backstage battles, though, they did manage—week after week, season after season—to get it up there on screen, and more often than not Penny and Cindy and Michael and David were funny, endearing, and silly, and to the millions of fans who tuned in faithfully they offered innocence and purity and, even, the possibility of grace.

Chapter Three

Guest Starring As . . .

WITH ENVIABLE SPEED Penny Marshall went from struggling unknown to working actress. Thanks to her comic gifts and her brother Garry, soon she was a universally known television star. Then, in 1988, just five years after her lengthy run on *Laverne & Shirley* was over and she was in her third decade in show business, Penny added Hollywood clout to her Hollywood fame, thanks to the $100 million box office draw for her second feature film, *Big*.

Marshall did struggle in her early career, taking small and insignificant parts, sometimes in obscure films produced by her brother or in TV shows written and produced by her brother or their pals. Later in her career, when Penny certainly didn't need the work for financial reasons, again she took small parts, in both TV and film.

"When I'm working, I'm obsessively working," Penny told *People* magazine in the mid-1990s, "I've lost all concept of what day it is." True enough. However, now that she's become a film director, it's apparent that she hasn't cared to work all that much, directing, on average, a movie only once every few years. (Woody Allen and Steven Spielberg, by contrast, can be reliably expected to direct at least one movie each year. In Spielberg's case he typically oversees one or more additional projects as a producer during the same period.) But doing cameos and taking small parts, usually in friends' projects—whether for James Brooks or Don Johnson—apparently is another matter, and those cameos do keep Penny clearly in the public eye.

Penny Marshall's TV and film career has been spiced with bit parts and guest-starring roles, from an early credit as Plaster Caster in the 1970 movie *The Grasshopper*, to a cameo as herself in the droll final scene of the film version of Elmore Leonard's Hollywood satire, *Get Shorty* (1995).

The Grasshopper, directed by Jerry Paris and starring Jacqueline Bisset, Jim Brown, and Joseph Cotten, is an artifact of late-1960s rock-star-mad pop culture. It was the first theatrical feature to be co-written and co-produced by Garry Marshall, then known only as a successful sitcom writer making his first foray into movies with his writing and producing partner Jerry Belson. Like many Hollywood pictures, *The Grasshopper's* somewhat excruciating production history says more about the ways of Tinseltown than it does about the particular individuals and creative elements attached to (or detached from) the project as it made its torturous way to the big screen.

The project was first announced in 1967, three years before the movie actually debuted. Movie rights to the Mark McShane novel, *The Passing of Evil* (1961), had been acquired by National General Corporation and it would be filmed, in England, from a script by Mel Chaitlin, under the title *Angel*. A search for a major director was under way. A year and a half later, the title and the script were both gone, as was the English setting. Now retitled *The Grasshopper*, the movie was, according to the *Hollywood Reporter*, set to roll "in mid-March (1969) in Las Vegas." The script was now credited to the film's tyro co-producers, Jerry Belson and Garry Marshall, who had been collaborating writers on more than one hundred series episodes, including such TV classics as *I Love Lucy* and *I Spy*. They also won an Emmy for their work on *The Dick Van Dyke Show*.

After the cast was assembled for *The Grasshopper*, but before the production got under way, the original director, Don Medford, bowed out, citing Hollywood's hoary dissolution cliché—creative differences. Belson and Marshall, the two producers from TV land, replaced Medford, a young TV director whose credits then included several episodes of *The Fugitive* and *Alfred Hitchcock Presents* (he would later direct installments of *Airwolf* and *Dynasty*), with Jerry Paris. Paris was another TV director, whose credentials also included *The Dick Van Dyke Show,* one of the seminal television programs on which Garry Marshall had learned his craft.

Paris would go on to direct episodes of Marshall's *The Odd Couple* and *Happy Days,* as well as the second and third *Police Academy* movies in the 1980s. He had once been an actor, and his film credits included small parts in *The Caine Mutiny* (1954), *Marty* (1955), and TV's *The Untouchables* series (1959–63), as well as the recurring role of Jerry Helper on *The Dick Van Dyke Show* in the 1960s.

Paris directed *The Grasshopper* with an uncommon sensitivity toward his cast, and the result was favorable notice for Bisset, a pretty young British actress who'd just made an impression on American moviegoers in the original *Airport* (1970). But his heavier, TV-trained touch was evident when it came to peppering the script with TV-style visual shorthand, such as the quick character-to-character camera pans and fast cutaways that punctuate many of the movie's sitcom-like scenes, as well as the vaudeville-level *shtick*. For example, in one scene, apropos of nothing, a morose, mop-topped Boy says to a clerically collared Priest at a party, where, clearly, both are out of place: "I hate my father, Father." As a result, *The Grasshopper,* originally intended as a serious, cautionary tale of an innocent girl's descent into show-business depravity, turned into an early example of the "dramedy," that hybrid form now so familiar on the small screen.

In the movie, nineteen-year-old Christine Adams (Bisset) escapes her boring existence in a small, picture-postcard Canadian town, only to fall in with Danny the Comic (Corbett Monica), who makes tired wisecracks, and his Vegas-by-way-of-Brooklyn (and the Bronx) cronies. Soon, Christine is living the fast life in Las Vegas as a topless showgirl. Her new friends introduce her to a lounge pop band, Ice Pack, and its two adoring groupies. They experience the joys of pot smoking, popper sniffing, and bad Japanese monster movies on late night TV. It's the beginning of a downward spiral that involves the no-longer-innocent Christine now involved with crass criminals, sugar-daddy millionaires, and, finally, murder and prostitution.

In the brief scene that introduces Ice Pack, the camera pans down from one of the guitarists, who is a *Brady Bunch* clone in a vest over a puffy-sleeved shirt with a huge collar open halfway down his chest, to . . .

Two groupies. Both are wearing matching orange sweatshirts, across the front of which are written in glittery, scrolling letters the words . . .

Plaster Caster.

There was a small group of female rock fans in the sixties who styled themselves as the Plaster Casters, and, as the movie went into production, their titillating doings were the subject of a 1969 *Rolling Stone* magazine story. Whether their activities were early examples of performance art or merely fanatic groupiedom, Cynthia Plaster Caster and her friends were real figures in the surreal rock world of the period, and what they did was make plaster casts of rock stars' penises.

Cynthia Plaster Caster was a Chicago art student in the mid-1960s and she loved rock 'n' roll. When an art school teacher assigned her to make a plaster cast of "something hard," she and her groupie friends decided to "immortalize the erections of rock stars," by casting them in wax, clay, and dental molds, among other substances. Among the rockers she cast were Jimi Hendrix, as well as the "members" of members of such groups as Led Zeppelin, Lovin' Spoonful, MC5, Procol Harum, and Savoy Brown. In the 1990s, she reappeared on the art scene, honored as a performance artist, and, now in her fifties, she's continued her casting among a new generation of punk rockers.

In the movie, as the camera pans down from the Ice Pack's mop-topped guitarist . . . There's Penny Marshall—pink-cheeked, fresh-faced, hair in a longer version of her Myrna Turner shag—in her orange Plaster Caster shirt. Next to her is another young woman, more glamorous, in an orange Plaster Caster blouse.

As the camera catches her, Penny is staring up. An adoring, twinkly, frankly lascivious look is on her young face. In Penny's hand is a tape measure. As she stares up, she pulls it out several inches, retracts it, and pulls it out again. At this visual punchline, there is, of course, a cutaway.

Penny appears once more in the movie, briefly, in the very next scene. This time it's an early version of what later will become the familiar Marshall character, albeit with only the merest trace of the Bronx accent that would serve her so well throughout her career. The Vegas club is quiet and nearly empty. The band is getting ready to leave after its set. In the foreground an Ice Packer sprawls indolently. Atop a nearby table sits the more glamorous Plaster Caster, a self-absorbed blonde staring into a pocket mirror, busily applying makeup. Into the middleground of this scene comes Penny, dejected, schlepping equipment.

"Do you want me to take this amp home or the other one?" she asks plaintively. A pained look crosses her young face. "I'll see you later at the paper," she says to the blonde.

And that's it.

The Grasshopper was the second film produced by the Marshall-Belson duo—two men in their early thirties. Their first movie, *How Sweet It Is!* (1968) was a comedy, starring James Garner and Debbie Reynolds. It was directed by Jerry Paris, and Penny had been given an even smaller part as a Tour Girl. And *How Sweet It Is!*, like *The Grasshopper*, didn't exactly light up the box office.

Just prior to *The Grasshopper* debut, Garry Marshall announced that he and his partner would next do a World War II comedy called *The Lunatic Patrol.*

"This time we're going to do heavy comedy, with moments of tragedy—not the other way round," he told *Daily Variety* in July 1969. However, that picture never materialized. Instead Marshall and Belson retreated from the big screen, returning to their strength—TV situation comedy.

Penny's earliest appearances on TV included a role as a Liberation Lady in the Barbara Eden-David Hartman TV movie, *The Feminist and the Fuzz* (1971). Marshall played the Stewardess on the 1972 episode of *The Bob Newhart Show* entitled "Fly the Unfriendly Skies." In the mid-1970s Penny also appeared on two entries of *The Mary Tyler Moore Show* playing Paula, and on a third as Toni. She also graced an installment of the Jack Albertson-Freddie Prinze comedy, *Chico and the Man*, in October 1975. Along the way, Penny took bit on-camera assignments on such TV series as *Then Came Bronson* (1969), *The Super* (1972), and *Banacek* (1973).

Before Penny's recurring role on *The Odd Couple* ended with that show's demise in the spring of 1975, she was featured as the sister-in-law in the short-lived series *Paul Sand in Friends and Lovers* (1974–75).

In January 1982, Penny Marshall guest-starred as herself on the final episode of *Bosom Buddies,* starring Tom Hanks, whom she later directed in *Big* and *A League of Their Own.*

The series, which debuted in November 1980 and ran for a year and a half on ABC-TV, was produced by the Miller/Milkis/Boyett creative team that had long been associated with Garry Marshall and his TV shows. Thomas L. Miller and Edward K. Milkis were executive producers and Robert L. Boyett was a creative consultant on *Laverne & Shirley.* (Miller and Boyett also went on to produce two more long-running series, *Family Matters* and *Full House.*) Their *Bosom Buddies* sitcom entry struggled with a rather thin, but high-concept, premise:

Artist Kip Wilson (Hanks) and writer Henry Desmond (Peter Scolari) work together in a droll advertising agency—named Livingston, Gentry &

Mishkin—and share an apartment. When their building is torn down and they have nowhere to go, the office receptionist Amy (Wendie Jo Sperber), who has a crush on Henry, suggests they stay at her hotel temporarily, which turns out to be . . .

The Susan B. Anthony Hotel for women. So of course . . .

Kip and Henry must dress up as women so they can stay there.

After Kip meets Amy's gorgeous roommate Sunny (Donna Dixon), he decides to stay at the hotel permanently to be near her and he convinces Henry to stay . . .

To write a book about his experiences living as a woman!

Among show-business professionals there's a telling, and certainly cynical, shorthand way to refer to the idea of high concept, and that's high con. There's an old rule of thumb about high con, popularity, and ratings: the higher the concept, the quicker the rise and then, inevitably, the faster the fall. A series that depends on a gimmick may catch the public's fancy and shoot up in the ratings, but gimmicks soon wear thin, and then the public turns elsewhere. This is particularly true of sitcoms, though other genres often turn on gimmicks as well: the *A-Team* (1983–87), for example, was a high-con action series.

After a year and a half on TV, *Bosom Buddies* finally bowed out, but not before Kip and the gang met Penny Marshall in their final episode, entitled "Cablevision." It was directed by Joel Zwick, who had helmed many *Laverne & Shirley* episodes. Interestingly, for the *Bosom Buddies* finale the cross-dressing gimmick is dispensed with entirely. Kip and Henry are trying to keep a client's account. However, there are no television shows the client wants to advertise in. The boys put on their own cable show, called *Bite the Big Apple*, which he agrees to consider sponsoring.

When their celebrity guest—Penny—doesn't arrive on time, Kip asks irately, "Where's Miss Superstar? Betcha if we had Shirley, she'd be here on time!" The cast improvises madly, and, in spots, amusingly: Kip and Henry juggle. Then they participate in a sketch that spoofs television history, from Ozzie and Harriet to Ed Sullivan to Archie Bunker. When Penny finally appears at the end of the second act, she's bound and gagged, and Kip carries her on stage, dropping her in a chair. Kip's first question to Penny is:

"Is it true that you and Shirley hate each other?"

To which Penny, now ungagged but still tied up, replies, "Why don't you be nice!" And she adds in rib-nudging fashion, "Doing a situation comedy can be murderous—even if you are part of a team. But you wouldn't know anything about that, would ya?"

Then, for their big show-within-the-show finale, Hanks and company bow out by singing *Laverne & Shirley's* theme song: *We'll do it our way, our way, and make all our dreams come true . . .*

A mildly ironic last word finds Kip and Henry assessing their cable-show losses. "Our first venture into television," says Kip, tongue firmly in cheek, "is a complete loss, a complete failure." And with that, *Bosom Buddies* went into the pop-culture history books.

That fall, in November of 1982, Tom Hanks—as if to return the favor—guest-starred on the "A Little Case of Revenge" episode of *Happy Days*, playing Fonzie's former classmate.

In 1985 Penny and fellow comedian Steve Martin made small special appearances in *Movers and Shakers*, a little-seen feature film written by Charles Grodin, starring Grodin and Walter Matthau in a gentle, almost wistful satire of the movie world. It is a story of a screenwriter (Grodin) and a director (Bill Macy of TV's *Maude*) recruited by a beleaguered studio production chief (Matthau) to turn *Love In Sex*, a best-selling sex manual (4 million copies sold!) into a blockbuster motion picture. Essentially a comedy of manners and morays set in the film business of the mid-1980s, its locations include the Paramount lot (standing in for the fictional film studio), a Malibu beach house, and mansions in Bel Air and Beverly Hills. The characters include a disappointed wife, a morose screenwriter, a droll studio head, and ambitious mid-level marketing executives maneuvering to stay on the right side in the intramural studio wars.

Martin, as seventy-year-old movie star Fabio Longio, who's being wooed for the movie, and Marshall, as his screeching harridan girlfriend Reva, have one scene, set in "Casa Longio." And unlike the rest of the low-key picture, it's played way over the top and for big laughs by director William Asher. Martin, hilarious in white wig and red smoking jacket, prances through the marble halls of the *casa*, using his best, Euro-accented wild-and-crazy-guy voice; Marshall, in a pink-feathered night dress over a pink teddy, screams out her few hectoring lines ("Everytime something goes wrong, you blame *me*! And it's always *your* fault!").

Though it was a heartfelt project for Grodin, who also co-produced, the film was generally decried, when it was noticed at all, as too inside. It was, the critics said, essentially a lark made by a talented cast—Tyne Daly, Gilda Radner, Vincent Gardenia, and Michael Lerner—best appreciated by their industry friends.

One of the first hits on the Fox Broadcasting Company, the new fourth network created in the late 1980s, was the witty sketch-comedy, *The Tracey Ullman Show*, starring the talented comedienne and directed by Penny's long-time friend and business partner, Ted Bessell. *The Tracey Ullman Show*, which debuted in 1987, was created and produced by James L. Brooks, another friend of long standing. It begat another early Fox hit, *The Simpsons* (1989–present), also from Brooks, an animated half-hour weekly series which started out as a brief, between-the-sketches animated interlude on *Ullman*, featuring the voices of the regular *Ullman* sketch players. Though *The Simpsons* continues on into its second decade as a critical and ratings hit, and a pop-cultural phenomenon, *The Tracey Ullman Show* was canceled after just three seasons.

A dispute over the lucrative merchandising rights to *The Simpsons* led to a lawsuit filed by Tracey against Brooks and Fox, which Tracey eventually lost. In Hollywood as elsewhere, a professional dispute can disrupt a professional family or a professional friendship, but not in this case. Penny guest-starred on both the first season of *The Simpsons* and on the 1998 season of HBO's Tracey Ullman series, *Tracey Takes On.* . . . And Tracey herself was a guest voice on one *Simpsons* episode "Bart's Dog Gets an F."

Penny's episode on the *Simpsons* was entitled "Some Enchanted Evening," which first aired May 13, 1990. In it, she's the raspy voice of Lucille Botzcowski. When Homer takes Marge out for a nice dinner at the Off Ramp Inn, the babysitter for Bart, Lisa, and little Maggie turns out to be psycho-killer Botzcowski, who's just been profiled on the *America's Most Armed and Dangerous* TV show. (The *Armed and Dangerous* reference in that installment is a sly dig at *America's Most Wanted,* another Fox show. Throughout its long run, *The Simpsons* has repeatedly poked fun at Fox, its executives, and its shows.)

A decade after Penny played herself in *Movers and Shakers,* she played herself again in a much more successful satire of Hollywood's Byzantine and back-biting ways, directed by Barry Sonnenfeld. In the final scene of *Get Shorty* (1995), Penny Marshall is the director shooting a film about a heroic, crime-busting moneylender. It is the ironic happy ending to the film story about the moneylender-turned-movie-producer protagonist, played by John Travolta, in the film-within-the-film. But this wasn't the last time she would play herself on camera.

She's quite obviously supposed to be playing herself as the Goody-Goody Shopper and the Nicer Cop in those popular Kmart commercials with Rosie O'Donnell that began airing in 1996. By then, Penny Marshall herself seemed every bit as created a character as Laverne DeFazio.

In 1998, fifty-six-year-old Penny played New York cop Iris Hellner on an episode of the CBS-TV cop series *Nash Bridges,* set in San Francisco and starring her 1980s pal Don Johnson. "Don's been asking me for a long time to do this, and eventually he wore me down," she said to *People* magazine at the time. The installment, entitled "Skin Deep," which aired during the February sweeps, is set in the world of high fashion and involves the hunt for a super-model's stalker.

Penny told *People* magazine that she'd insisted her on-camera character be from New York because she didn't have time to learn another accent. And from the uncomfortable way she handles her gun in the episode, it appears that she didn't have the time to learn how to properly handle the prop either. But actually, verisimilitude, the convincing appearance of reality in drama, is beside the point here; there's a smiley, in-joke feel to the proceedings, in which the story and the character take second place to—what else?—*shtick*.

In almost every scene in which she appears in her *Nash Bridges* episode, Iris is paired with Joe, the sidekick character played by Cheech Marin of the 1970s drug-humor comedy-duo Cheech & Chong (*Up in Smoke*). The con-tinuing joke is that Iris and Joe hate each other, and that Nash is reduced to refereeing their constant bickering as they argue over who gets to use the phone, who will sit in the car next to Nash, whose case it is (which leads to a brief arm-wrestling scene), and so forth. Rather than *San Francisco Vice* or *SFPD Blue*, the episode instead plays like *Cheech & Laverne*.

The one exception is a brief moment between Iris and Nash, in which she reveals that her husband of twenty-seven years, with whom she's had three children, has divorced her, by telephone, after paging her on a stakeout. Here, in this brief scene, as she says, "I'm too intense, at least that's what my ex-husband tells me," both her look and her tone are unexpectedly moving.

Chapter Four

MAKING MOVIES

W HY IS IT that so many TV sitcom stars from the 1970s made the transition to directing big-screen Hollywood movies? Opie (Ron Howard), Meathead (Rob Reiner), the Fonz (Henry Winkler), Louie (Danny DeVito) from *Taxi*, that guy in drag (Tom Hanks) who was one of the *Bosom Buddie*s and, of course, Laverne.

Encouraged by her brother, Penny Marshall directed some sitcom episodes, including four episodes of *Laverne & Shirley.* Then, when the opportunity arose, the training paid off—at least insofar as she was bold enough to take her shot.

Laverne direct a big studio movie? When, in the mid-1980s, director Howard Zieff (*Unfaithfully Yours*, 1984) abruptly pulled out of Whoopi Goldberg's *Jumpin' Jack Flash* in 1986, citing the usual creative differences, Penny Marshall, Whoopi's friend, was hired on a Friday and began her feature-film directing career the following Monday.

To her big brother, Garry, who gave Penny Marshall and many of her fellow actors—including Scott Baio, Ron Howard, Anson Williams, and Henry Winkler—their first opportunity to direct, it was the simple and rather solidly old-fashioned matter of keeping young people out of trouble by giving them something interesting to do.

"During the 1970s when you had a show that ran ten years, the concern was that young cast members would get antsy and drift into drugs or other trouble," Garry Marshall said to his journalist-daughter Lori in an Internet online interview a few years ago. "[We] were always looking for ways to keep the cast peppy without shoving something up their nose or smoking a funny cigarette. Whenever there was a break, we would teach them about other aspects of the business, which included directing. It was a hobby back then and now many have turned it into a career."

"I don't think they wanted us as actors anymore," was how Penny Marshall, deadpan, answered the same question in another forum (*Los Angeles Times*) in July 1998. She'd addressed the same puzzled query several times over the years, and this was just one variation. "Now they're paying a fortune for TV actors to go into movies. They didn't want us when we were all available."

A droll reply—self-deprecating and diffident—and typical of Penny Marshall, particularly after she became a feature-film director. Back in 1986, when she directed her first feature, it was "relatively rare to have a woman at the helm," she noted in June 1998, as she introduced the second annual Lifetime Women's Film Festival, a cable-television showcase for short first films by young female directors.

"Now, instead of being one of three or four women directing features, I'm one of five or six," she joked, adding, "In reality, there are many more women directing films today, and thousands more who want to."

However, a couple of years before, when her friend Rosie O'Donnell said that she wanted to direct after her TV talk-show career was over, Penny's response was simply: "Don't do it." Around the same time as the Lifetime program, when Penny guest-hosted on Rosie's talk show, there's this on-air exchange when Rosie asks Marshall if she is going to quit smoking:

"I'm going to," says Penny, a most Laverne-like edge of defensiveness in her nasally voice.

"How many times have you quit before?" Rosie inquires.

"Four or five," Penny sheepishly replies.

"And you always go back because . . . ?" Rosie prompts.

And Penny finishes the sentence: "I do a movie."

Between the short films shown on the 1998 Lifetime program, there were brief, interstitial snippets of conversation between Penny and the enthusiastic, young women directors, all of whom were at the beginning of their careers and most definitely did want to be doing it. Penny's on-camera remarks in these brief colloquies are as revealing of her oft-expressed diffidence, bordering on an outright antipathy, toward her chosen craft as anything else she's been caught saying over the years:

"Is there something you say to get you through each day?" Penny asks Dani Minnick, the director of a short film entitled *World Upon Your Shoulder*, "like, 'Please, let this be over?'" To Nicola Hart, writer as well as director of *Icebergs: The Secret Life of a Refrigerator*, Marshall remarks, "Writing seems like a lonely job, not that directing's not. When the crew goes home, you go, 'Where did all those people go?'" And to Paula Walker, a ballet-trained former dancer and the director of *Seed: A Love Story*, Penny notes that she had once been a precision tap dancer herself.

"Does it help you when you're directing?" she asks.

Yes, Paula replies, and Penny looks askance. "How so?" she asks. "It doesn't help me."

"Style of movement is part of the way I see a character," says the first-time director quite sensibly.

In response, Marshall offers Walker practical advice on how to handle actors. "Half of the job is groveling." Screwing up her face, she illustrates: "'Please say the words. Please come on time.' . . . They think it's a big power job," she concludes. "Basically, it's compromise."

Her on-camera advice to the thousands of women who want to direct movies: "Sometimes the best way to start is by making a short film." It was not, however, the way she herself started out.

Penny's first times in the director's chair were for four episodes of *Laverne & Shirley*, all of them airing during the second half of the ABC-TV show's lengthy run, and the final two as part of the California entries that came at the very end. Unlike feature films, however, series television is not a director's medium so much as it is a writer/producer's medium. Often, the visiting series-episode director hands over a less-than-complete rough cut of the program, leaving it to the show's creators—its writers and producers—to polish up.

In series TV—then as now—directors are usually merely the hired guns, going from assignment to assignment, from series to series. There are exceptions—Jim Burrows of *Cheers*, who directed almost every single episode of that hugely successful series, and Jerry Paris of *Happy Days* and *Laverne & Shirley*. It's most often the writer/producers who, in today's industry parlance, are the show runners. They guide the TV series over time, and along with the writers, design the show—the physical look and feel, the characters and their back stories, the plots of episodes, and the arcs of seasons. They and the camera and lighting people, the makeup artists, the costumers and other technicians comprise the working professional family that stays—week after week and year after year—with a weekly small-screen show.

Therefore, to direct an episode in series television means to come into a preexisting, more or less smoothly running, environment. TV directors, particularly sitcom directors, are typically handed a script, which they then run through with the actors at the initial reading (the so-called table read, at which director, actors, and writers all sit around a table, scripts in hand, cold reading through their lines—adding, cutting, making suggestions). Their job also includes guiding the subsequent round of rehearsals before shooting day and establishing rapport among the regulars and that week's guest stars, making certain the newcomers are reasonably comfortable in what is often a highly charged situation.

Directors work on sharpening the timing of the actors' delivery and particularly on those all-important punchlines. They make certain to get abundant coverage for each shot and scene, so each moment is filmed from multiple angles and views using multiple cameras. They're also responsible for getting the actors to hit their marks (actual little color-coded X's taped to the concrete floor of the sound stage), and the various cameras to glide to their spots, for exactly the right shots at exactly the right time.

Penny Marshall—a beginning TV director who was just learning her craft—exhibited preferences and tendencies in her *Laverne & Shirley* episodes that added up to a discernible film style. For one thing she directed herself only minimally, employing plot devices that got Laverne—and Shirley—out of the story, and off camera.

In an on-set environment where Cindy Williams was counting lines and measuring on-camera face time with a stopwatch to make sure she was being treated equally, it's perhaps too much to expect Penny to have used her first directorial opportunities to show generosity toward her costar. For example, instead of directing an episode in which, say, Laverne is out of town, leaving Shirley to cope alone, Penny chose to focus primarily on Lenny and Squiggy.

The title "Squiggy in Love," the first of the four episodes Penny directed, speaks for itself.

In the second, "The Duke of Squiggmann," Laverne and Shirley leave for a three-day wedding in Chicago at the beginning of the installment. They turn their apartment over to Lenny and Squiggy, who sleep in the living room. Carmine, who's being paid twenty-five cents an hour to keep watch over the dimbulb duo, gets to sleep alone in the bedroom. Laverne and Shirley leave and remain absent for the remainder of the episode.

The third episode, "The Dating Game" focuses on what happens when Lenny and Squiggy become Bachelor Number Two and Bachelor Number Three on *The Dating Game*, a daytime TV game show.

In the opening sequence, in which Shirley finds Laverne stretched out on the couch in a slinky, sexy, form-fitting dress, her shoulders bare except for spaghetti straps, Penny demonstrates a noteworthy care for her own image. The dress, which Laverne has just bought for $9.95 from Frederick's of Hollywood, is so tight, Laverne can't get out of it. So, she and Shirley, now entangled, spin and tug and hop around their apartment, in one of the bits of physical business they were so skilled at together, trying to get it off.

When their neighbor Rhonda (Leslie Easterbrook) finally comes to the rescue, pulling the garment off over Laverne's head, there's a brief but obvious cut (an edit to another version of the same moment), allowing Laverne's head to reappear with her hair only minimally—and attractively—mussed. After first-act *shtick* about Shirley trying to help Laverne wiggle out of a tight dress, the duo is only in a few second-act cutaways, watching the boys on TV from home.

And the fourth, "But Seriously, Folks," is all about Squiggy's attempt at stand-up comedy.

Penny's episodes have more than the usual *Laverne & Shirley* quotient of sentiment. In "The Duke of Squiggman," for example, Penny gives Lenny an opportunity to sing a lullaby and Squiggy a brief speech (about realizing that people really do dislike him). His words have a touch of genuine emotion (whether it's pathos or bathos, though, is for the individual viewer to judge), complete with tinkling piano accompaniment on the soundtrack.

In TV, unlike feature films, the director also tends to not learn the technology. For one thing, on a sitcom with standing sets used over and over, week after week, the various technical levels—for lights, sound, and so forth—are preset. What variation and innovation exist happen within very narrow, very defined parameters. If last week's entry began with a full shot of the living room that tracked toward a door as the main character(s) entered, chances are that this week's episode will not open with a flaming car crash or a shootout, but will be repeated angle for angle, shot for shot and lens for lens.

According to Rosie O'Donnell's biographer, James Robert Parish, when the "fledgling screen player" once asked Penny what she knew about various camera lenses, the latter responded in her familiar twangy New Yorkese, 'What lenses schmenzes? You hi-ah the D.P. [director of photography] ta know dat. You don't gotta know dat. You gotta know what's funny.'"

Penny brought that TV mindset and her sitcom-honed (or -dulled) sensibility to the world of theatrical-feature filmmaking, and time after time she was criticized for it. As the years have gone by, though, the movie-going audience has become ever more conditioned to both television subject matter and television techniques, including quick MTV-style cutting and multiple cameras. TV-trained sensibilities have gained ever greater currency and respectability. Meanwhile, precipitously rising movie production costs have meant that TV-trained directors, experienced at making do with tight budgets and condensed schedules, have become ever more prevalent in the movie world.

"It was a shock to me, on my first movie, to find out they didn't use multiple cameras," Penny said in May 1994 after directing her fifth big-screen movie. She further told *Millimeter* magazine, "I had to listen to the same words all day. . . . I mean, I'm used to doing forty [script] pages in one night because I'm from three-camera television.

"We do it for an audience [in television sitcoms]. The fact that movie people couldn't memorize more than four lines was shocking to me. And listening to these words over the single, the master, all day long for the same two pages, made me crazy."

Jumpin' Jack Flash

The "film's a mess," sniffed *Variety* on October 15, 1986. The influential show-biz trade paper's review pithily summarized prevailing opinion about Penny Marshall's debut as a big-screen film director by declaring that her *Jumpin' Jack Flash* was "not a gas," but a "bore."

The spy comedy was eagerly awaited by fans of Whoopi Goldberg, who, in the space of a few short years in the mid-1980s, had gone from hip stand-up comic, to Broadway monologist, to Academy Award–nominated actress. *Jumpin' Jack Flash* (1986) was her misbegotten follow-up to her dazzling performance as Celie in the Steven Spielberg film *The Color Purple* (1985), which had marked her own big-screen debut and had earned her a Best Actress Oscar nomination. But though *Flash* was a fizzle, it was not Hollywood's sophomore jinx or Whoopi herself who got the blame, even though it was widely noted that after the original director bowed out, it was Whoopi who suggested hiring her pal Penny.

The *Hollywood Reporter's* review (October 10, 1986) granted that Whoopi's performance was "sometimes shrewd," but the screen comedy itself was a failure and Penny Marshall's "lightweight direction" and the "sorry" script were judged the "main culprits."

In what was a distinctly minority opinion, the *Los Angeles Times,* Hollywood's hometown consumer, or general-circulation newspaper, allowed that even if *Flash* was merely "formula tongue-in-cheek thriller pabulum," as a director, Penny showed "promise."

A more typical verdict on the quality of Penny's direction focused on her TV background: *Jumpin' Jack Flash* had the "plodding humor of a bad TV sitcom," said the cineaste-minded *Village Voice.* "The audience gets just about every joke before the characters do. The film wallows in the predictable."

Although dismissive toward the new theatrical-feature director, the reviewers, consumer and trade press alike, generally noted that Penny had stepped into the production on short notice, after the original director departed. And despite taking a condescending tone toward the material, most critics gave Whoopi glowing notices (e.g., "If this film is even watchable, it's because Goldberg's so damn good," was how *Los Angeles* magazine summarized it).

The critics' generosity regarding *Jumpin' Jack Flash* extended to saluting the superior quality of Whoopi's supporting cast, which included Jim Belushi, Bob "Bobcat" Goldthwait, Phil Hartman, Carol Kane, Jeroen Krabbé, Jon Lovitz, Annie Pots, Jonathan Pryce, and Tracey Ullman. (Penny's brother and daughter had small roles, Garry as a detective and Tracy a secretary.) Unfortunately, when it came to reviewing Penny Marshall movies, complimenting the cast while disparaging the script and the director was the start of a trend.

What most of the contemporary critics of *Jumpin' Jack Flash* failed to notice was that Penny Marshall had come into a floundering big studio film project, and—because of her network of friends and industry contacts—within days had cast an uncommonly rich group of comics and character actors in all the key supporting roles. Instead of appreciation for that feat, or for the spunk she displayed by taking on the big-screen project at all, what she heard from most of the critics was scorn.

"Miss Marshall directs . . . as if she were more worried about the decor than the effect of the performance," proclaimed the *New York Times* in an utterly typical example of the kind of criticism that was heaped on the brand-new movie director. The type of criticism—easy and without nuance—persisted right through to the comedy's video release, when one trade publication called it "flat, predictable, and unevenly paced, thanks to the writing and Penny Marshall's direction."

What the critics who decry Penny's middle-of-the-road form of movie making persistently overlook is the fact that it is a choice, more than a lack of ability. Hers is a demystified, working class approach to directing, which, in many ways, harks back to the days of the studio system. No auteur, Penny Marshall is a clock-puncher, a craftsperson practicing a trade.

As Garry Marshall so memorably put it: "There's more to life than show business."

And as veteran actor Mickey Rooney once said, as he sat down for a meal at a Manhattan restaurant, expressing a view to which Penny herself might subscribe: "This is what you have to know how to say: 'Roll 'em. Cut. Once more. Lunch. Wrap.' There's nothing else to do. This fellow who sat us here at the table can make a picture."

Say what you will about the 100-minute, R-rated *Jumpin' Jack Flash,* it has a place in the history of movies beyond marking Penny Marshall's inauspicious feature-film directorial debut and Whoopi Goldberg's succumbing to Hollywood's famed sophomore jinx.

Jumpin' Jack Flash is also one of the top-ten computer networking movies of all time, according to NetworkWorld Abend, an Internet Web site which has compiled a list that includes such cyber classics as *Colossus: The Forbin Project* (1970), in which a computer tries to take over the world; *The Lawnmower Man* (1992), about a simple-minded gardener who becomes a super-intelligent, virtual-reality monster; and *Johnny Mnemonic* (1995), sci-fi noir in which a futuristic courier downloads dangerous information directly into his brain.

All lists like this are subjective, and invariably less than inclusive. For example, 1964's *Fail-Safe,* about a computer failure that nearly leads to World War III, is not on this list, though 1983's *War Games,* which has the same basic premise, is. However, it is noteworthy that *Flash* has the lightest-hearted touch of any of the films on the Network World list, and is the only out-and-out comedy.

Jumpin' Jack Flash is the story of Terry Doolittle (Whoopi), a cheery and whimsical computer operator who works in the international money-transfer department of a New York bank. When messages from someone code-named Jumpin' Jack Flash start appearing on her computer monitor, she finds herself in the middle of a complex espionage caper in which she has to save Jack, who turns out to be a British spy "trapped behind the Iron Curtain." Terry's spirited, impromptu rescue effort requires such unlikely maneuvers as listening to the title's Rolling Stones song in her cluttered and freezing-cold Manhattan apartment (to puzzle out Jack's key-code password) and dressing as Diana Ross, in full Supremes' drag (to crash a posh British Embassy party).

Viewed without the critical rancor that attended its opening, *Jumpin' Jack Flash,* while clearly not a good or successful picture (though it eked out a small profit) is—yes, thanks to Whoopi's charm and that strong supporting cast of colorful characters—quite entertaining. And for this the director certainly must deserve *some* portion of the credit.

The movie's biggest disappointment—also viewed with the benefit of hindsight—must be that the plot fails to treat Whoopi as it might have a Caucasian actress playing the same part; that is, there is no attempt made to introduce a romance between Whoopi's character and the dashing British spy whom she saves. And for this the director certainly must bear *some* portion of the blame.

The movie, which cost $15 million to make, was battered by the hostile reviews, and took in only $11 million at the North American box office. But theatrical revenues are only one factor in the new math of the new Hollywood, and *Jumpin' Jack Flash* eventually became profitable through international distribution and video-rental revenues.

It was the go-go mid-1980s and Hollywood was awash in Wall Street money. TV actors were bankable, screenwriters were replaceable, and blockbuster producers like Lawrence Gordon and Joel Silver and producer-directors like Steven Spielberg and James Brooks were king. No one sets out to make a bad

movie, and in the heady atmosphere of the period, the idea behind *Jumpin'
Jack Flash* must at one time have seemed irresistible.

If a bullets-and-brawn movie developed for Sylvester Stallone could be
turned into *Beverly Hills Cop,* a comic thriller starring Eddie Murphy that
was 1984's big summertime hit, then why not convert *Sweet Dreams* (also
known as *Knock Knock*), a movie that originally was supposed to star *Cheers*
TV actress Shelley Long (who dropped out, citing creative differences), into a
comic thriller starring Whoopi, who would promptly metamorphose into
the female Eddie?

Talented she was, versatile she was, but . . . *Whoopi Goldberg action hero?!*

Perhaps it could have worked, but as Whoopi told *Newsweek* magazine, as
many as eighteen different writers toiled on the script (though only four
were ultimately credited). Once the cameras were finally rolling, the screenplay was jettisoned anyway.

Then there was the problem of keeping the cameras rolling at all.
Filming first got under way in New York City in November of 1985, with
veteran director Howard Zieff at the helm. Three weeks into the shoot, he
and his entire staff were fired. Zieff explained to the *Hollywood Reporter,* "We
couldn't come to an arrangement about the script."

Handing the reins of a troubled picture to a forty-three-year-old first-
time director, and to one who'd directed only a few episodes of *Laverne &
Shirley,* might not have seemed like the best decision. However, Penny was
willing and available on short notice, the star was getting skittish and, as
Penny recounted it more than ten years later, she just happened to be the
star's first choice. So she and Whoopi took the idea to Joel Silver, who was
producing the picture with Lawrence Gordon, and he agreed to have Marshall
attached to the screen project.

How Penny got her first directing job became an oft-told story over the
years. Of course, usually she focused on her own insecurities and the advice
she'd gotten from friends and from big brother Garry: "I called my brother

and I called Jim Brooks [the producer of *The Simpsons*]," she said a half-decade after the fact, "and said whaddya think. And my brother said, 'They pay you to learn, strange business.' And Jim said, you have nothing to lose, if it doesn't do good it's not your fault, you didn't start it, and if you complete it, you've done good."

The tale of how Penny jumped precipitously into Twentieth Century-Fox's *Jumpin' Jack Flash* also centered on her friendship with Whoopi. In her 1996 *Premiere* magazine Q & A session with Rosie O'Donnell, Penny told an interesting variation on the story that she and Whoopi had taken the idea to the producers. In its undercurrent of bitterness lies probably more than just a hint of what really may have happened.

"I was in New York, and I ran into Whoopi at a restaurant and we hung out. I think the producers or the studio people saw us and said, 'Oh look, they're talking to each other. They must be friends. Let's make her do it.' I swear to God, I think that's what happened. . . . [And the first day on the set] I think Whoopi was so shocked. . . . But what was she going to say, 'Get out'? They put her in a bad position. All of a sudden they said, 'Marshall is coming.' She didn't want to say no. I thought she'd been asked."

Even while the film was still in production, Whoopi seemed less than thrilled by the direction it was taking under her tyro director.

"Don't ask," was her reply when she was queried by *Newsweek* magazine in December 1985 as to how the shoot was going. "It used to be [a spy story]. . . . This week it's a comedy. We're evolving."

Years later, Whoopi was still certain whose fault the failure of her second movie had been: "Penny wanted it big and broad. I like subtlety," she said on one occasion. She portrayed Penny as "standing behind the camera giving me nuances as I was working, as the camera was rolling, showing me what she wanted to see."

Big

With 1988's *Big,* her second time in the director's chair, Penny Marshall confounded almost every critical and industry expectation. After all, the conventional insider wisdom was: hadn't Laverne fallen flat on her face with *Jumpin' Jack Flash* just two years earlier?

As usual, insider Hollywood loved dining out on dish, and next to revenge, the dish it fancied most was *schadenfreude,* that delicious tisk-tisk gloating at someone else's expense. Insiders were quite capable of fixating on negative reviews and ignoring both a modest profit and the sheer accomplishment of—as James Brooks had counseled Penny—just getting it done.

How good could *Big* be, went insider thinking, the Disney studio hadn't even previewed it? That was a sure sign to the Hollywood *cognoscenti* that it would be another disaster. And it was going up against *Willow* (1988), the sure-fire new swords-and-sorcery movie produced by George "*Star Wars*" Lucas, and directed by Ron Howard who, with films like *Splash* (1984), had already left his Richie Cunningham and Opie identities behind.

Nevertheless, Penny Marshall hit a home run with a sensitive crowd-pleasing romantic fantasy that buried the competition and connected with the mass audience to the tune of $100 million at the box office. As the *Wall Street Journal* put it:

"Who would have thought that Penny Marshall, best known for her part in TV's *Laverne & Shirley,* would recover from her embarrassing film directing debut (*Jumpin' Jack Flash*) with something this sprightly and sure-handed?"

By 1988, the TV mentality had taken firm hold at the movie studios. The idiosyncratic visions of individual auteurs—directors like Martin Scorsese, Francis Ford Coppola, Brian DePalma, and Michael Cimino—had fueled an American film renaissance in the 1970s. Searching for a way to connect with the burgeoning youth audience, studio executives had tried film-school-trained,

European-style auteurs with their sociologically minded and character-driven pictures, arty and even experimental. Though the auteur movies of the 1970s were critical hits, often they were also box-office failures.

By the late 1980s that creative movement was history, though the auteurs themselves kept directing, generally making either commercial failures or middle-brow studio pictures. The reign of the auteur had been replaced by the event blockbuster. Both the idea and the terminology behind the blockbuster concept had been imported from the high-stakes world of network TV by new studio executives such as Barry Diller, Michael Eisner, and Jeffrey Katzenberg—all television-trained.

The one-time TV execs knew how to bring in the kids: high concepts, special effects, and amusement-park-style thrills! Easily promotable stories and familiar faces were imported directly from television. The once-maligned small-screen medium now offered a blueprint for the future.

TV was a medium with a message for the movie world: one hit show could become a must-see event, the tentpole lifting the ratings and the revenues for an entire night of programming. The same was true of the picture show; a movie could even become a franchise, a series—a formula repeated over and over, until the box-office well ran dry.

As in TV, imitation in movies soon became more than just simply the sincerest form of flattery: it was installed by the former TV executives running the studios as the industry's basic business practice. Sequels were in, genres were mined and mined until they were played out, then left fallow for a few years until it was their turn again. If one Robin Hood movie was worth making, then it was inevitable that two or even three would go into development. The same for prehistoric monsters, marauding aliens, exploding volcanoes, or hurtling asteroids.

And so it was that the year *Big* was released, 1987–88, not one but three movies on the same fantasy subject of role reversal made it all the way to the box office. They were: *Like Father, Like Son* (starring Dudley Moore and Kirk

Cameron, who became famous on TV's *Growing Pains*), *Vice Versa* (starring Judge Reinhold and Fred Savage, who became popular on TV's *The Wonder Years*), and *18 Again!* (starring Tony Roberts and Charlie Schlatter, who played the title role in the small-screen version of *Ferris Bueller*).

Role-reversal and body-swap fantasies have a rich cinematic history, dating all the way back to a silent version of *The Prince and the Pauper*. In 1977, for example, teenaged Jodie Foster and her mom, played by Barbara Harris, magically traded places in *Freaky Friday* (the same formula that *Vice Versa* and *Like Father, Like Son* repeated a decade later). In 1980, in *Oh, Heavenly Dog!*, Chevy Chase swapped places with a sheepdog! And under less fantastical circumstances, Dan Aykroyd and Eddie Murphy exchanged lives with each other in *Trading Places* (1983), as did Steve Martin and Lily Tomlin in *All of Me* (1984). Francis Ford Coppola's *Peggy Sue Got Married* (1986), starring Kathleen Turner, spun a distaff version of the essential *Big* story. There, its heroine, instead of wishing to grow big, is an adult married woman who finds that she's gone back in time to inhabit a teenage version of herself. (Ironically, when *Peggy Sue* was in development in the mid-1980s, there were two other directors attached before Coppola. Originally, the director was to be Jonathan Demme, who went on to direct *The Silence of the Lambs* (1991), *Philadelphia* (1993), and *Beloved* (1998); he was followed by a second director, who also left due to creative differences. That director was Penny Marshall.)

Perhaps the biggest reversal of all, though, was the one done by the critics. Their sneers at Laverne's nerve for trying to direct another big-screen film (and whose confident expectations were that *Big* would be the last small gurgle from an over-played, overly cute, and saccharine genre) turned into captivated smiles.

Big is the story of twelve-year-old Josh (David Moscow) who wishes to be "big." When that wish is granted by Zoltar Speaks, a carnival wishing machine, young Josh turns into adult Josh (Tom Hanks), but he's still a boy in a man's body. After his unsuspecting mother chases him as an intruder out of the house the next morning, Josh/Hanks finds his way to a job at a toy company, where his kid-like ways soon impress the boss (Robert Loggia), who promotes him, and a careerist female colleague (Elizabeth Perkins), who attempts to seduce him.

Preposterous as the premise might have seemed, the director's light touch and her cast's—particularly Hanks'—unwavering believability in every situation (from the dancing duo of Loggia and Hanks on the F.A.O. Schwartz walking piano to the dancing dialogue in the Hanks and Perkins overnight scene, in which he insists on being "on top" and then grabs . . . the upper bunk) made it work. Along with the critics, film-going audiences were transported.

Inevitably, there was a thorn or two among all the critical bouquets. A number of the reviewers, while praising both Penny Marshall and the script, duly noted that the director was the sister of one filmmaker and one of the co-screenwriters, Anne Spielberg, was the sister of another.

Throughout her career, Penny Marshall had been criticized for benefiting from nepotism, and clearly she owed both the start of that career and her big break to her big brother Garry. In her case, though, connections may have gotten her through the door and into the room where the players were, but it was still skill, pluck, and luck that kept her in the game. After her first picture, it might have been the easiest course to take her detractors' implicit advice and never direct another movie again.

Inside the business, people may have been jealous of the family connections that led to her opportunities, but most likely no one thought it improper. Naked nepotism—that is, the practice of granting business favors or patronage to relatives—was, and is, a commonplace in Hollywood. In fact, it may be looked down upon or even banned in other industries and other parts of society. In the awards-crazed Tinseltown of the 1990s, nepotism has now been elevated (by a branch of the American Film Institute) to the Platinum Circle Award, which honors the artistic contributions of an entire family.

The award's first winners were not the Fondas or the Carradines, the Bridges or the Baldwins, not even the Spellings or the Marshalls, but . . .

The Matthaus—father Walter (the Oscar-winning actor), son Charles (a director and sometime actor), and mother Carol (an occasional writer).

Nonetheless, for a brief and shining moment in 1988, nepotism was generally forgotten and even Laverne was forgiven. Seemingly overnight, Penny Marshall became the critical discovery *du jour*, and the very same reviewers who said that Marshall as a film director was a ham-fisted flash in the pan now chorused their approval, even when they didn't completely succumb all the way to the movie's gentle charms. "A formula fantasy movie that has been directed very tactfully, very gently, by Penny Marshall; she sleepwalks you through from start to finish," said *The New Yorker's* Pauline Kael, perhaps the most influential film critic of her time. Few others were as measured in their praise. (Except for the *New York Times* which gratefully said, "Miss Marshall minimizes the sentimentality and keeps things mercifully sweet.")

"She has a gracious touch," *New York* magazine noted, and, as the *New Republic* put it, "directed . . . with some communicated enjoyment."

Daily Variety, which, like the *Hollywood Reporter*, rarely had credited Penny with much of anything in the past praised her, "Credit goes to Penny Marshall for pulling it off so smoothly on screen." While the *Dallas Morning News* said flat out: "'Big' is a triumph."

For the delicacy and accuracy of his performance as a twelve-year-old boy in a thirty-year-old man's body, relative newcomer Tom Hanks also received the best notices of his career to date. Robert De Niro, known to be one of Penny's large circle of show-business friends, had originally been touted for the role and allegedly passed because he'd been offered only $3 million—just half of what Warren Beatty was then getting for a movie—to take the part.

Another truism in Hollywood is that casting is the most crucial ability any movie director can have, and this time Penny got the credit for smart casting—not only for Hanks, but for Elizabeth Perkins as his love interest and Robert Loggia as the president of the MacMillan Toy Company.

Big was shot mostly in and around New York City. According to the late Christopher Vaughn, a journalist specializing in the Big Apple's film and TV worlds, the "Zoltar Speaks" scene was filmed at an amusement park in Fort Lee, New Jersey. The toy company where Josh works was the offices of the Bozell, Jacobs, Kenyon and Eckhardt advertising agency, and the F. A.O. Schwartz piano dance was filmed at the famed toy emporium on Fifth Avenue.

In a business where directors are expected to be no-nonsense autocrats, Marshall's self-described method on *Big* was different: "I whine, then I sulk for a while. Then it comes around my way," she said in the July 1988 issue of *Life* magazine, which described her "crutches" as "cigarettes, White Tower burgers, [and] Pepsi mixed with milk."

Of course, that taste-bud-curdling drink wouldn't have come as a surprise to dedicated *Laverne & Shirley* viewers, who knew that Laverne's favorite drink, which she even tried to press on *Playboy*'s Hugh Hefner in one episode, was Pepsi mixed with milk.

In the late 1980s, upward-spiraling production costs resulted in one of Hollywood's periodic crises of profligacy, which of course meant that jobs in the lower echelons at the studios were being trimmed and the most visible symbols of out-of-control spending were (temporarily) curbed. This meant cutting back on the traditional lavish post-premiere party. These were not fetes for the cast and crew, except for the stars and the few crew members above-the-line (i.e., the director, the writer, perhaps the cinematographer and editor), as much as they were social gatherings for talent agents, execs, and the media. They were intended to stroke egos and attract the attention of the media cameras and the columnists. The costs could easily reach into the hundreds of thousands of dollars.

Big, however, had not just one but two premiere screenings, in June 1988. First, there was the klieg-lights-and-red-carpets media premiere in Westwood, the theatre-rich shopping district that serves UCLA and abuts Brentwood and the rest of the tony Westside of Los Angeles, where most of the top players in the film business resides. There was also a simultaneous screening at the Zanuck Theatre on the Twentieth Century-Fox lot a few minutes' drive away. The post-screening party for two thousand guests was held on the *Hello, Dolly!* street set on the Fox lot. To complement the film's amusement park theme, two hundred workers constructed a "football field–size carnival . . . complete with Ferris wheel, scrambler, merry-go-round, fifteen game booths, psychics, jugglers, and a dozen food stations with everything from fajitas to Philly cheese steak sandwiches."

What did throwing a big movie party in tough economic times signify? When Twentieth Century-Fox hosted the most lavish post-premiere party of the season for *Big,* it was widely seen as a vote of confidence in Penny Marshall's project, and a signal to Tinseltown's filmmakers and creative community: Come to us—the party was meant to convey—and we will treat you right.

By early in the new year, *Big* earned what was perhaps the ultimate late 1980s industry accolade: the concept was put into development as a pilot for a possible CBS series.

But did any of this bring a smile to the face of the dyspeptic sophomore film director? Penny had glumly chain-smoked her way through the *Flash* debacle, and that's exactly how she reacted in public to her *Big* triumph. The post-premiere party was attended by a Hollywood *Who's Who* that included Arnold Schwarzenegger and Debra Winger, as well as top producers and studio heads, and both her brother Garry and her former *Laverne & Shirley* costar Cindy Williams. According to the *Los Angeles Times* report, Penny was, "dressed in black . . . chain-smoking and doing a great imitation of a woman on the edge of a nervous breakdown."

Awakenings

And the nominees for Best Director are . . . Penny Marshall for Awakenings . . .

Not!

If Penny Marshall was bitter about being left out of Oscar's Best Director short list in a year when her 1990 *Awakenings* was one of the Academy of Motion Picture Arts and Sciences' nominees for Best Picture, she, perhaps uncharacteristically, did not show it. After all, she was a show-business trouper, and troupers know that whining is only attractive when it's funny; that is, when it's *shtick.*

But if the revelation of *Big* was that Penny Marshall was a film director with sensitivity, a revelation that overcame critical quibbles about her easy resort to sentimentality, then with *Awakenings,* the issue of distracting *shtick* itself became the problem for the theatrical-film director who had learned her craft all too well in her brother's TV sitcom laugh factory.

No doubt with *Awakenings* in mind, one veteran film critic, John Anderson (in a review of Robert Townsend's 1997 movie *B.A.P.S.*), even coined the term "Penny Marshall Syndrome" to describe a "good director of middle-brow comedy, [who] loses his composure when matters turn serious. The music swells. So do the tears. The buoyancy goes pooooof, and the film goes slack with sentiment."

In television, even the best situation comedies tend to turn all of human experience and the entire range of human emotions from joy to tragedy, into an occasion for *boom-bada-boom . . .*

Shtick.

Shtick, of course, is another show-business Yiddishism. The word means literally "a bit" or "a piece," and it has come to mean primarily "a piece of comic business." Vaudeville *shtick*, an early usage, describes the familiar ancient jokes and "bits of business" like selzer-spritzing and baggy-pants comics.

Whether it was Fonzie's posturings, Laverne's wide-eyed physicality, or Mork from Ork's rubbery, mime-based doubletakes and absurdist improvisations on TV's *Mork & Mindy* (1978–82), *shtick* was the specialty of the Garry Marshall sitcom house.

How far would a 1970s-era Marshall sitcom go for the easy laugh? As far as necessary, even to the toilet for repeated diarrhea jokes involving a fat tourist lady in "Not Quite South of the Border," one *Laverne & Shirley* episode directed by Joel Zwick.

At the other end of the *shtick* spectrum is "bathos," or overdone "pathos," which generally is defined as an "artistic representation evoking pity or compassion." Of course the line between the two is somewhat in the eye of the beholder, but ever since the singers of sad songs shared playbills with the comics back in vaudeville days, teary bathos has been another easy way to tug at an audience's emotions. *Laverne & Shirley* indulged in this easy-sentiment ploy from time to time, and even rose to genuine pathos in an episode entitled "The Slow Child," about the touching relationship between Edna's "retarded" daughter and Squiggy.

Perhaps the premier example of pathos sliding over into bathos in *Laverne & Shirley* is "Why Did the Fireman . . . ," another episode directed by Zwick, in which Ted Danson of *Cheers* guest stars as paragon-of-virtue fireman Randy Carpenter, who's so madly in love with Laverne that he intends to pop the question at the firehouse. Randy is consistently interrupted on the very verge of proposing—first by Shirley and Carmine, then by Lenny in a plastic raincoat and Squiggy in a yellow Macintosh. Then finally, when Randy is down on one knee, he is interrupted by the fire alarm.

Randy fights the fire heroically, between acts, and Act Two opens with the announcement of his tragic death. Most of the rest of the episode consists of a touching conversation between Laverne and her Papa Frank.

Shtick provides the quick smiles (or rather, snorts) of low humor and the even quicker tears of cheap sentimentality; it depends on proven audience reaction to the very familiar. That the consumers of pop culture have been trained to expect *shtick* is undeniable.

Many critics recommended *Awakenings*, praising both the actors and Marshall's direction, and the Academy of Motion Picture Arts and Sciences found it worthy of consideration for its biggest prize. However, the most influential of the critical voices found *Awakenings* overly sentimental and lacking in the gravity and complexity appropriate to its unbelievable-but-true subject matter. In short, they were put off by the film's overuse of *shtick*. As Janet Maslin summarized in the *New York Times*, the movie "both sentimentalizes its story and oversimplifies it beyond recognition. At no point does the film express more than one idea at a time. And the idea expressed, more often than not, is as banal as the reality was bizarre."

The fault, attributed equally to Marshall's direction and the formulaic script by Steven Zaillian (probably best known as the screenwriter of *Schindler's List*), was, in a word, *shtick*.

Awakenings starred Robert De Niro and Robin Williams. It was based on the book of the same name by neurologist Oliver Sacks, who also wrote *The Man Who Mistook His Wife for a Hat* and *The Island of the Colorblind*. The 1973 Sacks book, from which both a 1974 British documentary and a Harold Pinter one-act stage play, *A Kind of Alaska,* were also made, told the true story of a remarkable, but ultimately heartbreaking, moment in medical research.

In the mid-1960s, Sacks was a young researcher in a Bronx, New York, hospital, where a group of long-term sufferers of an encephalitis-caused sleeping sickness were warehoused. They had been in a motionless, speechless vegetative state, in some instances for decades—ever since a world-wide encephalitis epidemic in the 1920s.

And yet, some had remained internally lucid and aware of their immediate surroundings in the hospital. It was Sacks' insight that these living statues, who'd passed through the twitches and tremors of Parkinson's disease on their way to total immobility, might benefit from the new Parkinson's disease drug, L-dopa.

For up to a fourth of the sleepers, the results were nothing short of miraculous. L-dopa awakened an entire population of Rip Van Winkles! Movement, speech, life in the present-day world was restored. In many cases they'd gone to sleep as young men and women in the 1920s. To then be awakened in the 1960s as old people, with decades of their lives gone, was replete with confusion and stress. But, the "miracle" itself turned out to be short-lived. The drug was no cure. Gradually, one by one, their Parkinsonian tremors returned, and the statues went back to sleep.

The movie Penny Marshall made from the Steven Zaillian script based on this material smoothed the story down (some would say dumbed it down) in a number of ways. First, and perhaps most unavoidably, the story was now focused on the relationship between one patient, Leonard (Robert De Niro), and Doctor Sacks, inexplicably (given that the real Sacks was a consultant on the picture) renamed Doctor Sayer (Robin Williams). The book's equally fascinating stories of the other awakened patients turned into a parade of feel-good, poignant cameos by such veteran character actors as Anne Meara, Judith Malina, and jazz musician Dexter Gordon (who starred in the 1986 biofilm 'Round Midnight).

Responding to the widespread criticism that her *Awakenings* ignored much of the most fascinating material in Sacks' *Awakenings* to concentrate on a conventional Hollywood story, Marshall said, "There's so much fascinating material there because the book is based on eighty case studies and each chapter is a movie in itself. So we had to combine the cases. I think Oliver had done that himself. It was the only way because you still have to make a movie, otherwise you are making a documentary and we couldn't fit everything in."

Reasonable enough. And yet the movie also romanticized both the cure and the disease. "None of Sayer's patients who have reached the frozen end of Parkinson's road appears incontinent or drools," said UCLA neurologist Bruce Dobkin, who analyzed the film for the *Los Angeles Times* in January 1991. "Hollywood evaporates every feature of Parkinson's. . . . It seems unlikely that people who had spent more than twenty years in bed and wheelchair could maintain their joint mobility, muscle strength, and stamina to walk, without . . . therapy and conditioning exercises."

The movie character of Leonard is a romantic, a decent, sensitive, life-force kind of average guy in an extraordinary circumstance. In the book, the real Leonard was rude, abusive to those around him, particularly the women. And, under the influence of L-dopa, he was filled with a crude energy that turned him into an erotomaniac, who masturbated for hours, sometimes publicly, and eventually led him to rage against the scientists who had tortured him with false hope. Instead of presenting any of this humanly complex material, the movie works out a predictable Hollywood formula of emotional growth leading to a happy ending.

In the movie, just as Sacks awakens Leonard from his decades-long sleep, so too does the vibrantly alive Leonard awaken the emotionally frozen scientist to the possibilities of human connection and a richer, more expressive life. In other words, by fade out Leonard may be locked back into the prison of his body, but he's taught the good doctor a thing or two about being a complete human being, and—glory be!—the good physician has gained a girlfriend.

In yet another of her nuanced critiques, the *New Yorker*'s Pauline Kael isolated the basic problem in her February 11, 1991, review: "[Marshall's] talent is to work the audience. There's an underlying conflict between Marshall, who comes from a show-business family, and Sacks, the fabulist of illness. She exalts the normal, and she keeps zapping us to feel the humanistic, the obvious. (Her forte is to make blandness ring true.)"

Kael's exhibit A is a rather devastating claim. The producers sent Marshall the "do-gooding" script, which she agreed to direct before she'd ever read the Oliver Sacks book.

Why after the success of *Big* did Penny Marshall choose such an unlikely project as *Awakenings,* one with less than sure-fire commercial prospects, which had been nearly bludgeoned into a coma in a lengthy development process?

Though by the time she made *Awakenings,* Penny was savvy about the workings of the business of show business, she was "frightened about how I do another comedy," she readily admitted to *Time Out* magazine for its March 31, 1991, issue. She then explained the reasoning that had led her to take on the new project. "What if they think I'm supposed to do a comedy? And I'm no good at it! So I'll do a drama. Then if it's a drama and I fail, I'll say, well sorry, I do comedy. Basically it's a strange backward thinking that I have. I do it all the time."

There was one other reason the story appealed to her: her mother had suffered with Alzheimer's, a degenerative disease. In her last two years of her life, the woman who had been a vital dance teacher and demanding perfectionist lingered in a "sort of vegetative state."

At Marshall's urging, *Awakenings* was picked up by Columbia Pictures in turnaround from Twentieth Century-Fox, which had first optioned the book in 1979; which is to say, Columbia bought out Fox's interests and options in the project.

The expert Hollywood crew Marshall and her producers, Walter F. Parkes and Lawrence Lasker, assembled included production designer Anton Furst (who was responsible for the striking comic-book noir look of the 1989 *Batman* movie and who shocked Hollywood by committing suicide at the height of his post-*Batman* acclaim) and cinematographer Miroslav Ondricek (whose credits included *Amadeus* [1984] and *Valmont* [1989] and who would go on to film two more Marshall pictures, *A League of Their Own* and *The Preacher's Wife*).

On October 16, 1989, the *Awakenings* company began filming at the Kingsboro Psychiatric Center in Brooklyn. Production designer Furst retrofitted Kingsboro to resemble a psychiatric facility circa 1969. He said he'd been inspired by the images of Belgian surrealist René Magritte, in whose dreamlike paintings a giant boulder floats among the clouds and bowler-hatted gentlemen fall like rain from the sky.

In addition to its primary Kingsboro location, *Awakenings* also shot at the New York Botanical Gardens, the Julia Richmond High School on Second Avenue, and the Casa Galicia, site of the ballroom scene. Additional locales included City Island, the Bronx, where the Sayer's house was located nearby Sacks' actual home, in Park Slope, Brooklyn; an elementary school where the film's opening sequences of Leonard as a boy in 1930s were shot; and a Park Slope brownstone that became Leonard's mother's house.

Exactly four months after it began, production was completed. At one time, in the post-production process, Marshall's rough cut ran five hours, containing a complex subplot about the building of a hospital library by the "awakened" patients.

The studio's marketing department identified the *Awakenings* appeal as "upper scale," with a "slight skew to older and female audiences," according to Duncan Clarke, then a Columbia Pictures vice president based in New York. Of the movie's poster art, showing Robert De Niro, arms upraised, alone on a small rock surrounded by water, with Williams watching from a spit of land at the beach, Clarke informed *Screen International* (a trade journal), "It shows De Niro enjoying the simple joy of walking on a beach. That's the message: life's simple joys are what we should treasure."

Awakenings was released, cut to a more conventional final length of two hours and one minute (with the library subplot entirely eliminated), in December of 1990. It debuted with a charity-benefit showing and a post-screening dinner party and dance for eleven hundred guests that benefited the Cedars-Sinai Medical Center in Los Angeles. The red-carpet world premiere was held in Century City, the West Los Angeles enclave of high-rise office buildings and upscale shops that once was the backlot of Twentieth Century-Fox. The event raised approximately one half million dollars for the medical center from the companies (mostly Hollywood studios) that bought tables at the dinner. A later charity premiere in New York raised nearly $1 million for cancer research.

Though attended by Penny (with daughter Tracy), her friend actress/author Carrie Fisher, and costar Robin Williams, the Los Angeles evening was, according to the *Los Angeles Times*, "light on stars but heavy on behind-the-scenes powerhouses—producers Freddie Fields and Ted Field, [then Creative Artists Agency] chief Mike Ovitz . . . and Penny's brother, Garry Marshall."

Traditionally the holiday season was when studios released their most Oscar-worthy dramatic movies, and from the beginning—despite the film's early bumps—that's exactly how many of the nation's workaday film critics viewed the picture:

"One of the most Oscar-friendly of the Christmas releases," said the *L.A. Weekly*.

"This film is full of the kind of roles that often garner Oscar nominations," agreed *Screen International*.

"Daniel Day-Lewis won an Academy Award for pretending to have cerebral palsy in *My Left Foot* [1989]. Dustin Hoffman received the . . . Oscar for impersonating an autistic savant in *Rain Man* [1988]," the *Los Angeles Daily News* pointed out. "Now, Robert De Niro is going for the hat trick as lead sleeping-sickness victim in *Awakenings*."

"Any movie about mental disturbance . . . is likely to touch Academy members," judged *Time* magazine, "not so much because it treats a serious issue as because it parades the performer's craft. To watch De Niro shrink into the shadow of catatonia is . . . an awesome show that reveals more about De Niro than about the man he is playing."

For the *Hollywood Reporter,* while "critical bouquets and awards," certainly seemed in the offing, the more important point—as befits a trade paper—was that *Awakenings* "should enjoy a healthy box office as its emotional honesty strikes a responsive chord in the holiday season."

And so it did, pulling down an extremely wide-awake $53 million at the North American box office, and adding another $23 million over the years in video-store rentals.

And when, early in the new year, the Oscar nominations were announced very early one morning (to accommodate the morning TV chat shows, which aired live on the East Coast), *Awakenings* woke up in contention in three major categories—not only Best Picture, but also Best Actor for De Niro and Best Screenplay Adaptation for Zaillian, who would go on to write *Schindler's List* (1993), *A Clear and Present Danger* (1994), and *Amistad* (1997).

Penny's place on the list of Best Director nominees was taken by either Barbet Schroeder, who directed *Reversal of Fortune,* another docudrama, or Stephen Frears for the noirish con-man thriller, *The Grifters;* neither of which was a Best Picture nominee. The other Best Director nominees, whose offerings were in the running for Best Picture, were Francis Ford Coppola, for the third installment of his *Godfather* saga, Martin Scorsese for his stylish true-crime tale, *GoodFellas,* and Kevin Costner, who won for the expensive *Dances with Wolves.*

It turned out to be the year of *Dances with Wolves,* which won as Best Picture and Best Adapted Screenplay, and of Jeremy Irons (playing Claus Von Bulow in *Reversal of Fortune*) as Best Actor. *Awakenings* was shut out.

Penny Marshall got almost universal credit for her casting and for her exceptional sensitivity in her dealings with actors. As one critic put it, "she trusts her actors and lets them carry the ball."

In one of those annual flukes that make the Golden Globe Awards so consistently amusing to Hollywood insiders, it was Robin Williams, not Robert De Niro, who got the nomination for Best Actor in a Drama from the Hollywood Foreign Press Association (the tiny group that gives out the Globes, and is known for both its idiosyncratic picks and its checkered past). And Williams, like Hanks in *Big* before him, won some of the best critical notices of his career for the work that he did under Penny Marshall's diffident screen direction.

"You know [why] she talks so slow?" Robin Williams asked an *US* magazine reporter rhetorically in 1990. "That's just because she's thinking of all the other things she has to do before she finishes the sentence. She's the kind of person who always says, 'Gee, I don't know,' when she really knows exactly what she wants."

Marshall's shooting style was, as she has said herself, more is better, and she liked to let her actors go on and on, until they'd explored every nook and cranny of their characters and every interpretation of each scene. However, in one scene of *Awakenings*, clearly it would've been better if she'd yelled cut sooner:

During one take of a sequence in which the afflicted Leonard and Doctor Sayer have a scuffling fight, Williams' elbow connected with De Niro's nose. Williams recalled being horrified and yelling out, "Oh, no!"

"Everyone heard it crack," according to a person on set.

But not the director. Marshall recalled, "I'm going, 'Why is Robin overacting?' . . . And Bobby went on with the scene. He goes to the window, and only when we yelled 'Cut!' and I could get to the other side could I see the blood coming from Bobby's nose. We did nine more takes, because Bobby said, 'No, let's just keep going. . . . He knew the next day it would be worse and he would get black eyes, so we just shot."

The actor was rushed to the hospital, where he was X-rayed and treated for a broken nose. Of course, Marshall and company continued production, shooting around De Niro's character for a week until he was able to return.

Penny Marshall hit the interview circuit for *Awakenings,* making not only the usual domestic stops, but traveling to England, Australia, and Japan as well. Among the film's biggest boosters was its technical consultant, Dr. Oliver Sacks, who also flew to the British premiere to support the picture Hollywood had made from his book. (A revised edition, containing his description of the making of the movie, was even issued to coincide with the film's release.)

"My reservations are very small, because the essential truth of that time was conveyed," he informed the *Los Angeles Times* of December 23, 1990, responding early on to the critics of Hollywoodization and oversimplification. "My main reservation is the violence on Ward 5 [i.e., the Williams/ De Niro fight, added to the story for the usual dramatic purposes]. . . . I got very angry about it. In fact, I walked off the set."

There was an ironic, early 1990s sign-of-the-times coda to *Awakenings:*

While the film was still in theatres, Doctor Oliver Sacks became one of twelve-hundred health workers caught up in New York State's budgetary cutbacks. He was fired from his position at the Bronx Psychiatric Center.

A League of Their Own

Once again, Columbia Pictures had a Penny Marshall hit thanks to Twentieth Century-Fox . . . and to a half-hour TV show on public television.

A League of Their Own (1992) was derived originally from a true, if largely forgotten, chapter in American sports and social history. The event was the creation of an all-female professional baseball league during World War II. Though the All American Girls Professional Baseball League (AAGPBL) had been the subject of a recent PBS documentary also called *A League of Their Own,* this was a subject with many real—and potential—sources of stories.

Before litigation-sensitive studios would invest tens of millions of dollars in a production, all the *League* rights needed to be secured. For the movie *Awakenings,* which was based on a single source (the book titled *Awakenings*), the rights were purchased, thereby locking the story up.

Buying "life rights" from the participants in unusual real-life stories reported in newspapers and magazines is common Hollywood practice. A small cadre of Los Angeles lawyers, agents, and producers occupies this ripped-from-the-headlines niche in the local filmmaking ecology. No sooner does CNN-cable report on a baby miraculously rescued, or a female firefighter fired for posing in the nude, or a teacher seducing a student, or two babies being switched at birth, than the life-rights lawyers and agents are on a jet, contracts in hand.

The AAGPBL lasted from 1943 until 1954 and began essentially as a publicity stunt by Chicago Cubs owner Phillip K. Wrigley to maintain interest in the national pastime while many of its male players were away in the wartime military. (In the film, chewing-gum mogul Wrigley metamorphoses into candy magnate Walter Harvey and is played by Garry Marshall.) The girls, who played in short-skirt uniforms, turned out to be skilled athletes. The league became popular in its own right, eventually fielding fourteen teams, with names such as the Fort Wayne Daisies, the Battle Creek Belles, and the Grand Rapid Chicks that played throughout the Midwest. During the AAGPBL's heyday, in three seasons during and immediately after World War II, the teams drew more than one million paying fans (at a dollar-and-a-half per admission).

Decades later, documentarian and actress Kim Wilson and Kelly Candaele, the son of one player who joined the league with her sister, co-produced a half-hour documentary on the AAGPBL called *A League of Their Own*. When the documentary aired in California on the Public Broadcasting System, Penny Marshall was watching, and she proceeded to option the rights to it. She commissioned Candaele and Wilson, the documentarians, to write the story's treatment. (A *treatment* is movie-industry parlance for a present-tense short story, usually a dozen or so pages long, that outlines the plot of the movie-to-be, describing its characters and their story arcs and interactions. Customarily, there is little or no dialogue provided in a treatment; that becomes part of the mix only in the script, which follows the treatment stage.)

"It seemed the story just resonated with her on a number of levels," said Candaele, who, with Wilson, eventually got a "story by" credit on the completed film.

Meanwhile, two TV-movie producers, Ronnie Clemmer and Bill Pace of Longbow Productions (the company's titles included *An Unfinished Affair, Fighting for My Daughter* and *A Mother's Justice*), came across an article about the women's baseball league in the *Boston Globe*'s Sunday magazine while searching the nation's press for interesting stories to develop.

"We got on a plane, flew (to the AAGPBL's annual reunion in Ft. Wayne, Indiana) and met with their board of directors around a barroom table . . . and had beers with these 60- and 70-year-old ladies," Clemmer recalled.

Later, in the early 1990s, when the AAGPBL players were inducted into the Baseball Hall of Fame, Penny Marshall herself went to Cooperstown, New York, to attend the ceremony and meet the real players, as well as to option rights to their stories. There she learned that the rights to the AAGPBL itself were already in the hands of Clemmer and Pace and so she called the two TV-movie producers. "She asked if we wanted to join her project," Clemmer related later, "and showing we weren't brain damaged we said yes."

In due course, Pace and Clemmer, who maintained that Penny Marshall had always been their first choice for the material anyway, got producer credits on Penny Marshall's picture.

Marshall's own production company, Parkway Productions (named after Mosholu Parkway, the main thoroughfare through the Old Neighborhood in the Bronx), was then still located at Twentieth Century-Fox.

Although Hollywood studios make a wide variety of agreements with the talent, typically a director/actress of Marshall's stature will have some variation of what is generally known as a housekeeping deal. In return for providing her with office space, secretarial help, and so forth, she would agree to give the studio some sort of option—perhaps merely a right of first refusal—on any of the projects developed during the term of the agreement. And in return for the funding that turns a particular project into a multi-million-dollar feature film, the studio is given the right to distribute the movie and take a (large) percentage of its worldwide revenues. Typically, the rights also include making even bigger-budget sequels, licensing various merchandising and tie-in rights, and creating innumerable related products from Happy Meals and T-shirts to video games and amusement-park rides.

At first, the studio executives at Fox wanted to do Penny's female baseball-players story as a TV-movie-of-the-week. However, Marshall insisted on a big-screen feature, and she hired Lowell Ganz and Babaloo Mandel to pen the screenplay.

Ganz and Mandel, who by that time were already best known as the writing team behind such superior sitcom-like big-screen comedies as *Splash* (1984), *Parenthood* (1989), and *City Slickers* (1991), went back a long way with the Marshall family. Ganz had been one of the story editors on *The Odd Couple*, and they turned up—individually and together in various writing, producing, or consulting capacities—in the credits of both *Happy Days* and *Laverne & Shirley*.

"Basically, they tend to work for their friends," said *League* producer Clemmer. "They tend to work for Ron Howard or Garry Marshall. . . . So when Penny chose the material, they were interested right off the bat. . . . And, secondly, they fell in love with this very different arena."

The colorful tale that evolved out of the development process centered around two competitive baseball-playing sisters, who, after being discovered by a traveling scout (a part that was written with Jon Lovitz in mind), join a new team that's coached by a washed-up former big-league baseball player.

Twentieth Century-Fox, it turned out, had its own option on the baseball script. When it became clear that Marshall was going to be away filming *Awakenings* for rival-studio Columbia for the entire next year, Fox decided to go ahead without her. Following show-business custom, Marshall moved over to take a producer credit on the picture and the studio hired a new director.

Fox's *A League of Their Own,* directed by David Anspaugh (*Hoosiers*) and starring Demi Moore, Jon Lovitz, and Jim Belushi (in the role of the washed-up manager), came within weeks of beginning filming in May of 1990 with a budget of $18 million. Then Moore dropped out and a new regime, headed by filmmaker Joe Roth, was installed at Twentieth Century-Fox.

There are two truisms about new studio regimes: One, the new executives invariably redecorate the offices they've inherited from their predecessors, sometimes at great expense; and, two, they get rid of the old regime's projects in development, putting them all into turnaround. This is exactly what happened to Fox's female baseball-players movie. In turnaround, the graveyard of movie development, is exactly where Columbia picked it up, handing it right back to Marshall. At first she still intended only to produce, this time with the late Alan J. Pakula, whose films include *To Kill a Mockingbird* (1962), *Klute* (1971), and *The Parallax View* (1971), in the director's chair.

The budget went to $31 million, then climbed to as much $50 million, setting off alarms in the (once again) budget-conscious, but still enormously extravagant, town.

Once Madonna was part of the ensemble cast, she became the focus of the pre-release publicity drumbeat for the sports movie. Before Geena Davis finally took the role of Dottie, the older of the two sisters, Pakula had cast Debra Winger in the lead part. However, when the star of *Urban Cowboy*

(1980) and *An Officer and a Gentleman* (1982) dropped out, director Pakula soon left the project too. It was at that point that Penny took over.

Word spread around Hollywood, eventually finding its way into the gossip columns, that Winger had left the production to protest Madonna joining the cast—a rumor that Winger eventually was forced to deny.

In the late 1980s and early 1990s Madonna was at the height of her fame and notoriety. Her infectious pop songs and daringly staged music videos went straight to the tops of the charts, and remained there. Her elaborately staged concerts sold out stadiums all around the world. Her image—sometimes glamorous, sometimes wanton, but always immaculately crafted by the best professionals, whether the top fashion photographers or the highest-paid publicists, all spinning and snapping under her personal supervision—increased the newsstand sales of any magazine for which she posed. And she was rumored to be preparing an art book of sexually explicit photographs and poetry. Needless to say, it was as eagerly awaited as any other Madonna product or artifact of that period.

But there was one last bastion in the media-mad world of the 1990s that she'd not yet conquered, and it was the ultimate one: the movies.

Until then, like many music stars used to commanding the spotlight, she'd taken mostly lead roles, playing, typically, a femme fatale. However, there was only one part Madonna seemed capable of playing—namely, herself, or at least her pop-star persona. When she strayed from that persona, critics (and audiences) were not convinced and her reviews sometimes suggested (a) that she needed to stick to music and (b) that she would be well advised to take acting lessons.

There was one big exception to that chorus of negativity. In her debut Hollywood studio picture, *Desperately Seeking Susan* (1985), she'd not only stuck with her outrageous free-spirit persona—costumed, for example, in the same thrown-together street-rags she'd been wearing in her early music videos—she had also taken a relatively small supporting part.

The reviews were raves. *League* offered her a chance to repeat that screen formula.

When in post-production it became clear that Madonna's supporting role was a relatively small part, word spread through gossip columns around Hollywood that the director, finding Madonna's acting weak, had been forced to trim the pop star's scenes—a rumor that Penny Marshall eventually was forced to deny. Whatever the truth of the currents and counter-currents of rumor, gossip, and planted publicity items, there was no denying Madonna's diligence in preparing for her small *League* role—a fact attested to by Jon Lovitz.

"She'd never played baseball," Lovitz related to *People* magazine, with that insinuating vocal undertone that engenders a smiling doubt about practically his every assertion, "and she worked really hard. Before she came to practice, she'd run eight miles. Then she was out practicing after everyone was done. She would hit more. She's amazing."

Finally Madonna had a big-screen movie role well received by the critics. She was brazen ballplayer Mae Mordabito, and her lines were slyly crafted to resonate with Madonna's own brazen image.

Sample dialogue: Discussing how to attract more attention to the team, Mae suggests, "What if at a key moment in the game I go for a ball and—oops!—my bosoms come flying out?"

Replies teammate Doris tartly: "You think there's a man in this country who hasn't seen your bosoms?"

Funny lady Rosie O'Donnell, smartly playing Doris, was finally getting attention for more than her wise-cracking stand-up. Penny had seen her on TV and heard from Rosie's agent that she actually played baseball and knew her way around a batting cage. "I knew there was no other actresses in Hollywood who could lay down a bunt as good as me," Rosie said. "And it was really funny to see all these actresses [at the auditions at the University of Southern California] who had never played baseball who had lied to their agents and said, 'Oh, yeah, I can play.' Like you know, the really thin

Barbie-doll women. And I'm like 'Honey, hold the thin end of the bat, OK?'"

With her customary endearing acerbity, O'Donnell had declared. "When I read the script, I thought, 'If I don't get this part, I'll quit show business.' If there's one thing I can do better than Meryl Streep and Glenn Close, it's play baseball."

Her skill with a bat and a glove might have gotten her the part, which was originally written for a "hot, sexy girl," said Penny, but it was her acting in the movie that got the rave notices. And it was through the movie that Rosie became friends with both Penny Marshall and Madonna in real, albeit highly publicized, life.

The first meeting between Madonna and O'Donnell occurred at Penny's suggestion, and marked the first time Rosie and Penny teamed up to sell any-thing—in this case, they sold Madonna on the idea of appearing in the movie. According to two accounts published in *Rosie: Rosie O'Donnell Biography* (1997), the comedian's opening line to the Material Girl was either "Hello, I have a vibrator" or "Hi, my mom died when I was little, too."

By the time of *A League of Their Own,* interviewers had come to expect Penny's practiced catalog of amusing film production complaints, whether unforeseen complications of the actual shoot, such as one star breaking the other's nose, or acts of God, such as bad weather.

This time the curse was . . . The Curse. "It was a little tough during that women's cycle," Marshall alerted *US* magazine in August 1992. "*Everyone* gets a little testy at the same time."

There was a taste of testiness at *League's* premieres, too—all three of them.

In Los Angeles, where the world premiere was held at the Academy of Motion Pictures Arts & Sciences' Samuel Goldwyn Theatre, there it was dis-appointment over Madonna's non-appearance (she was said to be in New York recording an album). However, that disappointment was presumably mitigated for the eleven hundred or so guests who paid to attend the charity benefit (raising approximately $250,000 for the Westside Children's Center) by the presence of other celebrity attendees. Among those who managed to show up at the hoedown-style after-premiere party set up in the parking lot next door to the theatre, were the director, her brother and daughter, and Davis, Hanks, and most of the rest of the movie's cast.

That party's bill of faire included "pizzas, hot dogs, burgers, French-dip prime rib sandwiches, brownies, and cookies galore." And the sound system played not Madonna, who had performed "This Used to Be My Playground" over the film's end credits, but Ella Fitzgerald, the Andrews Sisters, and other period music from the 1940s. (Given Madonna's prominence it may seem odd that "Playground" was uncredited in the movie. The song was also omitted from the soundtrack album because Madonna was a Warner Bros., not a Sony/Columbia, recording artist.)

In New York at the East Coast premiere of *League*, it was the crashers who added an edge to the post-premiere party in the dining tent at Tavern on the Green, turning it into a free-for-all. In Evansville, Indiana, where the movie production headquartered during two-and-a-half months of location filming in Indiana, Illinois, and Kentucky, the locals had been promised that they would host the world premiere. It was a sense of disappointment and betrayal when, according to the *Wall Street Journal*, "it turned out that the Evansville premiere would be the Midwestern premiere instead of 'The' premiere. . . . And the stars, promised by Columbia Pictures 'if their schedules permit,' were, of course, elsewhere." The disappointed Indianians, "somewhat subdued" after seeing the movie, were mollified perhaps by thoughts of the estimated $10 million that the production had pumped into the Evansville economy.

Right before *A League of Their Own*'s July 1 opening on 1,782 screens around the country, *Variety* surveyed a producer, an agent, an exhibitor, and an attorney (none of whom were named), and got predictions from the Hollywood insiders about the film's future prospects such as a "solid double" and a "baseball film with no balls." At the same time an unnamed source described to *People* magazine the Columbia Pictures' marketing department as "all in a tizzy" after unfavorable test screenings. Then a newspaper analysis in the *New York Times* entitled "Budgets Bloat; Studios Worry" singled out *A League of Their Own* as a prime example of a movie that had grown so expensive in the development and production process that it "must be a major hit to earn money for the studio."

In addition to such factors as the cost of staging stadium-crowd scenes, the *Times* report cited the fees the above-the-line figures received: "One studio executive estimated that Mr. Hanks received $5 million, Ms. Marshall about $3 million, Ms. Davis about $2.5 million and Madonna at least $1 million. . . . Debra Winger . . . [who] dropped out . . . [received] $2 million anyway."

How much, if anything, all the pre-release negativity had to do with the fact that *League* went into production under one Columbia regime, headed by Frank Price, but opened under another, headed by Mark Canton, will never be known. Despite the dire predictions and sophisticated so-what shrugs at the prospects of a big-screen, big-budget period movie that fictionalized the story of long-forgotten female baseball players, the movie that Penny Marshall made from this material turned out to be nothing less than a bases-loaded home run.

In the mid- and late 1970s, television critics by and large dismissed *Laverne & Shirley* as mindless, middle-brow entertainment, without the redeeming social values of *All in the Family* and other celebrated sitcoms. But to young girls watching avidly at home, the premise of the simple situation comedy—two working-class girls living alone, not (really) dependent on men—was often revelatory.

Similarly, it was *A League of Their Own*—another innocent entertainment set in a beloved but bygone era—that made director Penny Marshall important to a new generation of girls and young women. Not only did she restore the AAGPBL and its female athletes to their proper place in the sports pantheon and expand the mythology of the all-American athlete, who it turned out could just as easily be a woman as a man, but she proved once and for all that a movie starring women (and of course, Tom Hanks) could strike gold at the box office.

Feminist-minded film critics included it in among the best, most progressive pictures of the first half of the 1990s, along with such other influential movies as Ridley Scott's *Thelma & Louise* (1991), Zhang Yimou's *Raise the Red Lantern* (1991), Allison Anders' *Gas, Food, Lodging* (1992), and Jane Campion's *The Piano* (1993).

A League of Their Own took in $107 million domestically in its initial feature release. Director Penny Marshall had her second $100 million-grossing movie, once again with Tom Hanks prominent in the cast. But, predictably, this latest triumph didn't seem to make her noticeably happier. Perhaps that was partly because *League's* critical acclaim often stopped just short of including the picture's director. Though she didn't say it publicly until a few years later, that grated on her.

In a chatty colloquy with Penny in a 1996 issue of *Premiere* magazine, Rosie O'Donnell, whom Penny elevated to a new level of fame by casting her in the movie, began to ask a rather innocuous question about how life changes for a director when a "movie does incredibly well, like *A League of Their Own*." But Penny, uncharacteristically, interrupted . . .

"And somebody else gets the credit."

Rosie, in the manner of an interviewer following her own previous thought or asking a pre-programmed series of questions, didn't respond to the answer, intriguing as it was, carrying on instead with: "Do you feel elation?" But for some reason Penny was determined to say it, to make the point: "Tom," she said of the actor who had starred in both of her big hit movies and would go on to become a two-time Best Actor Oscar winner, "got the credit."

The *Time* magazine review was typical of the criticism leveled at *A League of Their Own*. Without ever specifying that he was referring to Penny Marshall and to the Lowell Ganz and Babaloo Mandel scriptwriting team, the magazine's veteran critic, Richard Schickel, complained "if the people responsible for *A League of Their Own* had tried just a little harder to avoid easy laughs and easy sentiment, they might have made something like a great movie. As it is, they have made a good movie, amiable and ingratiating."

"Amiable and ingratiating." Another way of saying it was crowd-pleasing. Geena Davis, after the social phenomenon of *Thelma & Louise,* was perhaps the Hollywood actress most nearly an emblem of women's liberation. As Dottie, the dishy baseball-playing phenomena, she headed the large ensemble cast.

Asked why he'd taken the role of Jimmy, the overweight, over-the-hill, alcoholic manager—a supporting part—when he could have his pick of leading-man roles, Tom Hanks gave an answer that was amiable and ingratiating too: "I never had to shave. I was only in the make-up chair for three minutes. I got to take a nap every morning. I didn't have to watch what I ate. And I got to play baseball between shots. It was essentially like going to a baseball spa for the summer."

Almost lost in the large cast, which also included Lori Petty as Dottie's sister, was Teá Leoni as one of the ballplayers, and Harry Shearer as a newsreel announcer. Eddie Mekka, who played Carmine Ragusa, Shirley's erstwhile boyfriend on *Laverne & Shirley,* had, in a bit of nudge-in-the-ribs casting, a small part as Mae's Guy in Bar.

There was one more bit of noteworthy casting in *A League of Their Own.*

The picture ends in the present day of the early 1990s with Dottie, Mae, and the other players reminiscing at an AAGPBL reunion. Instead of filming these scenes with Geena Davis, Lori Petty, Madonna, and the others in (generally unconvincing) latex wrinkles and older makeup, Marshall instead cast women in their sixties, who were of the same facial structure and body type, then dubbed their voices for the final scenes. Of the actress who played Geena Davis's character, one of the movie's producers, Elliot Abbott (who was music coordinator on *Big* and collaborated on *Renaissance Man* and *The Preacher's Wife*), said: "We weren't just looking for someone who looked like her. . . . We also were searching for someone who had the same behavior, someone whose mouth moved the same way, who said the same words in the same way."

Abbott was also co-executive producer with Marshall in developing the subsequent TV show based on the movie, which was widely expected to air on NBC. Ironically, that initial plan broke down, not over finances, but rather because of the "casting process on the series."

General-audience-friendly, box-office smashes like *Big* and *A League of Their Own* almost automatically become candidates for a TV series. *Big* never made it beyond the pilot-episode stage, but within a few months of its release, *League*'s big-screen success bred a short-lived small-screen spinoff on CBS. It was also called *A League of Their Own,* with Penny Marshall producing the half-hour weekly program.

The TV version of *League* was rushed on the air in April of 1993, late in the TV season, and the critics, validating NBC's decision to bow out of the show, called it a strike out. Partly because the reviewers panned it and partly because the show aired on Saturdays, generally the lowest-rated night of the week, the home-viewing audience never tuned in. And, predictably, after only a few episodes, the show was pulled off the air.

The series is interesting on only a few minor accounts. As always, this Penny Marshall production was a family affair, with daughter Tracy in the cast and brother Garry reprising his role as candy-bar magnate Walter Harvey. The film's writers, Lowell Ganz and Babaloo Mandel, wrote the first two episodes of the show, and one of the series' producers was Jeffrey Ganz.

Penny herself directed the first episode, "Dottie's Back" (April 10, 1993), in which Dottie (Carey Lowell, in the Geena Davis role) rejoins the Peaches team after her husband is called back up to the military. Jon Lovitz also guest-starred in the first installment as baseball scout Ernie Capadino. Penny's production partner, the late actor Ted Bessell, directed "The Fat Boys of Summer," the second episode, as well as "Marathon," the sixth and last entry.

"The Monkey's Curse," the third episode, in which Jimmy (Sam McMurray, in the Tom Hanks role) wins a chimpanzee in a card game and the Peaches go into a slump, was directed by Tom Hanks, who, while "imitating (Penny's) distinctive nasal whine," explained his presence behind the TV cameras as a favor to a friend: "Penny called and said, 'Will you do it?' . . . I said, 'Yeah, but it has to be between these dates.' And she goes, 'Okay.'"

A profile by *TV Guide*'s veteran staff writer Mary Murphy of the period during which the TV show was being rushed to air paints a portrait of Marshall as a chain-smoking, ulcer-medication-swilling depressive. In the article, Mary Murphy depicts Penny as overworked and overstressed in the rush of preproduction, her unwashed hair pulled back into a ponytail, as she bemoans her decision to return to television—albeit this time behind the scenes—and her inability to find actresses who can play baseball without throwing and catching like, well, *girls*.

Marshall's only refuge at the time, according to Murphy's profile, was her bedroom, where one friend described her "in bed . . . propped up . . . scripts around her. There are usually a few . . . friends sitting with her. The phone rings every five minutes, there's a cigarette in her mouth . . . a bowl of chocolate pudding . . . tapes about serial killers on the VCR. And that's how she likes to live."

Years later, it was still how she liked to live . . . and even do business. In a 1994 "phone call" feature with Carrie Fisher for *Interview* magazine, in which Fisher was promoting her book, *Surrender the Pink*, and Marshall was touting *Renaissance Man*, Penny said she'd just had a massage, but it didn't help, and that she was in her bed, "in the fetal position."

In a 1998 episode of *The Rosie O'Donnell Show* on which Penny was guest host, actor Jason Priestley (*Beverly Hills, 90210*), who starred in *Calendar Girl*, a little-seen 1993 film that Penny executive produced for Columbia after *League*, was moved to remark that the last two meetings he'd had with Penny she'd been "propped up" in bed.

Renaissance Man

In the Hollywood world traditionally populated by females who are bombshells and babes, coy starlets or grasping femmes fatales, and not much more, Penny Marshall has occupied—perhaps chosen to occupy—a unique character niche. Long before the term was coined, she was a slacker.

At first, she was merely the slacker as celebrity—consistently amusing as the tired whiner, or as a bemused writer once described her, an Oscar Levant for our times. When *Laverne & Shirley* finally went off the air in the spring of 1983, she didn't do the things expected of a Hollywood workaholic. Instead she traveled to the kinds of destinations a slacker might choose, getting as far off the beaten path as Cambodia and Thailand.

When she returned, she reinvented herself as a Hollywood film director— a demanding, multifaceted, hyper-responsible position with hundreds of jobs and tens of millions of dollars at risk on every single picture in which she participated.

But only Penny Marshall—both as she's presented herself publicly, and as others have described her—had, seemingly willingly, become the very personification of the slacker as director. Not in subject matter, certainly, but in persona and attitude.

Even before the release of *Big* in 1988, the triumph that wiped away memories of *Jumpin' Jack Flash,* Penny, puffing incessantly on Marlboros despite an alarming hacking cough and despite bursts of neurotic energy and a self-deprecating charm, seemed to be just barely there—reclining on her couch, lifting her head only to answer the telephone or slurp her favorite drink, a bubbly concoction of milk and Pepsi.

"'I could just sleep forever,'" she sighed to an interviewer from the *Los Angeles Times* in mid-1988. The same reporter described her lying on a couch in her living room, groaning out a response to a question and "waving a limp hand in the air."

Penny was defined most often by what she was not—not a morning person, not a secure person, not a happy person, not a healthy person (she liked smoking and junk food too much for that). The same held true about her on the set—not a forceful person, not particularly a vocal person when it came to her opinions about how a scene should go, not even very informed about the various technical processes of filmmaking (*Lenses? Schmenzes!*). In sum, she was not a leader on the set in the conventional jodhpurs-and-riding-crop sense. What Penny most definitely was, though, was a loyal friend and a people person, the quintessential actor's director.

"I never aspired to be anything except to be around talented people," she said to *Time Out* magazine around the time of *Awakenings* in early 1991, echoing a comment she'd been making at least since as far back as *Laverne & Shirley*. "Both my brother and I have gotten called corny. Yeah, well I am. Kill me. Shoot me. I like to care about the people involved."

And corny was just what her new film was, as the critics all chorused. The PG-13-rated *Renaissance Man* (1994) starred Danny DeVito as Bill Rago, an unemployed ad man who is forced to take a job teaching basic comprehension to a colorful collection of Army recruits. As more than one reviewer complained, the comedy was an early 1990s throwback to those oddball Army squads immortalized in World War II propaganda movies, in which all-American misfits (one Italian-American, one Jewish-American, one black man from the South, one white man from the South, and so on) learn to get along and band together against the Nazis.

This time, though, the oddballs included a "disgraced jock, a manic punk New Yorker, an alienated black woman, a gangsta-rapper, a racist hillbilly, and a guy so emotionally beat that he's essentially a zombie," and now the war was against illiteracy.

The feel-good film, ostensibly based on an actual episode in the life of its screenwriter, Jim Burnstein, follows Rago and the eight racially and ethnically diverse recruits as they work out their personal problems. (The divorced Rago, for example, needs to earn his daughter's respect.) And, of course, the students, who have in common both a lack of education and a burning desire to become part of the Army, eventually do learn—not just about Shakespeare, but about the sheer excitement of learning—as they travel the road to becoming all that they can be.

This was material guaranteed to raise the hackles of *cineaste*-minded reviewers. Moreover, it instantly revived all the worst criticisms, progressively muted since *Jumpin' Jack Flash,* of Penny's easy resort to sitcom simplicities in her big-screen work.

To be sure, as with her other movies, it was still only the director and the script that the critics disliked. As for Danny DeVito, he "comes across as thoughtful, intelligent, even sweet," as one review (*San Francisco Chronicle*), emblematic of most of the rest, put it, but, "otherwise [the movie] seems to be an oddly unfinished yet overlong clunker whose brightest moments are tarnished by loose ends, episodic lard, half-baked sentimental drama, and an annoyingly manipulative military atmosphere."

Storyboards are drawings, more or less cartoonish, that depict individual camera shots, showing the actors or the action in the frame in relation to the camera's actual position at any given moment in the finished movie. In contrast to classic auteurs like Alfred Hitchcock—who was famous for storyboarding every shot in every movie well in advance so the actual filming was often anti-climactic—Penny's directing style was the ultimate in slacker filmmaking.

She rehearsed her actors repeatedly, had them construct back-stories for their characters' lives, then made them improvise in character after they finished their scripted lines. She filmed the way she learned in TV, with multiple cameras covering the action from every conceivable angle and assembling massive rough cuts. *Awakenings* ran five hours in assemblage. At one time, *Renaissance Man* was almost four-and-a-quarter hours long. Both were later honed in the editing room but were still taxing lengths.

"In *Renaissance Man* I had 17 classroom scenes with no props and the kids all in the same uniforms," Penny told a production-oriented trade magazine. "I had to figure out a way to make them interesting. In *A League of Their Own*, again, I had a million locker-room and dugout scenes. So to keep the characters alive, I had them make up their own history in conjunction with what their lines were, because I don't cut very well. After their written lines were finished, they had to continue the scene because I use a lot of that stuff."

From her first feature film directing assignment onward, Penny's making-it-up-as-we-go-along attitude was a big part of her actor-friendly technique, and it certainly extended to her view of the shooting script. She tended not to communicate very well with her writers, Penny said in the same trade-magazine interview. It was a problem she'd had since the *Laverne & Shirley* wars, and in *Renaissance Man* it was probably exacerbated by the fact that, in one sense, William Shakespeare was the uncredited writer on the script.

"Shakespeare always scared me," she explained to *Millimeter* magazine in May 1994. "I'm from the Bronx. They didn't do much Shakespeare in my neighborhood. I wanted to show that Shakespeare doesn't have to be intimidating, how what he wrote relates to our everyday lives."

Quite simply, the critics not only hated *Renaissance Man*, they often seemed to resent it on a deeply personal level, as if to say, *"Laverne" directing Shakespeare? How dare she!*

The movie reduces "Shakespeare to the literary equivalent of fast food," was the *Washington Post's* verdict. "The only aspect of the film that isn't wholly fraudulent [is Danny DeVito's performance], if only because his typical feisty abrasiveness protects him from sinking to the level of Marshall's mawkishness."

"A labored, unconvincing comedy that seems cobbled together out of the half-understood remnants of its betters," was another typically dismissive critical view.

Danny DeVito wasn't the only member of the cast to survive *Renaissance's* critical train wreck. As had been the case with Rosie and the baseball squad in *League*, Penny's shrewd casting of the movie's Army misfits squad launched yet another new movie career, this time even more unlikely.

Just before Penny Marshall cast Mark Wahlberg as Tommy Lee Haywood from Willocoochee, Georgia, the career of the Caucasian rapper then best known as Marky Mark was on the skids. Contributing to his apparent demise were weak sales for his second CD and a spate of bad publicity triggered by ill-considered and boorish bashing comments about both gays and Madonna.

Then, Penny Marshall, no doubt watching from the comfort of her bedroom at home, saw one of his rap videos on TV and invited him to audition for a part in her new movie. Typically, Wahlberg came to the audition for his big break something less than prepared. He hadn't read the script. . . . He only met with Marshall and the film's star, Danny DeVito, because he was a fan of theirs, not of film-making, according to Mark Wahlberg's biographer Frank Sanello.

"'I just wanted to meet Penny Marshall and Danny DeVito—I grew up in love with those two—I didn't want to be in the movie," Wahlberg said.

Boston-born Wahlberg, a beer-guzzling, blue-collar kid born in 1971, had grown up to be a slacker star himself. He was raised on the sitcoms of the 1970s and Laverne DeFazio was one of his personal heroes.

"By the time I walked out of the meeting, I wanted to try to be in their movie. Then I read the script . . . which I should have done beforehand," said Wahlberg. I was acting like I was interested [and had read the script], because I just wanted to meet them. . . . I could tell they really thought I could do it. Me. Not Marky Mark. That faith was everything."

That faith was demonstrated by a risky decision not to exploit Wahlberg's Marky Mark persona on screen, according to Wahlberg biographer Frank Sanello. "Wahlberg was subjected to enormous pressure by Disney, which [had] bankrolled the production, to lend his fame and name to the film and do an on-screen [musical] set. . . . Penny Marshall, unlike [Jeffrey] Katzenberg [then the number-two executive at Disney], didn't exert any pressure on the actor to rap on screen."

Instead, Wahlberg wrote and performed (but not on screen) several numbers for the film, including the squad's "Shakespeare Rap."

When the ploy worked—and Wahlberg got positive notices from the New York Times and others—in typical Hollywood fashion, his success turned out to have many authors. However, Mark understood the importance of the director's risky call, even if others did not.

"I literally owe Penny everything and I love her," said Wahlberg, adding in his ersatz-street-kid fashion, "She deserves some major butt-smooching."

Even before the movie came out, Penny, good trouper that she was, launched herself on the requisite multi-city publicity tour, the type that's inevitably described as grueling. And before that, she pitched in, too, when the studio—Disney—moved up its release date by six weeks. It was a decision she would later come to regret.

Slashing a full month-and-a-half off the post-production schedule of a major motion picture would create a major obstacle for any director, but especially for one who, slacker-like, molded her gigantic rough-cut assemblages in a time-consuming, trial-and-error process in the post-production editing bay.

Later, she told the *Los Angeles Times* that the picture actually wasn't finished until the very day of the traditional cast-and-crew screening, which customarily takes place just a few days before a picture's opening. She cited the stress of deadline pressure—rather than, say, her four-pack-a-day cigarette habit—for the health scare that punctuated that frantic post-production period.

Renaissance Man premiered at the end of May 1994. Just a few days before the premiere, Penny took a break from her publicity duties at the Long Island, New York, estate of Ronald Perelman, the chairman of Revlon Cosmetics who became a media mogul in 1989 when he purchased New World Communications, a producer of movies and TV. On May 28, while on the tennis courts at Perelman's home, Penny collapsed. Her symptoms were shortness of breath and chest pains. Paramedics rushed her to a nearby hospital, where she was kept overnight. The very next day, Penny Marshall, who, in the best of times could barely bring herself to rise from her comfy bed, resumed her publicity tour. She and her spokespeople, including her sister, repeatedly denied that she'd suffered a heart attack, saying the frightening symptoms were simply the result of fatigue and stress. And though the brevity of her hospital stay does seem to point away from a major health crisis, the widely held belief in Hollywood persists: In the rush to finish what became her least successful movie, Penny Marshall almost died.

The Preacher's Wife

In October 1996, during post-production in New York on *The Preacher's Wife*, her Christmas-holiday fable of hope, love, and faith that was due to open in theatres in less than two months, Penny Marshall again came face to face with the reality of mortality.

Sixty-one-year-old actor/director Ted Bessell, her friend and, since the mid-1980s, Parkway Productions partner, suffered a sudden and unexpected death.

An Emmy-winning director for his work on *The Tracey Ullman Show*, he was probably most famous to television viewers for his on-camera portrayals of two boyfriends in two different TV series. In the 1960s, Bessell was Donald Hollinger, Ann Marie's magazine reporter boyfriend in Marlo Thomas's series, *That Girl*. A decade later he was Joe Warner, Mary Richards' boyfriend in *The Mary Tyler Moore Show*.

When *Daily Variety's* senior columnist Army Archerd reached Penny by telephone for comment on Bessel's death, she was "overcome" and "barely able to speak." She did say, "He had been so supportive. He went over every cut I made on every picture. There wasn't a mean bone in his body. He was there for everybody. It's a great loss, personally."

And in a gracious, year-end tribute for *People* magazine, she remembered him as "so much more" than just the "guy from *That Girl*. . . . He wasn't a Hollywood type, but he was behind so many Hollywood people lending support."

At the time of his passing, Bessell was preparing to direct the big-screen version of TV's *Bewitched* (1964–72), which was to have been produced by Parkway. Upon learning of his death, Penny broke away from looping *The Preacher's Wife* to fly back to Los Angeles to attend the memorial service.

Two months later, in December 1996, in the midst of the publicity push for *The Preacher's Wife*, a *Washington Post* feature writer found Marshall, "stretched out on a sofa in her hotel suite," wearing "violet velvet lounging pajamas," with a "black enamel Victorian mourning locket" around her neck, in memory of a "good friend [who] recently died." On her feet were white sneakers. With the sole exception of her more elegant pants, the portrait of Marshall that emerged could have been drawn a decade, even two decades, before:

"In between chain-smoking Marlboros, Marshall talks in that nasal, clenched-teeth, Laverne-Kmart pitchwoman voice. Bits and pieces of words are swallowed up with each puff. She sounds like a caricature of herself," the *Post* writer observed.

The Preacher's Wife, starring pop singer Whitney Houston as Julia the minister's spouse, Denzel Washington as the angel named Dudley, and Courtney B. Vance as Pastor Harry Biggs, was a remake of 1947's *The Bishop's Wife* in which Loretta Young, Cary Grant, and David Niven played the equivalent roles.

A remake in one form or another had been under consideration for years, but it was only when Denzel Washington, Best Actor Oscar winner in 1990 for *Glory* and an eminently bankable actor, got involved that the project moved onto the fast track. After Washington was attached, Marshall signed on to direct.

"Penny was the absolute perfect idea for director," Washington was quoted as saying in an unsigned feature story, posted on the Internet, that had the smooth, burbling aura of a publicity release. "She knows comedy and she knows how to bring warmth and lightheartedness to material. Her films leave audiences with a good feeling. And since this was new territory for me, as an actor, I wanted to work with someone I trusted. I knew I could trust her 100 percent."

In the same story, Penny herself, sounding very un-Penny-like, is quoted as saying, "Denzel is one of the most accomplished actors in films today. Working with an actor of his level of accomplishment is thrilling and challenging. And with Whitney in the title role we had the wonderful opportunity to use music in a way that is organic to the film."

And with Whitney on board, the picture was, as they say in Hollywood, a "firm go."

The Christmas fantasy, distributed by Disney, seemed a natural, and the elements for another Penny Marshall family-picture breakthrough seemed in place. The movie was a sentimental fantasy, derived from a beloved holiday classic. Its casting was impeccable. An Oscar winner and a multi-platinum-selling pop diva were in the lead roles (in contrast to multi-platinum-selling pop diva Madonna, who in *A League of Their Own* merely had a supporting part). The African-American filmgoing audience was large and ready to line up to support its films. The same was true about the audience for family movies. There was even something of a religious rebirth in Hollywood film-making, according to *USA Today*, which took note of the fact that not only was Penny Marshall making *The Preacher's Wife*, but at roughly the same time, her brother Garry was directing a film called *Dear God* (1996).

The Hollywood religious-movie trend was "not about God so much as having faith, having good morals," Penny declared to a national newspaper, adding with a kind of comic censoriousness, "I'm talking about the movies, not the people, but a couple of them could use it in their own lives."

Despite only gently critical and some outright positive reviews, which this time even occasionally (albeit grudgingly) praised the movie's director, *The Preacher's Wife*, like *Renaissance Man*, worked no miracles at the box office.

In fact, when asked in late November 1997 by *TV Guide* to name the biggest "turkey" in her career, Penny didn't mention *Jumpin' Jack Flash*, her first film, or even the execrable *Renaissance Man*, her worst-performing and worst-reviewed picture. Instead, she awarded that dubious distinction to *The Preacher's Wife*. "I made the movie because I like gospel music," she said. "I'm not sure why Whitney Houston or Denzel Washington made it."

During preproduction, Penny toured churches in Black neighborhoods, scouting locations and getting a feel for the rhythms of African-American church life.

"I went with Whitney to Whitney's mom's [singer Cissy Houston] church," she said, a year after filming was completed, "and I went with Denzel to [church in] Los Angeles, and I watched a lot of video stuff given to us by Reverend Bingham of the Georgia Mass Choir.

"But during the filming in the church in Newark, New Jersey—the interior of the church was in Newark, the exterior was in Yonkers—when we were doing the end song, 'Joy to the World,' when we were doing the wider shots, with Whitney and the band and the whole congregation, the Spirit did come, and it was quite thrilling. That was just quite exciting."

When Penny made the film, she shot and shot and shot, as usual: "There'd be these big scenes showing the entire congregation, Whitney and the choir and everyone would get going and it was like, 'Jesus is in the building.' There was no yelling cut," she recalled to the *Washington Post*. "It went on for 30 minutes. . . . It was quite thrilling."

And after it was all over and she'd assembled her movie, she compiled her list of production complaints, which, this time, were more serious than just the inclement weather. There was a blizzard during the shoot in New York and an unseasonable heat wave while filming an ice-skating scene on location in Maine.

Tragically, a fire in an apartment building near the Yonkers church where the movie was filming killed two children.

"We were in Yonkers, not in a great neighborhood, shooting a scene between Denzel and Jennifer Lewis," Penny told Rosie in their *Premiere* magazine Q & A in 1996, "and I heard a noise. I finished the take, which I always do, because God forbid I yell, 'Cut!' And I said, 'Who started up a truck during that?' Then I turned around and saw smoke pouring out, two buildings down. So the grips and the electrics ran into action with the ladders."

With that, the death of her friend Ted Bessell, and a respiratory infection that plagued her throughout the filming, finishing *The Preacher's Wife* must have seemed a small miracle.

The Preacher's Wife is the story of an overworked and preoccupied preacher trying to save his church, his beautiful but neglected wife, and the suave angel who works his small miracles, saving them and restoring their faith—not simply in a Higher Power, but in themselves and each other. Those plot elements were taken directly from 1947's *The Bishop's Wife*, and transformed by Marshall and her writers, Nat Mauldin and Allan Scott, into a modern African-American milieu.

Marshall and her writers weren't content with a mere remake of the original, a rather austere fantasy. Instead, they piled on what in Hollywood is called the "rooting interest," giving the audience a sitcom-worthy menagerie of characters to root for (or hiss at):

There's the greedy real-estate speculator (Gregory Hines). He wants to raze the old church and lure Pastor Biggs out to a brand-new church in the suburbs, far from his flock in the Old Neighborhood.

There's Pastor Bigg's boy, Jeremiah (Justin Pierre Edmund). He's separated from his young friend, Hakim, who, just before the holidays, has been taken to a foster home.

There's the Preacher's mother-in-law (Jennifer Lewis). She just can't stop smoking.

There's the troubled teenager trying to go straight, who is wrongly accused of a crime.

And there's the Preacher's secretary, a single mother, struggling to raise three children alone and looking for a husband.

The film begins with voiceover narration by little Jeremiah, who recalls the "Christmas I learned all about miracles."

When Pastor Biggs, dejected after a sermon that netted only $96 and a button in the collection plate, raises his eyes to heaven and asks for help, the dapper Angel Dudley appears. He is garbed throughout in an elegant pearly-gate gray suit (and matching coat, hat, tie, and silk neck scarf). Dudley, in the Cary Grant mode of the original, is a most low-key celestial being, demonstrating his heavenliness not so much with miracles (though he does fix Jeremiah's toy ambulance so that it's better than new), but with a stellar smile and a heart-warming handshake that reminds the mortals who grasp his hand of "Springtime and Mom's home cookin' all rolled into one."

Pastor Biggs is a good man, but he's lost belief in his own ability to make a difference. His beautiful wife Julia leads the choir and has the gift of soul. She still loves Pastor Biggs, but is dejected by his neglect.

There's barely a non-African-American face to be seen in front of the camera. However, when the subplot about the unjustly accused teenager begins to unfold, both the cops who arrest him and the liquor-store owner who accuses him are white—adding a touch of verisimilitude. For the most part, though, the world in which *The Preacher's Wife* exists is very much a fantasy of the Old Neighborhood—that same romanticized place from which Penny and her brother Garry hailed.

"The story is so predictable and the setting so romanticized that it's a wonder this film can hold the interest it does" was the verdict of the *San Francisco Chronicle*, which praised not the director but the "heavenly performances" of the "engaging" cast.

Calling the plot "noble sludge," *Time* magazine said of Penny's direction: She "binges on cuteness. . . . The audience is so many Strasbourg geese, force-fed treacle." *USA Today* gave Penny's direction a rather blunt, backhanded compliment, in effect saying that she was right for the sitcom-level material. "Penny Marshall . . . may not be the fanciest director, but she knows the way to our hearts, and the unflashy virtues of her holiday film feel audacious in their steadfast old-fashionedness." *Boxoffice* magazine, on the other hand, put a velvet glove over the same backhanded slap, saying Penny's direction "consistently attains genuine sentiment without the usual melodramatic excess," even though "criticizing a film like *The Preacher's Wife* seems a little like criticizing a useless Christmas gift. In both cases, it's the thought that counts."

Before *Preacher's Wife*, Whitney Houston had starred in *Waiting to Exhale*, a 1995 film that proved to mainstream Hollywood that there was an audience for films about middle-class Black life, and that made more than $66 million at the domestic box office. And in 1992 she starred in the film *The Bodyguard*, a small romantic thriller that became a box-office phenomenon—taking in almost $120 million domestically and an incredible $410 million worldwide.

Compared to that, *The Preacher's Wife*, not an inexpensive film to have made, must be accounted a failure. Its $48 million domestic box office is almost $10 million less than *The Bodyguard* made in video rentals alone.

Penny and Rob Reiner in Malibu, at the Challenge of the
Network Stars in the 1970s.

Laverne & Shirley—making faces.

Laverne & Shirley, episode #92: "What Do You Do with a Drunken Sailor?" featuring Ed Begley Jr.

Penny and Tom Hanks during an impromptu
script conference on the set of *Big* (1988).

Penny checking out a shot during the filming of *Big*.

Penny as Michael J. Fox's agent in *The Hard Way* (1991).

Penny coaches Mark Wahlberg in military preparedness
on the set of *Renaissance Man* (1994).

COURTESY OF FOTOS INTERNATIONAL/ARCHIVE PHOTOS.

Penny and Danny DeVito at the *Renaissance Man* premiere.

COURTESY OF LEE/ARCHIVE PHOTOS.

Penny and Steven Spielberg at the Golden Globes, 1980.

COURTESY OF FRANK EDWARDS/FOTOS INTERNATIONAL/ARCHIVE PHOTOS.

Penny with brother Garry at the
1997 Television Academy "Hall of Fame" Ceremony.

COURTESY OF FRED PROUSER/REUTERS/ARCHIVE PHOTOS.

Chapter Five

CARRYING ON

Rosie, Kmart, and Victoria's Secret

REAL LIVES ARE not tidy narratives, except perhaps in retrospect, and even then it's the exceedingly rare life that provides the neat climax and the moral uplift that Hollywood has taught us to expect. If Penny Marshall's story was a morality tale, filmed by Hollywood, it would end after *Big* (1988), when, at a stroke, that charming fairy tale's box-office triumph wipes away the years of critical condescension toward Laverne. The epilogue perhaps would include the lesser, but still substantial, critical and financial successes of her next two movies, *Awakenings* (1990) and *A League of Their Own* (1992).

But Penny Marshall continued on . . . to make *Renaissance Man* (1994) and *The Preacher's Wife* (1996), two feature films that were much weaker at the box office than their predecessors. And once again the critics have generally sneered. Despite critical condescension, the public is the final arbiter, and the public continues to have an overwhelmingly positive feeling—warm and fuzzy—toward Penny the person. Perhaps it is because they remember Laverne the lovable character, or perhaps because of Penny's persona as a normal, and even normally neurotic, girl from the Old Neighborhood.

There's no better indication of this continuing public affection for Penny than her successful stint as a pixieish corporate pitchwoman, part of the Penny and Rosie duo, for Kmart, the giant discount retailer. When companies like Kmart, which spends nearly $50 million each year on TV advertising, commission celebrities to represent them, they pick people for qualities that are beyond simply a famous face and a recognizable voice. Those particularly desirable qualities in a spokesperson are likability and familiarity. For years they've been measured and codified in something called the TVQ Score.

Naturally the mass medium of television is where those with the most familiarity are to be found. Recent corporate spokespersons with high Q scores include such television performers as Candice Bergen (*Murphy Brown*), John Lithgow (*Third Rock from the Sun*), Paul Reiser (*Mad About You*), Lea Thompson (*Caroline in the City*), and Janine Turner (*Northern Exposure*). Not surprisingly, one of the highest Q scores of all time belongs to the immensely likable and familiar pitchman for Jello (among many other products), Bill Cosby.

The fact that Penny and Rosie represent the Kmart chain in a variety of cute and funny ads written by Rosie, which began airing for the 1995 Christmas holiday season, and continue on TV to the present day, says volumes about the duo's likability. It also denotes their down-to-earth appeal to the kind of working and middle-class families that Kmart wants as customers.

Those first November 1995 commercials featured Penny and Rosie as bargain-hunters finding all their Christmas gifts at Kmart—everything from bedroom slippers to diamond bracelets. And backed by a new "Celebrate the Magic" theme and coupon savings offers, the ads were critically important to the giant chain's corporate welfare.

With its stock at a thirteen-year low, Kmart needed to prove to Wall Street that it could convince customers that it was an excellent Christmas shopping destination.

"People tend not to think of Kmart as a gift store," said Kenneth Watson, Kmart's executive vice-president of marketing and product development, at the time. "We will really drive home the idea that Kmart has tremendous value. . . . We're combining the price aspect along with the idea of a special product—be it a diamond tennis bracelet, Lego, or a CD player."

According to the Kmart executive vice president, Penny and Rosie were picked as the spokespersons for this crucial, make-or-break campaign because of their "down-to-earth yet savvy qualities." Or as Penny put it: "Rosie and I are people who seem blue-collar, I think. We're regular people."

"The customer," Watson explained, "can really relate to Rosie, if they're younger, or Penny if they're a bit older."

The Kmart ads, said Rosie on the *Today* show in early autumn 1998 as part of the publicity push to promote her revamped TV talk show's third-season debut, were "anti-sell." It was as good a description as any of their essential appeal.

What did a down-to-earth, regular-person, with blue-collar sensibility look like after two-and-a-half decades of Hollywood success? A late 1996 *People* magazine profile, part of *The Preacher's Wife* publicity drumbeat, provided a glimpse:

There was Penny, looking spent, Marlboro in her mouth, Pepsi in her hand, in her "sprawling, antique-filled" Hollywood Hills house, which seemed to be not merely a home but a kind of shopper's paradise warehouse, with rooms nicknamed "The Mall" and "The War Room." In the Mall was where Penny kept the presents she accumulated and planned to give as future gifts. In the War Room was the World War II-era memorabilia she started collecting after *Renaissance Man*.

As a compulsive collector, on locations Penny unwound by "sweeping the area for antiques, armed with a walkie-talkie to communicate with the set."

Oddly enough for someone who trades on a blue-collar persona, she allowed herself to be photographed as she stretched out—cigarette in her mouth, cell phone at her ear—in the back seat of a limousine.

"I don't drive," said Penny, who by then had lived in the city of Los Angeles for nearly three decades, to the *People* writer, who characterized her as "living the hectic life of a Hollywood hotshot." "Do you?"

Two years after the crucial Kmart campaign began, the *USA Today* headline—*Women Like Kmart's Rosie and Penny Ads*—didn't quite say it all. By then, though, the Kmart turnaround was well under way and Rosie was a daytime talk-show host. Her chatty mix of show tunes and talk and confidences (seemingly) shared while the audience just happened to be tuned in, was an ingratiating throwback to the pre-tabloid-TV days of Merv Griffin and Mike Douglas, and was the ratings sensation of the syndication world.

When Penny appeared on the show for the first time during the 1996–97 season, Rosie prompted Marshall to relate how, while they were shooting the commercials, she'd asked Kmart execs, "You don't mind if we take a few things, do you?" Her Kmart booty, Marshall continued, included a "microwave oven, refrigerator, cappuccino machine, roller blades, and lots more."

True story or not, it had the added benefit of reinforcing Penny's image as a lovably kooky but commonsense, thrifty, average person, the kind of blue-collar person who just couldn't pass up a freebie. It also served to boost Kmart's image as the kind of company whose 2,126 stores nationwide would sell everything from a microwave oven to a cappuccino machine, "and lots more."

It was the kind of added value exposure that was a godsend for any advertising campaign. And, as it turned out, the media blitz's appeal went well beyond women. It included "most consumers—rich, poor, young, or old—[all of whom] feel comfortable with the comediennes," the chief creative officer of the Minneapolis ad agency Campbell Mithun Esty, which created the Kmart campaign, told *USA Today*. "When you see the ads, you feel like they are just like the folks next door, not celebrities."

Six months later, Kmart introduced yet another Penny-and-Rosie ad from the Campbell Mithun Esty agency. It turned the "folks next door" into the Price Police, uniformed and badged, who, in the words of a company press release, "approach a shopper about Violation 421, unnecessary disbursement of domestic funds. As they review her sales receipt, they point out that, had she shopped Big Kmart, she could have saved on several items."

Kmart launched its conversion to the larger Big Kmart store format in 1997. Nearly twelve hundred of its stores were scheduled to be turned into either "Big" or "Super" Kmart shopping centers by the beginning of 1999. In 1998, another Price Police Kmart ad started appearing on television. In this one Penny and Rosie are at a diner counter, talking to a waitress and sitting comfortably among real police.

Familiarity and likability were surely what made late-night so special on February 14, 1996, for NBC. That was when Rosie O'Donnell guest-hosted, and Penny Marshall guest-starred, on *Saturday Night Live*. It turned out to be the highest-rated *SNL* episode in more than two years (with a ten rating and a twenty-five share). Of course, it didn't hurt that Whitney Houston was the musical guest or that Beavis and Butt-Head, America's favorite animated slackers, made a cameo appearance to promote their new movie.

Rather than the single grand entrance, to surprised oohs and delighted applause, of most other *SNL* guest stars, Penny popped in throughout the program. During Rosie's opening monologue, she waxed eloquent and nostalgic for the virtues of the TV shows she grew up with, saying, for example, "to me, TV is what football was to O. J. before he killed his wife." Afterward, Penny and Whitney joined Rosie to sing "I Got You, Babe," in a tribute to *The Sonny and Cher Show.*

Later, in a Mary Katherine Gallagher (Molly Shannon) sketch, Penny was piano-playing Sister Maria, who was due at a Gamblers Anonymous meeting. In another routine, Penny was the neighbor who got into a kicking war with Rita Delvecchio, the Porch Lady (Cheri Oteri).

There aren't many $100 million movie directors to whom the average salaried working stiff can readily relate, just as there aren't many $100 million movie directors who themselves would readily relate to the idea of doing a TV commercial in the first place. However, Penny Marshall is one of them. Certainly there aren't many A-list movie directors who, back at the beginning of the 1990s, had a sense of the importance of cable shopping channels, especially to the marketing of a big-screen movie. In fact, the first one probably was Penny Marshall.

Back in the summer of 1992, "in a movie marketing first," Penny appeared live on the Philadelphia-based QVC Network to "promote the sale of licensed merchandise connected to her upcoming film," *A League of Their Own*.

QVC touted the appearance as part of a "Block Party Weekend," in which the twenty-four-hour-a-day channel sold such *League* merchandise as crew jackets, baseball caps, and jerseys. The tie-in was part of a deal between the cable channel, the studio (Columbia Pictures), and Parkway, Penny's production company, that also included *Calendar Girl*, another Columbia film produced by Penny's company, and starring *Beverly Hills, 90210* heartthrob Jason Priestley.

In another example of Penny's marketing prowess, in February of 1993 when *League* was released on home video, with 500,000 units expected to ship, there was a tie-in campaign with Contadina, the ketchup and tomato sauce company, offering *League* video renters who also purchased two Contadina products a $3 rebate.

Was all this commercial activity, particularly the on-camera pitches for Kmart, somehow beneath a big-time film director like Penny Marshall? Not according to the big-time film director herself:

"All of a sudden, I'm a big Hollywood director!" she scoffed when asked the question online. "Usually, I'm just Laverne, that happened to be directing. Now, I'm a big Hollywood director and Kmart's beneath me? Wait a second. I don't get it. Yell at Candy Bergen. Yell at Whoopi. Leave me alone. Meryl Streep did American Express. Spike Lee's doing those commercials. All right? Leave me alone. I'm having a good time with Rosie. That's all I know. And I get free toys for my grandson."

She was right about the other performers doing commercials and about the film directors like Spike Lee (*Do the Right Thing* and others) directing commercial TV spots (Nike ads in Lee's case) between big-screen projects. In fact, one of these directors was Penny Marshall, who, in mid-1997, directed a widely seen commercial for Victoria's Secret entitled "Heavenly Angels."

The spot featured well-known models Tyra Banks, Helena Christensen, Karen Mulder, Daniella Pestova, and Stephanie Seymour all wearing sexy underwear and diaphanous angel wings. While sitting on clouds they talked about Victoria Secret's Angel Collection with comedian Dennis Miller, who joked and interacted "extemporaneously with the models," according to the company's press release announcing the ad campaign. The company's release also saluted "Penny's fresh and inventive directing approach (that) brought an engaging and entertaining spontaneity to the actors' performance."

On the Road to 2000

Laverne and Shirley meet the royals?!

However unlikely the match-up seems, that has been the big-screen concept floating around Hollywood for the past few years, ever since the *Laverne & Shirley* reunion TV special of the mid-1990s.

Hollywood, like Washington, is a city of trial balloons—show-business trade-paper stories and newspaper and magazine gossip-column items that offer a carefully worded wish as if it was almost a fact. It's a time-tested way for those in the business to communicate, if sometimes in a kind of insider code. The producer who wants a certain actor whose bankability will help raise financing for a project; the actor who wants to be considered for a certain important part; the studio that wants the town's A-list players to know it's no longer consumed by executive in-fighting and is now able to listen to project pitches and is ready to make high-profile deals—these are some of the sources of (and reasons for) Hollywood trial balloons.

For example, after his success in *Titanic* (1997), Leonardo DiCaprio was suddenly the star of the moment, in demand at every film studio. He was touted as about to star as, variously, a "cowboy, a Hemingway hero, a yuppie murderer, a schizophrenic law student, and . . . a wanderer who's in possession of a map to paradise." *The Beach*, the story of the American backpacker with the map to Eden proved most likely to be the first post-*Titanic* DiCaprio project. Whether or not he takes on any other of those roles, or whether any of the other scripts eventually make it beyond the development stage, is, at this writing, an open question. In the overheated post-*Titanic* climate, however, they all (like *The Beach*) started out as trial balloons.

And a trial balloon is exactly what the teasing mentions of a big-screen *Laverne & Shirley* movie seem to be. The telefilm was the first occasion for column items about a potential $50 million big-screen Paramount movie, starring Penny and Cindy, possibly to be directed by brother Garry. Ever since, intermittent trial balloons have tested the atmosphere. Penny and Cindy think the screenwriter "should be someone who was a major fan of the sitcom, says a source . . ." went a typical, "planted" item in *People* magazine in the mid-1990s.

A few years later in 1998, Penny floated the idea again, this time in the *Los Angeles Times*, saying, "Don't know if they want us in it, or a young us. All I know is they want it for cheap." She also observed, "All that's being done is TV shows made into movies or blowing things up."

True enough, as any regular moviegoer can readily attest. TV shows that have been made into feature films include—in addition to the various *Batman, Superman,* and *Star Trek* movies—*The Avengers, Beavis and Butt-Head, The Brady Bunch, Dennis the Menace, Flipper, The Fugitive* (and its sequel, *U.S. Marshals*), *George of the Jungle, Leave It to Beaver, Lost in Space, McHale's Navy, Mission: Impossible, Mr. Magoo, The Saint, The X-Files,* and *Zorro.*

Among the shows, like *Laverne & Shirley,* that are still in the trial-balloon phase or that have made it into the early development/production pipeline, and most likely will be coming soon to a multiplex near you are: *The A-Team, Babylon Five, Battlestar Galactica, Bewitched, I Dream of Jeannie, Gilligan's Island, Green Acres, The Green Hornet, Have Gun Will Travel, The Honeymooners, The Incredible Hulk, The Love Boat, Magnum, P.I., The Mod Squad, The Partridge Family, The Adventures of Rocky & Bullwinkle, Run for Your Life, The Six Million Dollar Man, South Park, The Wild, Wild West,* and *Wonder Woman.*

Whether or not the *Laverne & Shirley Meet the Royals* script, which, according to yet another trial balloon, actually has been completed, ever gets made or not is, at present, very much up in the trial-balloon air. However, as the sometimes excruciatingly slow development process inches forward, the likelihood diminishes that the original Laverne and Shirley will ever be back in their old roles.

Asked who might play Laverne if she didn't do it herself, Penny suggested maybe Marisa Tomei (*My Cousin Vinny, The Slums of Beverly Hills*).

In the 1990s, Penny Marshall continued to go her own way, producing four films, very occasionally guest-starring on TV, and acting in small roles in movies like the 1991 action-comedy *The Hard Way.*

Both *The Hard Way* and the Gulf War "opened" the same weekend, and, predictably, the film became a box-office flop. Potential moviegoers stayed home to watch TV for news of the war. In *The Hard Way,* a method-acting movie star (played by Michael J. Fox) shadows a tough New York cop (James

Woods), to prepare for a role. Quite obviously modeling herself after 1970s super-agent Sue Mengers, Penny plays the movie star's tough-broad agent, who retorts to her client's complaint that all she gets him is parts in movies with Roman numerals in the title, "they made *Henry V*. It won awards for that little Scottish guy!"

Throughout the mid- and late 1990s, Penny seemed just as likely to turn up in a Kmart commercial, or in the gossip or society columns, as on a casting call or a Films in Production sheet. To the cynical, seen-it-all wiseguys of the entertainment press, those with a finely honed sense of who's a has-been and who's on the A-list, she had become part of the will-turn-out-for-the-opening-of-an-envelope set. Of course, John Travolta, among others, had once been similarly disparaged, too. It took just one box-office smash to wipe away (for a while anyway) the condescension.

Until then, though, she'd become one of that cadre of celebrities who could be relied upon to turn out for premieres and parties, making the short walk from the limo along the red carpet to the theatre or the ballroom, past the TV cameras and the paparazzi, basking in the brief attention. These celebrity-studded events ranged from charitable and artistic benefits to the openings of movies like director John Dahl's *Rounders* (in the company of such media-friendly folks as Alexis Arquette, Benicio Del Toro, Robert Forster, Gina Gershon, Michael Keaton, Swoosie Kurtz, Martin Sheen, and Ben Stiller), and the thirtieth anniversary reprise of the original *Planet of the Apes*.

Despite her accomplishments behind the camera, when she did show up at a public event, Penny was still likely as not to be dubbed one of the "mondo '70s tagged stars," just as she was when she appeared at a Vistas for Blind Children party in 1998. And still, after almost two decades, she was identified as "Penny 'Laverne DeFazio' Marshall."

Inevitably, some of her many personal appearances also took on the aura of farce. One such was her turn at New York's Fashion Cafe to promote the debut of Kmart's *Sesame Street* line of children's clothes. Twirling down the runway with the Public Broadcasting kids' show characters, Penny lost her balance—and, according to *Entertainment Weekly*, "much to her horror . . . not to mention that of the predominantly preteen crowd,"—when she grabbed for balance, "Marshall latched on to Big Bird's right wing and promptly tore it off. . . . Later, Marshall vowed to 'never again' work with puppets."

It was an incident that could have happened to anyone, but it would have fit so well as a piece of business—as *shtick*—on *Laverne & Shirley* that a suspicious and cynical mind familiar with the ways of the Hollywood hype machine might wonder if the whole thing was a publicist's inspired invention.

More often, though, Penny was mentioned in the press in a more dignified way, more befitting a major Hollywood motion-picture director, in society columns about various charitable galas and fêtes benefiting good feminist and liberal causes. When the Artists Rights Foundation honored director Milos Forman (*One Flew Over the Cuckoo's Nest* [1975], *Amadeus* [1984], *Valmont* [1989], *The People vs. Larry Flynt* [1996], and others) for his work on their behalf and for opposing such common TV practices as colorization, pan-and-scan, time compression, and cutting for content, those making special appearances at the gala included Sid Caesar, Annette Bening, Martin Scorsese, Kevin Spacey, Anjelica Huston, James Woods, and . . . Penny Marshall.

Studio and network insiders, stung by protests from gay-rights activists, formed an organization called Hollywood Supports to end discrimination on the basis of sexual orientation within the industry, and to monitor its often insensitive portrayals of lesbians and gays. The prestigious Board of Trustees, a veritable *Who's Who* of the famous and powerful, included everyone from Steve Martin to Sylvester Stallone, and . . . both Garry and Penny Marshall.

And when A-list stars, including Tom Cruise, Barbra Streisand, and Daryl Hannah, publicly petitioned, in a *New York Times* newspaper advertisement, to end the practice of clear-cutting in the temperate rain forest of British Columbia, Rob Reiner signed . . . and so did his ex-wife, Penny Marshall.

Probably the most exclusive of the events at which Penny turns up annually is the one she's been hosting since the mid-1970s. Or rather, hosting in conjunction with Carrie Fisher, her long-time best friend, who shares her October fifteenth birthday. Their annual party, usually an unpretentious and casual, home-cooking kind of affair, which is held as often as not at Penny's house in the Hollywood Hills, attracts not just the A-list, but A-list crashers. In 1995, for example, at Penny's house for the annual party were Warren Beatty and Annette Bening, Meg Ryan and Dennis Quaid, Michael Keaton, Sean Penn, Garry Shandling, Rita Wilson (Tom Hanks' actress wife) and celebrity du jour Christopher Darden of the O. J. Simpson criminal prosecution team. That year's celebrity crasher was comedic superstar Jim Carrey.

"He said, 'I crashed.' I said, 'Fine,'" recalled Penny a year later. "I didn't think he'd steal anything."

In late 1998, just two weeks after their joint birthday, Reuters wire service reported that Carrie Fisher had checked herself into a drug treatment program for an addiction to prescription medication. According to Fisher's publicist, the actress/writer who'd fictionalized her own battles with cocaine addiction and an earlier stay in drug rehab in her bestselling novel, *Postcards from the Edge*, entered the program after dental surgery.

"The combination of the prescribed medication required for manic depression and the pain medication prescribed to her recently from getting dental implants caused her to recognize the problem early on and act immediately," the publicist was quoted as saying in the Reuters report.

Like Penny, Carrie Fisher, the daughter of actor/singers Debbie Reynolds and Eddie Fisher, entered show business because of her relatives. Like Penny, she is now firmly ensconced in what the Business is pleased to call the Community. Like Penny, she is both loved and valued in the Industry, in her case not simply as an actress and a novelist, but as a highly paid script doctor as well. She, too, is undeniably a good citizen when it comes to taking high-visibility public stands, and her personal missteps and idiosyncrasies will continue to be understood and forgiven, as will Penny's.

But Penny Marshall's own most recent *fin-de-siecle* column-item mentions were bizarre by any standard—even Hollywood's.

At the end of this century, as at the end of the last, more often than not the typical lifestyle-of-the-rich-and-famous column item celebrates conspicuous consumption. Or it looks askance at dangerous, disreputable, or just plain weird behavior.

To pick just one among literally scores of possible examples: In the summer of 1998, Penny's ex-husband Rob Reiner found himself peripherally entangled in the Phil Hartman murder-suicide story. He probably would have preferred to be in the news to promote his movies or for his commendable efforts in behalf of programs that benefit children's health and encourage early childhood education.

When comic actor Phil Hartman was murdered by Brynn, his disturbed and drug-addicted wife, who then killed herself, Rob was widely mentioned in tabloids and TV news shows as someone who had once dated Brynn Hartman, and had even given her a small role in *North* (1994), his least-successful movie.

(In typical tabloid fashion, the *Globe's* headline of June 10, 1998, was, "Meathead's Eerie Link to Phil Hartman Murder," and the story under it began, "Rob Reiner's blood runs cold when he thinks of the horror he narrowly escaped.")

A hundred years ago it was the railroad and steel barons, with their yachts and castle-size seaside cottages who made the social columns or the scandal sheets. In our own era, it's the moneyed Hollywood A-list and corporate Wall Street darlings. For example, who could be richer than Microsoft's co-founder Paul Allen, and what consumption could be more conspicuous than rounding up a few hundred friends and jetting them off to Alaska for a birthday party or to Venice (Italy, not California) for a little celebration in honor of a sweet business deal?

The occasion of the Venice fest was the sale of Allen's share of Ticket-master to the Home Shopping Network, and, according to a newspaper columnist quoting a *New York* magazine report, to commemorate it, the multibillionaire offered about 300 of his best pals, including actor Michael Keaton and tennis player John McEnroe, a chartered jet flight overseas for the big party.

Some of the favored 300, however, who traveled via Allen's chartered plane, according to the report in the *St. Paul* (Minnesota) *Pioneer Press*, thought the in-flight accommodations weren't quite up to snuff: The plane "turned out to have small coach seats and unappetizing coach food. So this group of rich and famous people were complaining. . . . They became very rebellious and refused to comply with basic requests."

Ringleader of the rebels, according to the report, was none other than "timid," "insecure," "eager-to-please" Penny, who was the first among them to fire up an illegal cigarette. Then, "others followed in breaking the plane's no-smoking rule. . . . Smokers in the bathroom set off alarms, apparently to no concern of the partying celebs."

Penny Marshall?!

However that kind of behavior may sound in the retelling, it apparently wasn't enough to disturb Penny's place on the super-rich's A-list. When Paul Allen decided to fete Bill Gates, Microsoft's co-founder and reputedly the "richest man in the world," on the occasion of his birthday in Summer 1998, he arranged to jet "more than 500 of the world's most famous, well-to-do, and well-connected" to Juneau, Alaska. He threw a top secret party aboard the Crystal Harmony, a 960-passenger ship, which cruised Glacier Bay and the Inside Passage. Aboard the ship were Dan Aykroyd, Candice Bergen, James Cameron, Jeff Goldblum, and Debbie Reynolds, among others.

Guests arrived in Juneau on approximately twenty planes, "most of which stayed far from the passenger terminal," and then they were "whisked by bus" to the ship. But first they stopped off in nearby gift shops for a little spree. Her long-time pal Carrie Fisher "bought a sweatshirt and a Russian lacquer box." Per the Associated Press, "director Penny Marshall got so caught up buying furs [at the Alaska Fur Gallery] that she delayed the ship's departure."

If all that seems hard to believe of go-along-to-get-along Penny, consider this: pro-basketball bad-boy Dennis Rodman and Penny buying lap dances at a strip club?!

Attired in a Rodman jersey, Penny watched Game Four of the 1988 National Basketball Association finals from a front row seat. After the Chicago Bulls' victory, she and the tattooed and technicolor-haired, cross-dressing basketball star allegedly headed for Chicago's Crazy Horse Too strip club. At the club, as the *National Enquirer* rather breathlessly reported it on June 30, 1998, "the pair had a harem of chesty charmers frolicking all around them as Dennis peeled off $50 bills. He even paid to have a lass do her thing in Penny's lap!"

Because the report first appeared in a tabloid newspaper, it's easy to discount—unless, that is, you closely follow the increasingly surreal world of Hollywood scandals and see how often the *National Enquirer* and its ilk are right (as well as first) when it comes to titillating celebrity news. It was the *Enquirer*, after all, that tipped police to the identity of Ennis Cosby's killer, and the paper was the first to publish damning photos of O. J. Simpson in those "ugly ass" Bruno Magli shoes.

In Hollywood, celebrities regularly decry the intrusion of the paparazzi and the tabloids into their lives. Just as regularly, they—or perhaps a wily publicist in their pay—will tip or plant the tabloids with stories, even the titillating ones, just to keep their names and images on the covers of those huge-selling weeklies so omnipresent at the supermarket checkout lines. How, for example, did the tabloid learn the plot of the season-opening episode of your favorite TV series, the one that solved the mysteries of last season's cliffhanger, in advance? More than likely, the show's producer himself slipped it to them to hype the show's flagging ratings!

Among the many rules governing the complex relationship between Hollywood celebrities and the tabloids is: Bizarre behavior breeds bizarre behavior. In other words, once a celebrity comes to the attention of the tabs, it becomes ever more likely that such attention will persist, and every little miscue and misstep will become public knowledge, and an occasion for tisk-tisking in print.

Another rule: the tabloids are like old-fashioned neighborhood back fence gossips, in that what they like most of all are the cautionary stories with a moral . . . stories in which the rich and famous, the beautiful people with beautiful lives, are brought low. That deliciously enjoyable feeling of superiority that comes to tabloid readers head shaking over the misfortunes of others, particularly those better off or more famous, is best described as "malicious joy"—from the utterly apposite German word *schadenfreude*.

So with those rules and relationships well in mind, consider the oddly elliptical cautionary tale spun by the *National Enquirer* for its issue of September 22, 1998, under the screaming headline, "ROSIE'S AGONY: She prays for best pal Penny Marshall." Perhaps coincidentally, it appeared the same early-autumn week when the highly touted third-season debut of Rosie O'Donnell's TV talk show was getting under way.

Rosie was "upset and frightened," said the tab, "caught in an agonizing dilemma."

At a charity auction the month before, the tabloid reported, quoting a "friend" and an "insider," Penny had "repeatedly raised her hand and jumped to bid on auction items," even interrupting the auctioneer in mid-spiel and pushing her way into an interview Rosie was doing with *Access Hollywood*.

Most damning of all, though, at the filming of their latest Kmart commercials that same month, Penny had seemed "out of it," forgetting her lines, screaming, *"You're all trying to get rid of me!"* According to the insider, unnamed execs had decided to shoot Penny and Rosie separately. (In fact, in the subsequent new TV commercials, which began airing in fall of 1998, Penny and Rosie did appear for the first time in separate ads. They were back together in time for the Christmas-season ad campaign, though.)

Still later, the omnipresent insider reported to the same tabloid, at a women's basketball game in New York, Rosie was "too flabbergasted, too embarrassed" to reply when an "agitated" Penny suddenly turned up and began yelling: *"What are you trying to do to me? Why are you cutting me out of the Kmart commercials?"*

As other examples of Penny's bizarre ways, the tab cited the *Sesame Street* fashion-show incident of the year before, giving Penny's slip on the runway a sinister interpretation. It also told the well-known Kmart-shoot story, the one in which Penny, with what theretofore was considered delightful kookiness, had loaded up with free toys for her grandson and other young relatives. This time, though, the charming little tale was reinterpreted by this dark new bit of information: the toys, the tabloid now revealed, had been earmarked allegedly for one of Rosie's favorite charities and Rosie had been "upset" by Penny's peculiar selfishness.

"I'm worried sick about Penny" said Rosie, in a direct quote supplied to the paper by a "friend," "but I don't know how to help her."

In the aftermath of the bizarre behavior Rosie was said to be "praying" for Penny Marshall.

If these seem like surreal incidents, bordering on the unreal (and some may in fact be nothing more than the hot air of Hollywood puffery), in fairness we should consider that the modern celebrity lives with a fundamental contradiction. On one hand, they are constantly on display in the fishbowl world of tabloids and TV; but, at the same time, they are protected within the confines of the high-powered Hollywood hype machine—a behind-the-scenes engine that functions to benefit the celebrity, to control and manipulate the media spotlight. When things get a little out of hand for you and me, if perhaps we tie one on or spend time in some dubious person's company, our lapse is not instantly memorialized and magnified by censorious tabloid hyperbole and the media's all-seeing eye. And, of course, from time to time, the modern celebrity, just like the average working stiff, has to face more worrisome issues than mere unwanted publicity.

That happened to Penny as far back as March of 1981, when, in her own Hollywood Hills home in the middle of the night, Penny came face to face with a bizarre version of what today is called a home-invasion robbery. Hearing noises outside as she prepared for bed, Penny tripped a silent alarm, then two teenaged burglars dressed as Japanese Ninja in hooded masks confronted her, threatening to kill her with a Samurai-style sword while they ransacked the house, according to a police report of the March 13, 1981 incident.

Setting off the silent alarm was a cool, self-possessed move that Laverne might have envied. In the *Laverne & Shirley* episode, "Fake Out at the Stake Out," she and Shirley are robbed by the Milwaukee Masher (a cross-dressing thief who steals Shirley's poodle skirt and Laverne's favorite sweater). After the girls tiptoe around the apartment with baseball bats, with only Boo Boo Kitty (Shirley's beloved stuffed animal) hiding under the bed, Laverne agrees to be a police decoy in the park that night. Why? Because Norman, the cop who shows up on the case (and becomes her sometime boyfriend for a few subsequent episodes), is cute, of course.

In real life, when police with helicopters and dogs responded to the alarm, the black-clad youths fled Penny's house, hiding in the brush of a cliff about sixty yards away, where they were eventually discovered. According to the police report, they had to be plucked from the cliff with a fire truck ladder.

When the two teenagers were captured, the police found knives and nun-chaku sticks (typically two thin wands made of either lacquered hard wood or metal that are used as weapons in Asian martial arts). Police never found the sword.

The two young robbers, aged eighteen and nineteen, were held in lieu of $20,000 bail, and were charged with counts of burglary, armed robbery, and possession of dangerous weapons (the nunchakus). Penny appeared at the two teenagers' preliminary hearing, testifying that one of them had apologized when he realized they had broken into the home belonging to the star of *Laverne & Shirley*. The would-be teenage ninja had gushed to her that he liked the TV show.

Seventeen years later, in February of 1998, Penny Marshall's name surfaced in the trial of another potentially violent criminal. The previous July, a man had been arrested outside of Steven Spielberg's Pacific Palisades' mansion for reportedly stalking the Oscar-winning director. In the man's car, police reportedly found handcuffs, duct tape, a box cutter, razor blades, and a notebook filled with photographs of Spielberg, his actress wife, Kate Capshaw, and their seven children.

The man had intended to rape the director, police said.

According to a *Reuters* news service report at the time, "No one before has ever come into my life in a way to do me harm," Spielberg said in his subsequent testimony at the trial of the thirty-one-year-old man, whom prosecutors described as "obsessed" with the filmmaker.

"I've had fans and I've had people who have been a little pushy before, but not people with handcuffs and duct tape and knives and maps to my home," he added, fearfully voicing the deepest fear of the modern celebrity. "I feel to this day that I am prey to this individual."

A police officer testified that he had found a "shopping list" of sado-masochistic sex aids among the man's belongings, as well as writings that mentioned President Clinton, cable mogul Ted Turner, and two other movie directors . . . Ron Howard and Penny Marshall.

With weird and potentially dangerous events like these, does it seem so strange that Penny might have gone out for a wild time with NBA wild man Dennis Rodman? Or that the same month her name became part of the record at the Spielberg stalking trial, Penny was at the Hard Rock in Las Vegas, living it up at a semi-private Rolling Stones concert?

It wasn't her first Stones concert. A few months before, in November of 1997, she'd been in Dodger Stadium in Los Angeles, part of a celebrity contingent that had included Jennifer Aniston, Gabriel Byrne, Naomi Campbell, Jim Carrey, Peter Fonda, Dennis Hopper, Alanis Morissette, Jack Nicholson, Keanu Reeves, and Billy Bob Thornton. Unlike their stadium show in Los Angeles, though, the last stop on the North American part of the Rolling Stones' world tour was a concert for a mere fourteen hundred fans. Fans had paid scalpers up to $2,000 per ticket to be part of the small audience in the Hard Rock's Joint nightclub, in relatively close proximity not only to the Stones but to the hard-rockin' celebrities in the front rows, as well.

Right up there with Carol Alt, Drew Barrymore, Johnny Depp, Leonardo DiCaprio, Pamela Lee, Jenny McCarthy, Brad Pitt, Elisabeth Shue, and Sting was . . .

Penny, again, who this time "donned a cap that blinked 'Rolling Stones' in red as she oo-oo'ed along to 'Miss You.'"

Meanwhile, in 1996, Penny's Parkway Productions moved from Sony, which owns Columbia Pictures and TriStar Pictures, in Culver City, across the Cahuenga Pass through the Hollywood Hills, to Universal City. There Parkway joined Danny DeVito's Jersey Pictures and Demi Moore's Moving Pictures, as well as Ron Howard and Brian Grazer's Imagine Entertainment and Steven

Spielberg's Amblin Entertainment on the sprawling Universal Pictures' lot.

The year before, MCA, Universal Pictures' parent company, had been sold by Japanese hardware manufacturer Matsushita Electric to Canada's Seagram Company, founded and controlled by the Bronfman family.

Around Hollywood it was widely assumed that Universal's new head, Edgar Bronfman Jr., the young scion of the Bronfmans and a sometime songwriter himself, was most passionate not about films or TV, but about the music industry. That view was validated when one of the new owner's first acts was to acquire Interscope Records, an expansion of Universal's Music Entertainment Group that promptly moved it up from last place to first place in album market share.

In 1997 and 1998, film development at Parkway accelerated, and in the trade papers and elsewhere, development and preproduction trial balloons were ascending. Not surprising—from a production company newly based at a studio known for its owner's interest in the music industry, and in this era of multi-platinum movie soundtrack albums—two of the first new Parkway projects were music-related.

As if on cue, the trades reported that Penny Marshall was attached to direct *Wild Oats* and was developing *Saving Grace*, both for Universal.

Oats was a spec screenplay, meaning it hadn't been commissioned by anyone before it was written. It was finished on speculation by a writer who hoped for a later sale, rather than being sold first as a verbal pitch—in today's Hollywood the more common form of sale—that only later would be set down in script form. The writer, a former musician and record company executive, told the story of the lifelong love-hate friendship between two rock stars. *Saving Grace*, to which Penny also was at one point attached to direct, was an equally high concept—a romantic comedy, by Jeremy Miller and Daniel Cohn, about a playboy record producer who discovers that he has a son from a long-ago love affair.

Later, echoing the *A League of Their Own* development process, Marshall stepped aside as *Saving Grace* director, and another director stepped in. Mimi Leder, a former TV director (*ER*), was hot after her big-screen directing debut in *The Peacemaker* (1997), a big-budget, high-tech thriller, starring George Clooney and Nicole Kidman, that was the first picture from Dream-Works, the fledgling studio headed by yuppie moguls Steven Spielberg, David Geffen, and Jeffrey Katzenberg.

Leder's second picture, *Deep Impact*, one of two earth-gets-slammed-by-a-giant-rock disaster pictures from Summer 1998, did far better than expected at the box office, and suddenly the hot new director was incandescent. By fall 1998, Leder was also detached from *Saving Grace*, opting instead to direct *Still Life*, a family drama starring Michael Douglas and Meryl Streep as an estranged couple who, after the death of their daughter, are forced to confront their past and their relationship with one another while trying to raise their grandchildren.

Both *Grace* and *Life* are Universal Studio projects, so Leder's move from one to the other is less likely a reflection of their relative quality than a function of Streep and Douglas's availability, and the studio's desire to put a big-star picture on to the preproduction fast track.

By late 1998, Parkway had several other projects in various stages of development, including: *The Boys of Neptune, Delancey Street, Live from Baghdad, Cinderella Man*, and *The People's Choice*, a political satire based on a first novel by Cable News Network TV news analyst Jeff Greenfield.

Although scripts in early development are often well-guarded secrets, at this stage, it seems likely that *Baghdad* will be produced. It is based on *Live from Baghdad: Gathering News at Ground Zero*, a 1992 memoir by Cable News Network's executive producer Robert Wiener, who tells of covering events in Iraq prior to and during the Gulf War. The *Neptune* and *Delancey* projects will return Penny to her East Coast Old Neighborhood roots.

Delancey Street is a real location in New York City and was one of the great immigrant gathering places early in this century. The Delancey Street of the immigrant era was a vibrant, crowded block where Italians and Sicilians lived cramped in tenements one stoop over from Russians and East European Jews, all of them in pursuit of the same American Dream.

The Neptune Club, actually a small company called Neptune Glass in Coney Island, New York, was allegedly a gathering place for a later generation of ethnic Americans—an erstwhile social club that was often associated with the Mafia and organized crime, and particularly with John Gotti Jr., the son of the imprisoned Teflon Don. "The feds say Gotti took over Neptune Glass through extortion," according to one newspaper article. A Mafia-related Penny Marshall picture?

Of all these projects, however, probably the most un-Penny-like, but seemingly closest to her heart, is *Cinderella Man*, a film biography of boxer James J. Braddock.

Braddock, whose nickname was "The Cinderella Man," is best known to fight fans as the man Joe Louis defeated when he became heavyweight champion, knocking him out in the eighth round in Chicago, Illinois, on June 22, 1937. Braddock had held the title for two years since upsetting Max Baer, who in turn had taken the title from Primo Carnera a year before, in a fifteen-round decision.

"One script I want to do is the Jimmy Braddock story, a boxer during the Depression. A Cinderella story, a reluctant hero," Penny said to the *Los Angeles Times* in early July 1998, in a kind of terse show-business shorthand. Industry wags took to calling the project Penny's *Raging Bull*.

And then there's *Riding in Cars with Boys*, based on a book by Beverly D'Onofrio. In late spring 1999 it was touted in the trade papers that Penny was "close to committing" to directing this comic drama about a young mother who once gave up her baby boy and is now struggling to become a

writer. Drew Barrymore was hyped in industry publications as the likely star
of this big-screen project.

The April 1998 issue of *Vanity Fair,* in a full-page cartoon by Barry Blitt,
offered the following casting for the inevitable Monica Lewinsky scandal
movie (entitled, of course, *All the President's (Se)Men*): as the President, Nathan
Lane; as Kenneth Starr, Chevy Chase; as Monica, Shoshanna Lonstein; as
Hillary, Ellen DeGeneres; as Lucianne Goldberg, Angela Lansbury, and as
Linda Tripp . . . Penny Marshall.

But in the overheated media atmosphere of the late 1990s, supermarket
tabloids and glossy, up-market magazines alike could play this game. When the
National Enquirer cast its presidential-sex-scandal movie, for its March 28, 1998,
issue, the scenario was "First Lady Julia Louis-Dreyfus defending her beleaguered hubby George Clooney—all because special prosecutor Bob Newhart
alleges that President Clooney had an affair in the Oval Office with Courteney
Cox!" And the tabloid pick as a Linda Tripp . . . *still,* Penny Marshall.

Penny had directed supermodels playing angels for Victoria's Secret, and
now the role she agreed to take was not as the wiretapper near the center of
a presidential scandal, but as an archangel in a small independent romantic
comedy entitled *The Calling.* Budgeted at only $5 million, and starring Sean
Young and Nell Carter, it is to be the "story of a young woman chosen to
bear God's child." The movie marked the writing and directing debut of
Ken Carlson, who produced *Wild Bill: A Hollywood Maverick,* a recent documentary about the director William Wellman, whose many movies ranged
from *Wings* (1927) and *The Public Enemy* (1931) to *Battleground* (1949) and *The
High and the Mighty* (1954).

At about the same time (April 1998), *Vanity Fair,* tongue in cheek, suggested a
role she might take in the Monica Lewinsky "movie." Penny herself, in aviator
sunglasses, turned up at the magazine's fifth-annual Oscar party at Morton's,

perhaps the most inside of all the Hollywood insider restaurants, where guests from Sean "Puffy" Combs to Nancy Reagan, Madonna, and Brad Pitt were watching the ceremony on wall-mounted TVs.

At the Academy Awards, it was the year of *Titanic*. Outside the party were scores of paparazzi; inside, as the magazine put it, was a "palpable longing for the smart, acerbic talkies that Hollywood used to churn out by the bushel."

In short, movies without sentimentality, but with a superior sitcom zip— just the kind of movie that Penny Marshall seems so well positioned to direct, but has yet to make. However, an early review of *With Friends Like These . . .* , a show-business satire produced by Parkway that was developed under the title *Mom's on the Roof*, suggests she may be edging closer.

The movie, written and directed by Philip Meson, won the Audience Award at the Santa Barbara Film Festival in March 1998. It is "blessed with a great premise," according to an early, and almost uniformly positive, *Daily Variety* review. The plot involves four middle-aged actors, all friends, all from New York's Old Neighborhood but now living in Los Angeles. They specialize in the kind of ethnic character roles that fill out cop shows like *NYPD Blue*, and who idolize the great ethnic New York method actors—De Niro, Pacino, Hoffman—all up for the same part of "Al Capone" in Martin Scorsese's next movie.

With Friends Like These . . . stars Adam Arkin, Amy Madigan, Laura San Giacomo, Beverly D'Angelo, Elle Macpherson, and David Straithairn, among others, but was made for a minuscule $2.5 million because Penny, according to the *Los Angeles Daily News*, convinced a "lot of good friends to defer their salaries." Playing cameos in the picture are Bill Murray as a cheap producer, Scorsese as himself, and . . . Tracy Reiner and Garry Marshall.

"All the showbiz details are wonderfully handled," said *Daily Variety*, "the gossip, hearsay and commotion over new films and roles, the dealings with agents, the backstabbing that seems like an automatic reflex even when friends are involved."

Though it was *from* Penny Marshall, not *by* Penny Marshall, it seemed a good omen, a project taking her in the right direction.

What *is* the right direction for Penny Marshall the one-time sitcom star and the much-maligned director of big-budget, (generally) money-making Hollywood movies as the millenium approaches?

Since her behind-the-camera debut with *Jumpin' Jack Flash* in 1986, Penny's directed a feature film every two years. But *The Preacher's Wife* in 1996 was her most recent film, and 1998 came and went without a new helmed-by-Penny-Marshall picture.

Of all the movies she has directed thus far, only one—her first—was R-rated; all the rest were PG or PG-13. When telling sentimental stories or charming fables, that's not an issue. However, mature artists are expected at some point in their career to tackle mature and difficult themes, which becomes problematic if your movies aspire to be merely "entertainment for the whole family." The best directors bring passion to their mature projects, not simply G-rated sentiment.

What would Steven Spielberg be, for example, if his reputation rested only on the likes of *E. T., Raiders of the Lost Ark,* and *Hook*? What if he'd never made *Schindler's List, Amistad,* or 1998's *Saving Private Ryan*?

Perhaps it's presumptuous to hope that Penny will stretch professionally, that she'll make *Cinderella Man,* the Braddock boxing movie, and that it really will be her *Raging Bull.*

Despite the spotty record of her movies, Penny Marshall remains, unlike most of her fellow directors, internationally recognizable, her name a household word. That's one legacy of the much-maligned *Laverne & Shirley,* and she's benefited from it in her movie-directing career. So despite the failures of her most recent pictures, she probably still has the clout to make the pictures she wants to make.

Since her sitcom days, Penny Marshall has been a figure of accomplishment and a token of possibility for younger women, both in and out of show business. *Laverne can be on her own and make a living*, little girls sitting in front of their flickering TVs thought in the 1970s, *and maybe so can I.*

And after the successes of *Big* and *A League of Their Own*, a new generation is able to point to Penny as proof that a woman can make it to the very top echelon of the closed world of show business.

What will Penny's name and reputation mean in the new century? Will she be Laverne forever? In the ultimate evaluation of her career, will Penny ever be more than Garry's little sister, who made it on luck and continued on through pluck and by the grace of good friends and good connections?

Unlike other famous close relatives who have turned to vicious infighting (Barbara versus the kids after the death of Frank Sinatra, comes to mind), Penny and big-brother Garry have always remained commendably true to each other and the rest of their family, with never a hint of jealousy or back-biting. In fact, when Garry was finally honored in 1998 by the Academy of Television Arts and Sciences and inducted into its Hall of Fame—along with James L. Brooks (*Taxi, The Simpsons*), Quinn Martin (*The Fugitive*), Diane Sawyer (*Primetime Live*), and former MTM and NBC executive Grant Tinker—his presenter was not Julia Roberts or Richard Gere, or even Robin Williams or Henry Winkler, but his sister Penny.

Maybe the sweat and the dedication, and even the sacrifice, that making a movie masterpiece requires is, at this stage of her life, more than she can or cares to summon, particularly after her mid-1990s collapse on a Long Island tennis court. Maybe she'll be content with her commercials and her cameos and with directing movies that critics dismiss as corn.

After all, Penny gives every evidence of doting on her grandson, Spencer, and pining more for the kind of home life she once had with Rob Reiner before they were both caught in the hot white light of fame. "I have no social life," she told *Woman's Day* in 1992. And despite the routine appearances at black-tie galas, which are more about business and networking than about actually having a social life, and despite the occasional escapade, that still seems to be the case today.

"At times, I still feel that if I found a guy, I'd give it all up. I'm probably kidding myself. But as I get older, I would like to have somebody to share my life with. I don't want to have . . . Tracy pushing me around the set in a wheelchair when I'm seventy."

So perhaps all a well-wisher can do ultimately is to hope that she gets her wish, whatever that may be, and that her luck—which, together with her gift, has brought her extraordinarily far—continues to hold. And, of course, that she finally quits smoking.

Chapter Six

A Final Word

W<small>HEN I BEGAN</small> this book, I sent Penny Marshall a letter, telling her about the project and about myself, expressing my intention to write a "serious and reflective work," one that wasn't particularly concerned with "fluff or trash," and asking for her cooperation and an interview. After three months had gone by and I hadn't heard from her, I sent the letter again.

In the meantime, I prepared a short list of questions—the basics of what I was interested in—just in case I picked up the phone one morning and on the other end was that familiar nasal whine. Of course, that never happened—I didn't really think it would—and my letters went unanswered too. Just to be sure, I called her office on the Universal lot, explaining to the intern who answered about the letters and my project. A few days later, I heard from a woman who said she was Penny Marshall's assistant, and she asked me to fax the letter directly to her office. I did, and a few days later I called again. There was no decision on an interview yet, said the assistant, so I said I'd phone back in another week. When I did so a week later, I was told the assistant was out of the office. I left a detailed message, but never heard from her or anyone else in Penny Marshall's office again.

But now that the book is done, I think I can answer these few basic "opening" questions myself, and if you've followed along on this journey, then so can you.

1. *Do you feel locked into your 1970s persona?*

2. *Generally, have the critics been fair to you or not?*

3. *Have the benefits of your career been worth the costs?*

4. *Are you taking care of yourself or do you still smoke and eat junk food?*

5. *Are you happy yet?*

THE *LAVERNE & SHIRLEY* EPISODE GUIDE

THERE ARE A TOTAL of 178 *Laverne & Shirley* TV series episodes, the final sixty-five of which are set in California. With the exception of the occasional visit to the Old Neighborhood in New York, the other episodes take place in Milwaukee, Wisconsin.

Though the show, like *Happy Days* (1974–84), from which it was spun-off, is set in a blue-collar brewery town, it often seems to exist in an idealized version of the same Bronx ethnic neighborhood in which Penny and Garry Marshall were raised. It seems to be populated primarily by Jewish and Italian immigrants and their offspring, all of them smitten by the kind of contagious show-business infatuation that invariably results in everyone trying out for the annual factory talent show.

The series premiered on January 27, 1976, and aired on ABC-TV until May 9, 1983. After the 158TH episode, Cindy Williams left the show in a dispute over how her real-life pregnancy would be accommodated into the shooting schedule. Shirley was said to have married an army medic, who was assigned overseas. For its final twenty episodes, *Laverne & Shirley* was actually *The Laverne Show.*

The following summaries are adapted, with his kind permission, from Robert Hoey's excellent episode guide. Hoey, a dedicated *Laverne & Shirley* fan, is a computer software engineer living in Scotland, who first came upon the show at the age of six or seven. He recalls his rather charming introduction to the series this way: "I can distinctly remember me asking my mother, 'Why does that lady have a pound sign (£) on her jumper?' From then on I was hooked."

Like many fans, Hoey likes the show's era, as well as the 1950s and 1960s music that's always present, if often only in snippets, and the fact that it's about "two ordinary women . . . wandering into the most ludicrous (at times) comedic situations."

Robert's own favorite episodes include: "Debutante Ball," in which we learn about Lenny's background and discover that he has a "bit of a soft spot if not a crush" on Laverne, and "The Bully Show," in which Lenny and Squiggy stick their necks out to help Laverne. Like many other dedicated fans, Robert's favorite character is Shirley—"the cutest"—and his favorite bits are mostly the ones involving Lenny and Squiggy.

And so, with a final tip of the tartan to Robert, here are the episodes as he has memorialized them. (Some have been edited for space reasons.)

Season One (1976)

1. "THE SOCIETY PARTY"

Laverne and Shirley attend a posh dinner party at the Shotz mansion with Fonzie. The girls don't have nice dresses to wear so they ask Lenny and Squiggy for help. Lenny (Michael McKean) and Squiggy (David L. Landers) arrive later with two dresses, which they rent to the girls, telling them the dresses are from Squiggy's uncle's wax museum. When the girls get to the party they are accused of stealing the dresses, which prompts them to take their gowns off and storm out in their slips. Henry Winkler guest stars.

2. "THE BACHELOR PARTY"

Laverne rents out her father's (Phil Foster) pizza parlor to Fonzie for a bachelor party. The girl hired to jump out of the cake falls sick and after much pleading Shirley agrees to take her place. When she comes out of the cake and Carmine (Eddie Mekka) sees that it's his "Angel Face," he gets protective. The revelers threaten to smash up the place until Fonzie steps in. Henry Winkler guest stars.

3. "BOWLING FOR RAZZBERRIES"

In the Shotz employees' canteen, Laverne tries to avoid Karen, who always refers to her scornfully as unskilled labor. Shirley talks Laverne into beating her with dignity (instead of with a ketchup bottle) by beating Karen's team in the company bowling tournament. However, Laverne comes down with a cold. Carmine gives medication the doctor prescribed. The pills make her sleepy, not perky. Laverne's team wins anyway, and Laverne, now barely conscious, asks Shirley to blow a razzberry in Karen's face for her. Good-sport Shirley instead wishes Karen better luck next year. Back at the apartment, Laverne refuses to take her medicine because Shirley ruined her chance of revenge, so Shirley obligingly delivers Laverne's razzberry by phone.

4. "FALTER AT THE ALTAR"

Laverne's new boyfriend Sal asks her to marry him. Shirley, however, suspects that Laverne doesn't really love Sal at all and announces this at the wedding rehearsal. Eventually, Laverne realizes that she doesn't really love Sal. She tells him the news. He takes it well, promising to write. Al Molinaro guest stars.

5. "A Nun's Story"

Shirley is busily organizing her annual high-school reunion, when Laverne informs her that she's not coming because Shirley's reunions are dull. In fact, she says, they stink. Laverne refuses to go until Shirley gets a letter from the girls' old best friend, Anne-Marie, memorable as the ringleader of all their wildest high-school fun. Laverne now is eager to go to the reunion, and Carmine spreads the word to everybody that good-time Anne-Marie is coming this year. When Anne-Marie turns up, Shirley answers the door and is shocked to find that Anne-Marie has become a nun. Greg Antonacci guest stars.

6. "One Flew Over Milwaukee"

Shirley is driving everyone crazy worrying about her pet canary that has escaped, so Carmine secretly buys a replacement bird. When Carmine's canary finally flies in the open window, Shirley seems happy that her beloved bird has come home. However, we discover that she knew all along that it was a different bird, and when her own canary returns she keeps them both.

7. "Dog Date Blind Dates"

Laverne and Shirley meet two extra-strange guys on a blind date. The dates proceed to take Laverne, Shirley, Lenny, and Squiggy hostage while they try to rob the bank next door. Fred Willard guest stars.

8. "Did She or Didn't She (a.k.a., Once upon a Rumor)"

Shirley is changing her skirt in the brewery lunchroom. When Squiggy walks in, Shirley's zipper is stuck and Squiggy fixes it, but not before Lenny opens the door and sees what he sees. Squiggy lets Lenny fuel the rumor that he's gotten further with Shirley than anyone else. Shirley is in tears at the brewery until she overhears Squiggy finally telling the truth about what happened.

9. "IT'S THE WATER"

Laverne and Shirley both try out for a new job as a Shotz beer taster. Because it comes with more perks and pay, everybody wants it. When it's Shirley's turn, she takes a small sip from one beer bottle, feels sick and has to go home. In contrast, Laverne drinks every beer offered her without getting a buzz and telling the boss which beers were good. Despite all, it's Shirley who's made the new beer taster. She soon wishes she were back on the bottle-capping line.

10. "DATING SLUMP"

Shirley's boyfriend dumps her for another girl, so Laverne tries to snap her out of the depression by getting her out of the house. While out on a date at a pool hall, the girls end up getting into a fight. Carol Ita White and Mark Harmon guest star.

11. "FAKE OUT AT THE STAKE OUT"

Laverne becomes a decoy in the park to help catch a thief who has stolen Laverne and Shirley's favorite clothes. This episode introduces the policeman who's her boyfriend for a few shows. Bo Kaprall guest stars.

12. "HI NEIGHBOR"

Lenny and Squiggy move into Laverne and Shirley's apartment building. Laverne and Shirley have to vouch for the boys before Edna Babich, the landlady (Betty Garrett), will accept them as tenants.

13. "HOW DO YOU SAY . . . IN GERMAN? (A.K.A., HOW DO YOU SAY "ARE YOU DEAD?" IN GERMAN?)"

The German-speaking pizza delivery man faints in Laverne and Shirley's apartment. When they find out that he's an immigrant who's been taken for all his money, and that he's just been fired, Shirley wants to raise money for him. Laverne isn't happy about giving him charity, which leads to an argument. However, in the end Laverne comes through, getting him a busboy job at the Pizza Bowl.

14. "SUDS TO STARDOM
(A.K.A., THE FIRST ANNUAL SHOTZ TALENT SHOW)"

After losing several Shotz Brewery talent contests, Laverne and Shirley take dancing lessons from Carmine. This is the episode with the Calypso number in which Garry Marshall plays drums with the band.

15. "MOTHER KNOWS WORST"

Shirley receives a telegram from her mother saying she's coming for a one-day visit. Shirley begs Laverne to always stay with her while her super-critical mother is there. Mrs. Feeney is such a nag that Laverne tells her that her actions are ruining Shirley's life. Eventually mother and daughter agree to try to be more tolerant toward each other. Pat Carroll guest stars.

Season Two (1976–77)

16. "DRIVE SHE SAID"

Shirley offers Laverne driving lessons in exchange for money to buy a new car, but whenever she goes out driving, Laverne terrorizes the neighborhood's pedestrians. Laverne then disappears for a few days, announcing when she returns that she's been away taking driving lessons from her father and has gotten a temporary license. Bo Kaprall guest stars.

17. "ANGELS OF MERCY"

Laverne and Shirley become hospital volunteers and end up trying to change bed sheets with a "fat guy" still on the bed. Charles Frank guest stars.

18. "TWO WEIRDOS
(A.K.A., TWO OF OUR WEIRDOS ARE MISSING)"

Lenny and Squiggy want to talk, but Laverne and Shirley rush out instead to go for a ride in Rosie's new Cadillac. The next day Shirley finds a note on a paper bag saying that Lenny and Squiggy have run away to join the circus. Laverne and Shirley find them rehearsing and offer to help them out with all their problems, proving to Lenny and Squiggy that their friends do care. Carol Ita White guest stars (returning this time as Rosie, a recurring role).

19. "GOODTIME GIRLS"

Laverne and Shirley get plenty of offers for dates after Hector puts their names and phone number on a men's room wall in Vinnie's Pool Hall, so they raid Lenny and Squiggy's closets for clothes to dress up as guys and get into the men's room to remove their names. Greg Antonacci guest stars.

20. "BACHELOR MOTHERS"

Laverne and Shirley agree to babysit Fonzie's godson, but when they get an invitation for a big date only one of them can go, so the other has to stay home and watch the baby—who soon disappears. Henry Winkler guest stars.

21. "BRIDAL SHOWER"

Laverne and Shirley get an invitation to a bridal shower, but they're afraid to go because they're the only ones left unmarried. Carol Ita White guest stars.

22. "STEPPIN' OUT"

The girls have big dates. Now, if only they can get themselves together in time.

23. "EXCUSE ME, MAY I CUT IN?"

Shirley acts nice to Richie so he'll ask her and Laverne to the dance, but the real reason is that Laverne wants Richie to ask Potsie, who's the high school's best dancer. When Potsie is injured and can't dance, Laverne teams up with Richie instead for the big number. Ron Howard and Anson Williams guest star.

24. "LOOK BEFORE YOU LEAP"

After a drunken party at the brewery, Laverne wakes up to find she's wearing a pair of men's boxer shorts. When she starts feeling ill in the mornings, she fears that she's pregnant, so Lenny and Squiggy flip a coin to see which one will ask Laverne to marry him. Lenny wins and, in a touching scene, proposes. Of course, Laverne turns out not to be pregnant.

25. "DEAR FUTURE MODEL"

When Laverne and Shirley find the men at the Pizza Bowl drooling over a bowling beauty, they decide to become high-fashion models. Shirley sends away for a home-modeling course, and when it arrives the package contains potions, creams, and a book, which Shirley insists they're going to follow to the letter.

26. "CHRISTMAS EVE AT THE BOOBY HATCH"

Laverne and Shirley and the gang put on a Christmas Show at the hospital—which turns out to be the *mental* hospital. The revue the gang puts on has Edna doing a song and playing a small guitar, Carmine offering "Jingle Bell Rock" and tap dancing, Lenny and Squiggy performing "The Jolliest Fat Man," and Laverne and Shirley baton-twirling and singing. That's Garry Marshall, playing the drums in the band. Howard Hesseman guest stars.

27. "GUILTY UNTIL PROVEN NOT"

In a posh store, Laverne accidentally takes an expensive scarf and the snooty salesman is delighted to press charges. Laverne's bail is set at $500, so Shirley goes off to raise the money, with Lenny and Squiggy helping. Louis Nye guest stars.

28. "PLAYING HOOKEY"

Laverne and Shirley both call in sick to Shotz Brewery and decide to have some fun. At the movies, they see a couple of guys, whom they run into again later in the park. The dates turn out to be undercover vice cops.

29. "GUINEA PIGS"

The girls become scientific guinea pigs to raise money to go to a cocktail party. Laverne is allowed to sleep for only a few minutes at a time, and Shirley has to eat dirt.

30. "TOUGH IN THE MIDDLE (A.K.A., LONELY IN THE MIDDLE)"

Shirley is promoted to supervisor and the other workers hate her for it. She tries to introduce some time-saving ideas that don't go down very well.

31. "CALL ME A TAXI"

Laverne and Shirley take jobs as taxi dancers when they get laid off from the Brewery. Shirley pads out her bra to enormous size with tissue paper to get more customers.

32. "BUDDY CAN U SPARE A FATHER"

Shirley goes to a sleazy bar to look for her father.

33. "HONEYMOON HOTEL"

When Shirley wins a vacation at a hotel for newlyweds, she and Laverne plan to use Carmine to fool the hotel staff into letting them stay.

34. "HI NEIGHBORS"

Laverne and Shirley reluctantly agree to go out with Lenny and Squiggy after their dates cancel on them, so Lenny and Squiggy take them to a very fancy

French restaurant. This episode was written by Michael McKean and David L. Lander (Lenny and Squiggy).

35. "FRANK'S FLING"

Laverne asks Lenny, Squiggy, and Carmine to dress up as gangsters to scare away a gold digger who wants to marry her father.

36. "HAUNTED HOUSE"

The girls want new furniture, so they go after a used couch Lenny and Squiggy know about that's in a haunted house about to be torn down. Of course they start disappearing one by one, until they discover that the owners of the house are trying to scare people away so they won't have to move.

37. "CITIZEN CRANE"

Milwaukee's most prominent citizen, Charles Feister Crane, makes Laverne and Shirley his newest singing discovery, a duet called the Rosebuds. Severn Darden guest stars in this *Citizen Kane* (1941) spoof.

38. "ANNIVERSARY WRAP-AROUND (A.K.A., THE BIRTHDAY SHOW)"

While Laverne and Shirley are stuck at a train station in Canada, the rest of the gang is waiting for them, so they can have a surprise birthday party at the Pizza Bowl. To pass the time they reminisce—in flashbacks of previous episodes.

Season Three (1977–78)

39. "TAKE MY PLANTS—PLEASE"

Laverne and Shirley are laid off temporarily and they're wondering what to do. Laverne suggests welfare and a rest, but Shirley wants to do something.

Lenny and Squiggy also have been temporarily laid off, but they have a plan—to use the time to develop their invention, the radiobrush, a combination radio and toothbrush. Unbeknownst to Laverne, Shirley invests their two final paychecks in buying plants wholesale to resell at retail.

40. "CRUISE, PART ONE
(A.K.A., AN AFFAIR TO FORGET, PART ONE)"

Laverne and Shirley take a job dressed as Jack and Jill to sell children's shoes to earn extra money for their Great Lakes holiday-cruise vacation. Aboard ship at last, they say goodbye to the gang, only to find out that the stowaways on the ship are none other than Lenny and Squiggy. This two-part episode was co-written by Babaloo Mandel, who with his later writing partner Lowell Ganz (who also became a producer of *Laverne & Shirley*), went on to write Penny Marshall's *A League of Their Own* (1992), among other feature films.

41. "CRUISE, PART TWO
(A.K.A., AN AFFAIR TO FORGET, PART TWO)"

While on their Great Lakes cruise, Lenny and Squiggy are caught as stowaways and Shirley falls for one of the ship's crew.

42. "AIRPORT 1959"

Laverne and Shirley go on their first plane trip and end up at the controls when their pilot faints.

43. "TAG TEAM WRESTLING
(A.K.A., IN THIS CORNER)"

Laverne and Shirley team up to enter a charity wrestling match that turns into a grudge match when one of their opponents turns out to be a woman Laverne has called bananaface.

44. "THE PACT"

Laverne and Shirley get into a fight after Shirley's new boyfriend asks Laverne out. The girls finally swear to never again let a guy come between them.

45. "ROBOT LAWSUIT"

A giant robot attacks Laverne in a toy store, so she sues the toy company.

46. "LAVERNE & SHIRLEY MEET FABIAN"

Fabian's concert is sold out, but the girls impetuously bet Rosie that not only will they meet Fabian, but they will have their pictures taken with him as well. Rosie agrees, promising that if she loses she'll clean the girls' apartment with her toothbrush. Soon Rosie is scrubbing away. Fabian guest stars.

47. "LAVERNE'S ARRANGED MARRIAGE"

Laverne's father arranges her marriage to a wealthy cheese manufacturer who turns out to be in the underworld.

48. "SHIRLEY'S OPERATION"

The gang is rehearsing a production of *Alice in Wonderland* when Shirley, in Alice costume, faints and is taken to the hospital. Shirley panics and disappears, but she needs an emergency appendectomy, so the gang sets off to find her before her appendix bursts.

49. "THE STAKEOUT"

Carmine is suspected of being a counterfeiter, leading the F.B.I. to use Laverne and Shirley's apartment in a stakeout to catch him in the act.

50. "THE MORTICIAN"

Laverne has a crush on a mortician who is more interested in her dead than alive. So to help her get to know the mortician better, she asks Shirley to pretend she's dying.

51. "THE SLOW CHILD"

Edna's "retarded" daughter is left with Laverne and Shirley, but later disappears with Lenny, who falls for her. Edna is angry when she finds out that her little girl was out walking with Lenny, then realizes that her daughter is more capable than she thought. This is one of the few *Laverne & Shirley* episodes to be critically acclaimed for dealing with an important social issue.

52. "NEW YEAR'S EVE 1960"

It's New Year's Eve and Laverne is dumped by her date, Shirley has a cold, and Squiggy becomes a human fly.

53. "THE HORSE SHOW"

Shirley rescues Buttercup, a horse from a glue factory, and hides it in her bedroom. Lenny and Squiggy find a farm with a nice pasture where the horse can live out the remainder of its days.

54. "THE DENTIST"

Laverne has a chipped tooth and goes to Shirley's dentist brother. The only problem is he's an awful dentist. This episode was written by Babaloo Mandel.

55. "SHOTZ TALENT SHOW (A.K.A., THE SECOND ALMOST ANNUAL SHOTZ TALENT SHOW)"

Mr. Shotz wants the girls to find a spot in the talent show for his no-talent nephew.

56. "BUS STOP"

The girls take a bus to a distant city to visit two medical students who leave them stranded.

57. "DRIVING TEST"

Unless Squiggy passes his driving test, he'll lose his job. The girls reluctantly agree to help, because if they don't Lenny will be forced to move in with them.

58. "OBSTACLE COURSE"

Shirley tries out for a volunteer policewoman's job. However, the policeman in charge thinks Shirley is too puny, so Laverne helps her train.

59. "DEBUTANTE BALL"

Laverne and Lenny attend a debutante's ball where Lenny learns he's eighty-ninth in line for the Polish throne. For a proper ball gown, Laverne gets Lizzie Borden's dress from Squiggy's uncle's wax museum and Lenny wears a magician's tuxedo, which comes complete with a pigeon.

60. "THE DANCE STUDIO"

The girls try to help Carmine get financing to open his own dance studio. But it's one disaster after another, and in the end Frank and Edna have to lend him the money that the banks won't.

61. "2001: A COMEDY ODYSSEY"

Laverne dreams she and Shirley are in their eighties, still living together and still single. But so are Lenny and Squiggy, which leads to marriage.

62. "BREAKING UP AND MAKING UP: EDNA AND FRANK"

Laverne and Shirley try to get Frank and Edna back together after they break up when Edna's ex-husband comes to town. This episode was co-written by Marion Zola and Phil Foster (who plays Poppa Frank).

63. "A DATE WITH ERASERHEAD"

Shirley has a blind date with Eraserhead.

Season Four (1978–79)

64. "Festival, Part One"

The girls go to New York for an Italian festival and to visit Laverne's grandmother, who is estranged from Poppa Frank, her son, but she takes a liking to Squiggy.

65. "Festival, Part Two"

Poppa Frank enlists the gang to try to win the greased-pole climbing contest so he can win a trip to Italy for his aged mother.

66. "The Quiz Show"

Laverne and Shirley appear on a game show called *Be Silly for Dollars*, and they are.

67. "The Robbery"

Laverne's date with a tough guy goes bad when he robs a grocery store.

68. "Playing the Roxy"

Shirley gets amnesia and thinks she's a stripper named Roxy. She finds herself on stage at a lodge meeting going through her act when her memory comes back. This is the first episode directed by Joel Zwick, who became the show's main director.

69. "Laverne and Shirley Go to Night School"

Shirley wants to become a medical assistant, so she convinces Laverne to go to night school with her. At school, the teacher tells Shirley that he's going to boot Laverne out because she's hopeless and never does her assignments. Shirley begs him to give Laverne another chance. Hans Conried (probably best known as Uncle Tonoose on *The Danny Thomas Show* and the voice of

Snidely Whiplash on *The Adventures of Rocky and Bullwinkle*) guest stars in this episode directed by Lowell Ganz.

70. "THE BULLY SHOW"

Lenny and Squiggy are forced to make a date between Laverne and their foreman, but they come to Laverne's rescue just in time.

71. "CHORUS LINE"

Laverne dreams of being on Broadway when she auditions for *West Side Story* in Chicago.

72. "LAVERNE AND SHIRLEY MOVE IN"

Shirley remembers how she and Laverne first moved in together.

73. "VISIT TO A CEMETERY"

Laverne comes to accept the death of her mother by visiting her grave for the first time.

74. "DINNER FOR FOUR"

The girls inadvertently cook dinner for the girlfriends of their dates, who actually only wanted to hire them to be maids for the evening.

75. "IT'S A DOG'S LIFE"

Shirley handcuffs herself to a homeless dog at the pound to protest its impending death. Carmine comes to the rescue, offering free dance lessons to anyone who adopts a dog.

76. "O COME ALL YE BUMS"

Laverne and Shirley become street performers to raise cash for Frank's annual holiday hobo dinner at the Pizza Bowl, after Frank has to take a job as a department store Santa Claus to raise money to pay for the traditional charitable event. Their various money-making schemes don't work out, but the hoboes themselves show up anyway, each one bringing a gift of food. Lenny and Squiggy arrive with a huge turkey and stuffing that saves the Christmas dinner.

77. "SUPERMARKET SWEEP"

Laverne wins three minutes of free grocery shopping and everyone wants something, including Bosco for Lenny and Squiggy. At the big event, the girls start grabbing items from the shelves; once the cart is full they start stuffing goods down their pants and in their shirts, getting so greedy they can hardly walk.

78. "WHO'S POPPA?"

When she realizes that everyone else in her family is tall and blonde, Shirley tries to find out if she was adopted.

79. "LENNY'S CRUSH"

Lenny falls in love with Laverne after misunderstanding what she has told him. This episode was directed by Carl Gottlieb, who also wrote *The Jerk* (1979), starring Steve Martin and directed by Carl Reiner.

80. "TALENT SHOW
(A.K.A., THE THIRD ANNUAL SHOTZ TALENT SHOW)"

This time Laverne and Shirley perform as human puppets.

81. "FIRE SHOW"

One of the firemen who arrives to put out the fire in their apartment is attracted to Laverne, but Shirley falls for him, testing the girls' friendship to the limit.

82. "FEMININE MISTAKE"

Shirley tries to make Laverne more beautiful to impress a guy, but Laverne just ends up doing an imitation of a southern belle. Jay Leno guest stars.

83. "SQUIGGY IN LOVE"

Laverne and Shirley try to help Squiggy by telling him that his latest great-looking girlfriend is just using him to help her move into and decorate her apartment. Squiggy admits he knows he's being used, but what other chance does a guy like him have with a beautiful girl like that? Of course he eventually tells off the gold digger. This is the first episode directed by Penny Marshall.

84. "TENANTS ARE REVOLTING"

The girls believe they are doing a good deed by calling in a building inspector to make repairs, until Edna has to fix the building before a deadline or pay a huge fine. Laverne and Shirley organize the building tenants to make repairs and end up stranded on the roof. When the inspector finally passes the building before the deadline, Edna raises the rent.

85. "SHIRLEY AND THE OLDER MAN"

Shirley's friendship with a rich older man is resented by Carmine, who is jealous, and the man's daughter, who is suspicious of Shirley's intentions. Robert Alda (Alan "Hawkeye" Alda's father) guest stars.

86. "INDUSTRIAL ESPIONAGE
(A.K.A., THERE'S A SPY IN MY BEER)"

No one believes Laverne saw an industrial spy in the brewery, so she takes it upon herself and Shirley to prove the truth. Both girls end up soaking wet in a huge vat of beer waiting to entrap the culprit.

Season Five (1979–80)

87. "UPSTAIRS DOWNSTAIRS"

A fight over returning a wrongly-issued check sets the girls to dreaming about Shirley in heaven and Laverne in hell. Dick Shawn guest stars.

88. "FAT CITY HOLIDAY"

The girls get jobs at a weight loss camp. Sally Kellerman guest stars.

89. "SHOTGUN WEDDING, PART TWO"

The girls pretend to be engaged to Richie and Fonzie to avoid a shotgun wedding. (Part One of this episode aired as a *Happy Days* installment.) Henry Winkler and Ron Howard guest star.

90. "ONE HECKUVA NOTE"

Shirley finds an old love note written to Laverne from Carmine and the girls' friendship nearly ends.

91. "BAD GIRLS"

The girls arrange for Edna's niece to join their old club, only to learn that it has now become a thieves' gang.

92. "WHAT DO YOU DO WITH A DRUNKEN SAILOR"

Shirley's brother returns home from the Navy, an alcoholic. Ed Begley Jr. guest stars.

93. "THE WEDDING"

Edna accepts a marriage proposal from Frank, and Laverne and Shirley sing in a gospel choir at their wedding.

94. "You Pushed Me Too Far"

Lenny refuses to have anything to do with Squiggy after he's pushed into a garbage can from their second-floor apartment window, but Laverne and Shirley get the two friends to make up in Squiggy's uncle's wax museum.

95. "Testing Testing"

Mr. Shotz hires a psychiatrist to evaluate job aptitudes at his brewery. Everyone is terrified that some deep dark secret or a neurosis is going to be revealed when they visit the company shrink.

96. "Shotz Talent Show
(a.k.a., The Fourth Annual Shotz Talent Show)"

Laverne and Shirley are in charge of selecting the acts for talent night. Frank auditions with his ventriloquist act, which includes Laverne and Shirley dolls. To please Mr. Shotz, the gang comes up with a skit that features Lenny as a little boy asking Father Time (Squiggy) questions about American history and the girls singing "Boogie Woogie Bugle Boy from Company B."

97. "In the Army, Part One
(a.k.a., We're in the Army Now, Part One)"

To get even for a missed promotion Laverne and Shirley enlist in the Women's Army Corps. Vicki Lawrence guest stars.

98. "In the Army, Part Two
(a.k.a., We're in the Army Now, Part Two)"

Laverne and Shirley regret their decision to join the military. Vicki Lawrence guest stars.

99. "Take Two, They're Small"

Lenny and Squiggy fix Laverne and Shirley up with computer dates, who turn out to be vertically challenged.

100. "NOT QUITE SOUTH OF THE BORDER"

The girls can't wait to go on a vacation to "Near" Mexico. Their resort turns out to be equipped only with a plastic kiddie's wading pool and they find one wall missing from their hotel room.

101. "YOU OUGHTA BE IN PICTURES"

The girls jump at the chance to be in a movie, not knowing that the film they will be starring in is an Army hygiene film. When the cameras start rolling, they discover they're playing hookers and that Shirley's leading man is gay.

102. "BEATNIK SHOW"

The girls' coffeehouse performance attracts a band of beatniks. This episode features the Shirley Feeney scarf dance. Art Garfunkel guest stars.

103. "WHY DID THE FIREMAN . . ."

Laverne falls hard for a fireman who dies heroically in the line of duty before he has a chance to propose to her. Ted Danson (*Cheers*) guest stars.

104. "THE RIGHT TO LIGHT"

To protest having their electricity turned off, the girls chain themselves inside the light-and-power company building, little knowing that another disgruntled customer has planted a bomb in the very room where the girls have entrapped themselves.

105. "MURDER ON THE MOOSE JAW EXPRESS, PART ONE"

The girls are riding the Moose Jaw Express when a murder is committed aboard the train. Charlene Tilton, Scatman Crothers, Wilfred Hyde-White, and Roger C. Carmel guest star.

106. "MURDER ON THE MOOSE JAW EXPRESS, PART TWO"

Laverne and Shirley angle to uncover the murderer's identity. This episode is narrated by Michael McKean.

107. "THE COLLECTOR"

The girls try to talk Carmine out of going to work for a loan shark. Billy Sands guest stars.

108. "THE DUKE OF SQUIGGMAN"

When Squiggy sleepwalks, he turns into a wealthy, demanding, upper-crust duke. Only Lenny's lullaby, accompanied by guitar-strumming, can soothe him back to dreamland. This is the second episode directed by Penny Marshall.

109. "THE SURVIVAL TEST"

Mean WAC Sergeant Plout returns to take the girls on a wilderness survival test, in which they have to compete against a very macho man. Vicki Lawrence guest stars.

110. "DANTE THE DARING"

Laverne and Shirley find a strange man asleep on their sofa. Laverne arms herself with a baseball bat to hit him. But just when she decides to kiss him awake instead because he's gorgeous, Edna and Frank arrive, informing Laverne that the sleeper is her Italian cousin Antonio, in Milwaukee to find a job. Ed Marinaro, who also plays Sonny St. Jacques in the California episodes, guest stars as Antonio.

111. "SEPARATE TABLES"

Laverne wants to go to the movies, but Shirley is building a lollipop-stick model of her dream house and just wants to be left in peace, so she tells Laverne to go on her own. Laverne is afraid to go out by herself, so Shirley books them both separate tables at a new Chinese restaurant to cure Laverne of her phobia. Julius La Rosa and Pat Morita guest star.

112. "THE DINER"

When Lenny inherits a greasy spoon diner called Laslo's Place, Lenny and Squiggy immediately rename it Dead Laslo's Place and hire Laverne and Shirley to cook and waitress. The place is soon packed—with members of the Purple Fiends gang. Laverne is getting the orders all wrong while Shirley is being run ragged and pinched by the customers.

Season Six (1980–81)

113. "NOT QUITE NEW YORK"

After being fired from the brewery, the girls decide to move to California. However, the only way they can afford to get out there is to have Lenny and Squiggy drive them in an old ice cream truck.

114. "WELCOME TO BURBANK"

The girls are ready to return to Milwaukee after experiencing an earthquake on their first night in Los Angeles. Leslie Easterbrook and Ed Marinaro guest star, playing the new continuing characters of Rhonda and Sonny.

115. "STUDIO CITY"

Laverne and Shirley are hired to play stunt women in a Troy Donahue movie. Troy Donahue guest stars.

116. "GRAND OPENING"

To pay Shirley back some of the money she owes her, Laverne agrees to be the target in Sonny's knife-throwing act at Cowboy Bill's grand opening. When Sonny breaks his arm and is unable to go on, Shirley takes over the knife throwing, which understandably makes Laverne extremely nervous.

117. "CANDY IS DANDY"

The girls finally get a job in the gift-wrapping department at Bardwell's Department Store. On their first day, Laverne gets tipsy after eating candy laced with alcohol.

118. "THE DATING GAME"

Lenny and Squiggy appear on the television show *The Dating Game*. Jim Lange guest stars. Penny Marshall directed this episode.

119. "THE OTHER WOMAN"

Shirley finally gets to date a doctor, but the problem is that she looks exactly like his old wife.

120. "ROAD TO BURBANK"

There is a dispute over who should pay the bill for Lenny and Squiggy having trashed a hotel room on their way to California. The boys try to blame it on Laverne and Shirley. This leads to two different versions of what happened that night—one in which Lenny and Squiggy are chasing the girls, the other in which the feisty girls are pursuing the boys.

121. "BORN TOO LATE"

Lenny and Squiggy imagine that they are the stars of black-and-white silent movies.

122. "LAVERNE'S BROKEN LEG"

After she has to miss a party because of her broken leg, Laverne sits at home alone and falls asleep while watching *It's a Wonderful Life* on TV, and she dreams what life would be like for her friends and her family if she had never been born.

123. "LOVE OUT THE WINDOW"

After learning Laverne fears for his safety, Sonny quits his job as a stunt man and takes a position selling insurance.

124. "MALIBU MANSION"

The girls are hired to housesit at the Malibu beachfront mansion of the owner of the Cowboy Bill's restaurant chain. While he is away for the weekend, the girls throw a beach party that is crashed by a biker gang. Richard Moll and Stubby Kaye guest star.

125. "TELL THE TRUTH (A.K.A., TO TELL THE TRUTH)"

Stuck at home on a rainy night with nothing to do, the gang play a game of Truth or Dare. Within minutes, everybody ends up arguing and a chocolate pudding ends up in Shirley's face. But most shocking of all, the fact that Shirley stuffs socks down her bra is revealed.

126. "I DO, I DO"

The girls almost marry two British rock stars after eating brownies laced with marijuana. Eric Idle and Peter Noone guest star.

127. "BUT SERIOUSLY, FOLKS"

Carmine's new stand-up comedy act is not a big hit with his friends when he starts to make fun of them. Penny Marshall directed this episode.

128. "BARDWELL CAPER, PART ONE"

Laverne writes an insulting letter to her boss, thinking she and Shirley have been passed over for a raise.

129. "BARDWELL CAPER, PART TWO"

After learning that they're getting a raise after all, the girls try to retrieve the nasty letter Laverne wrote to the boss. The only problem is, his office is guarded by a state-of-the-art security system.

130. "HIGH-PRICED DATES"

Laverne and Shirley turn to Edna for advice when their dates expect rewards.

131. "ANNIVERSARY SHOW (A.K.A., THE FIFTH ANNIVERSARY SHOW)"

Laverne and Shirley host a fifth wedding anniversary party for Frank and Edna at their trailer, which has a broken jack.

132. "A. W. O. L. (A.K.A., OUT, OUT, DAMNED PLOUT)"

Sergeant Plout goes A.W.O.L. and hides out at Laverne and Shirley's apartment. Vicki Lawrence guest stars.

133. "GUITAR SHOW (A.K.A., SING, SING, SING)"

Laverne asks Carmine to give her singing lessons so she can sing for Hoot Night at Cowboy Bill's. This episode was directed by Cindy Williams.

134. "CHILD'S PLAY"

Because Squiggy is forgetful, Laverne and Shirley must play all the parts in Shirley's play, *Murder in Mother Goose Land*, which is attended by a Broadway producer.

Season Seven (1981–82)

135. "NIGHT AT THE AWARDS"

When Lenny and Squiggy get backstage at a televised awards show, they suddenly find themselves on stage with sexy actress Joey Heatherton. Joey Heatherton guest stars.

136. "THE MOST IMPORTANT DAY EVER"

Trying to help Lenny and Squiggy's new talent agency, Laverne and Shirley end up on television as part of a Latvian acrobatic act.

137. "IT ONLY HURTS WHEN I BREATHE"

Recalling their high school days, Laverne and Shirley find themselves embroiled in a slugfest that leaves Laverne with a broken jaw.

138. "DEFIANT ONE"

Shirley finds herself mistakenly handcuffed to a bank robber who is forced to take her with him when he escapes from the police. Richard Moll guest stars.

139. "SOME ENCHANTED EARRING"

Laverne accidentally loses one of her mother's diamond earrings.

140. "FRIENDLY PERSUASION"

While they're gift wrapping at Bardwell's store one day, an actor comes in and chats to the girls. Laverne mistakenly thinks he's asking her out and she invites him over. Shirley thinks he's after their gift-wrapping jobs at Bardwell's, so she's mean to him that night at dinner. Charles Grodin guest stars.

141. "TEENAGE LUST
(A.K.A., YOUNG AT HEART)"

The girls attend a wild fraternity party and realize they're not as young as they once were.

142. "MOVING IN"

Laverne's new boyfriend asks her to move in with him, but Shirley disapproves because Laverne isn't marrying him. Nonetheless, Laverne convinces Shirley to cover for her with her father, and not long after Laverne leaves, Frank turns up looking for her. Paul Sands (of *Friends and Lovers*, the short-lived series on which Penny was featured in 1974–75) guest stars.

143. "LIFE IS THE TAR PITS"

While out at the local tar pits, Squiggy sees a nice-looking girl reading on the lawn, but it's Lenny who asks her out on a date, and this starts to make Squiggy feel left out. Weeks later, Lenny and the girl are still together, and Squiggy is sure that she's going to ruin his friendship with Lenny.

144. "I DO, I DON'T"

Shirley tries to convince Carmine to marry her after she wins a complimentary wedding reception. Once Shirley has her free wedding, she tricks Carmine into meeting her at the hotel where the ceremony will take place.

145. "WHATEVER HAPPENED TO THE CLASS OF '56?"

Laverne, Shirley, and Carmine return to Milwaukee for their high school reunion. What they don't know, however, is that the gang in the old neighborhood thinks that the girls are famous movie stars and that Carmine is a noted Las Vegas singer. Carol Ita White guest stars again as Rosie.

146. "Rocky Ragu
(a.k.a., Rocky Roger)"

Carmine is in the girls' apartment when Rhonda comes in saying she's just landed a role in a new movie musical about a famous ex-boxer and that Carmine should audition for the lead part. Squiggy then offers to represent Carmine, but when Lenny, Squiggy, and Carmine arrive at the audition there are lots of actors waiting to try out for the part.

147. "I Wonder What Became of Sal?"

Laverne's old boyfriend Sal, who she almost married in Milwaukee, comes to California looking for her. Sal is a millionaire businessman and once again he proposes to Laverne.

148. "An Affair to Forget"

Laverne is dating a guy but doesn't know that he's married. When he takes her to a restaurant for dinner, his wife shows up. Mayhem ensues. Anjelica Huston guest stars.

149. "Watch the Fur Fly"

After Shirley yells at Rhonda for wearing a coat made of animal fur, Laverne unknowingly sets Shirley up on a date with a furrier. Jeff Goldblum guest stars.

150. "Star Peepers"

Laverne and Shirley vow revenge on an obnoxious singing star who was rude to them at Bardwell's department store. They decide that the best way to get even is to take incriminating pictures of him and sell them to a tabloid.

151. "Helmut Weekend"

Squiggy's long lost father suddenly shows up and wants to spend time with his perplexed son.

152. "Perfidy in Blue"

When Shirley loses Laverne's favorite purse, she is afraid to tell her because she didn't ask if she could borrow it. Later, Shirley dreams that Laverne is trying to kill her because she knows that Shirley lost her favorite purse and lied about it.

153. "Ski Show"

Laverne and Shirley go on a weekend skiing trip to meet men, after they decide they're not getting anywhere at the single bars. When Laverne wants to impress a guy, she lies about her skiing ability, but she can't even mount the ski lift.

154. "Lightning Man"

The girls are in the kitchen at Cowboy Bill's. In wanders Carmine, smoke wafting from the top of his head, his clothes burned. A TV news crew that spotted Carmine being struck by lightning arrive on the scene, and soon he's on the air, when in walks a robber who orders Frank to empty the cash register.

155. "Crime Isn't Pretty"

Frank and Carmine set traps in the girls' apartment to catch a burglar who's been stealing their things.

156. "That's Entertainment"

Frank and Carmine argue about whether today's music is better or worse than that of yesteryear. In this musical episode Carmine sings "It's not Unusual," Rhonda sings "Blue Moon," Carmine and Laverne tap dance, and Lenny and Squiggy duet. There's even an opera spoof.

Season Eight (1982–83)

157. "WINDOW ON MAIN STREET"

Laverne and Shirley agree to live in Bardwell's main show window for a weekend to demonstrate the House of the Future.

158. "THE MUMMY'S BRIDE"

Shirley Feeney marries Walter Meeney. This is the last episode of *Laverne & Shirley* in which Cindy Williams appears.

159. "THE BABY SHOW"

Sergeant Plout shows up on Laverne's doorstep again. This time she's pregnant and looking for a place to stay. Plout and Laverne enter a mothers-to-be contest and then visit a funeral home to pay their respects to one of Frank's buddies. While there, Plout goes into labor. Vicki Lawrence guest stars.

160. "THE PLAYBOY SHOW"

Laverne reluctantly goes downtown to pick up a *Playboy* Bunny application form for Rhonda. The audition is already packed with beautiful women when Laverne arrives, and the woman in charge, a hypochondriac, says she has a fever, so Laverne starts handing out the application forms for her. Laverne becomes friendly with Kathy, one of the applicants, and despite her insecurities, she decides to try out herself. Carrie Fisher and Hugh Hefner guest star. Michael McKean directed this episode.

161. "SHORT ON TIME"

When Frank finds a note from Edna saying she has left him, he goes to Laverne to talk about it. Laverne, who doesn't know that Edna has left, asks her father to stay at the apartment and babysit Little Chucky the Chimp, because she won a chance to sing with the Spinners in a contest. The Spinners guest star.

162. "PLEASE DON'T FEED THE BUZZARDS"

After Lenny and Squiggy return from a swap meet, they discover that inside the old suitcase they bought is a map with an "X" on it. Carmine and Frank join the expedition, and soon the four of them are wandering aimlessly in the hot desert.

163. "THE FASHION SHOW"

Laverne doesn't believe that the beautiful, temperamental model her fashion-photographer boyfriend has to sweet talk means nothing to him. To find out the truth, she sneaks into the fashion show where he's working. Naturally, she ends up being one of the procession of models. Anjelica Huston guest stars.

164. "DO THE CARMINE"

Carmine and Squiggy are sitting at Cowboy Bill's where Carmine complains that nobody likes his new record "Do the Hotfoot." Squiggy notices that Bobby Bitts, King of the Hits, is sitting at the next table, so Squiggy tries to talk him into playing Carmine's record on his TV show. Jay Leno guest stars.

165. "DEFECTIVE BALLET"

Squiggy is mistaken for a Russian ballet dancer who is trying to defect to the United States.

166. "LOST IN SPACESUITS"

Out of a job and desperate for money, Laverne asks Frank's old army buddy to get her work at an aerospace plant. Her new job turns out to be testing gravity boots. When everyone else goes for lunch, a coworker named Chuck convinces Laverne to try on a secret experimental anti-gravity spacesuit.

167. "DEATH ROW, PART ONE"

Carmine, dressed as an ear of corn, is tired of his singing telegram job, so it's easy for Laverne to talk him into helping her scam new dinnerware from her bank, which is giving away dishes to anyone who opens a new account. Meanwhile, a bank robber and his moll, Sheba, plan to use Laverne as the patsy for their planned robbery. Laraine Newman and Timothy Stack guest star.

168. "DEATH ROW, PART TWO"

Having been mistakenly arrested for the bank robbery, Laverne and Sheba are confused with the murderers who are to be executed at midnight. When Frank finally finds out about the mix-up, he rushes to the jail, where a priest is hearing Laverne's last confession. Anne Ramsey and the Greenwood Gospel Singers guest star.

169. "THE NOTE"

Laverne gets depressed, then angry, after she finds a very short note from Shirley saying she has left to go overseas with her new husband. Laverne just can't believe that Shirley would leave with only a few words on paper to say goodbye. To cheer her up, each of the gang tries to find Laverne a new room-mate. But things turn out okay when Laverne finds the rest of Shirley's farewell note under the bed.

170. "OF MICE AND MEN"

Laverne's plan to restore her cowardly boyfriend's self-confidence backfires. Jim Belushi guest stars.

171. "JINXED"

When Laverne is convinced she is jinxed after refusing to answer a chain letter, her friends send a gypsy to help her. Carol Kane guest stars.

172. "THE ROCK AND ROLL SHOW"

Laverne convinces her wacky musician friend Chuck to form a band. Chuck's new group turns out to be a bunch of geeky classical musicians, but Laverne convinces them they'll all make big money if they play rock 'n' roll, so they all quit their jobs to become rich and famous. Jack Mack and the Heart Attack guest star.

173. "THE GYMNAST"

Laverne is convinced that the former trapeze artist she's dating is out to kill her. Adam West guest stars.

174. "HOW'S YOUR SISTER?"

Carmine, dressed as a doctor, is ready to quit his singing-telegram job, when Squiggy appears and offers him $200 to date his bizarre sister, Squendolyn. When Squendolyn arrives at Laverne's, however, she takes an instant shine to Carmine.

175. "THE MONASTERY SHOW"

Laverne is in a torn dress in a confessional, telling a priest she hasn't made confession in fifteen years, but she woke up on an aircraft carrier and all the sailors saluted her. The priest suggests penance at the local convent, where she can contemplate the meaning of her actions. Louise Lasser guest stars.

176. "THE GHOST STORY"

Carmine and Rhonda are examining the wiring in Laverne's apartment, when a wrench and other items start floating around the room by themselves. Carmine and Rhonda flee in terror. When Laverne returns, she doesn't believe her apartment is haunted until her backpack floats off her back.

177. "HERE TODAY, HAIR TOMORROW"

Rhonda tells Frank she fears Carmine is about to commit suicide: He's packed all his stuff, turned off the gas, and even disconnected his phone. But Carmine arrives to say he's moving to New York to try his luck on Broadway. Rhonda and Frank lend him money, but not quite enough to get him there.

178. "COUNCILMAN DeFAZIO"

At Cowboy Bill's, Frank is making his usual cash "contribution" to the local councilman, who, after getting Frank's money, says he plans to tear Bill's down and build a high-rise there instead. Frank decides the only way to stop the corrupt councilman is to run against him. In the end, the councilman is defeated. He shows up to unscrupulously suggest going ahead with the destruction of Cowboy Bill's anyway. He'll give Frank a huge discount on the new building that will be built on the site, because his sister owns the company that has the contract to build it! However, Frank throws him out, and so ends the final episode of *Laverne & Shirley*. This last installment, with its nepotism theme, was co-written by Dottie Archibald and Phil Foster (Poppa Frank), from a story by Foster, Archibald, and Perry Williams.

Appendix B

FILMOGRAPHY

Director

JUMPIN' JACK FLASH

TWENTIETH CENTURY-FOX, 1986. COLOR, 100 MINUTES. R-RATED.

Producers, Lawrence Gordon, Joel Silver; associate producers, George Bowers, Richard Marks, Elaine K. Thompson; director, Penny Marshall; assistant director, Beau Marks; assistant director/second unit director, Richard Greenberg; story, David H. Franzoni; screenwriters, David H. Franzoni and J. W. Melville, Patricia Irving and Christopher Thompson; production designer, Robert F. Boyle; computer effects supervisor, Steve Grumette; costume designer, Susan Becker; original music, Thomas Newman; supervising sound editor, Robert Grieve; cinematographer, Matthew F. Leonetti; editor, Mark Goldblatt.

Whoopi Goldberg (Terry Doolittle); Stephen Collins (Marty Phillips); John Wood (Jeremy Talbott); Carol Kane (Cynthia); Jonathan Pryce (Jack); Annie Potts (Liz Carlson); Peter Michael Goetz (Mr. Page); Roscoe Lee Browne (Archer Lincoln); Sara Botsford (Lady Sara Phillips); Jeroen Krabbé (Mark Van Meter); Vyto Ruginis (Carl); Tony Hendra (Hunter); Jon Lovitz (Doug);

221

Phil Hartman (Fred); Lynne Marie Stewart (Karen); Ren Woods (Jackie); Tracy Reiner (Page's Secretary); Chino 'Fats' Williams (Larry, the Heavyset Guard); James Belushi (Sperry the Repairman); Paxton Whitehead (Lord Malcolm Billings); June Chadwick (Gillian); Tracey Ullman (Fiona); Caroline Ducrocq (French Embassy Guest); Jeffrey Joseph (African Embassy Guest); Julie Payne (Receptionist at Elizabeth Arden); Deanna Olive (Karen at Elizabeth Arden); Carl LeBove (Earl the Guard); Donna Ponterotto (Pedicurist at Elizabeth Arden); Matt Landers (Night Guard at Bank); Jamey Sheridan (N.Y. Officer); Charles Dumas (N.Y. Officer); James Edgcomb (Lincoln's Aide); Gerry Connell (Lincoln's Aide); Miguel A. Núñez Jr. (Street Tough); José Santana (Street Tough); Bob Ernst (Street Tough); Benji Gregory (Harry Carlson Jr.); Kellie Martin (Kristi Carlson); Kim Chan (Korean Flower Vendor); Antony Hamilton (Man in Restaurant); J. Christopher Ros (Hairdresser); Heidi Lund (Woman in Restaurant); Kenneth Danziger (Embassy Computer Man); Eric Harrison (Embassy Computer Man); Edouard DeSoto (Superintendent); Garry Marshall (Detective); Teagan Clive (Russian Exercise Woman); Tom McDermot (Minister); Hilary Stern (Customer); George Jenesky (Man with Umbrella); Mark Rowen (Cab Driver); Michael McKean (uncredited: British Party Guest).

BIG

TWENTIETH CENTURY–FOX, 1988. COLOR, 104 MINUTES. PG–RATED.

Producers, James L. Brooks, Robert Greenhut, Juliet Taylor; co-producers, Gary Ross, Anne Spielberg; director, Penny Marshall; first assistant director, Thomas A. Reilly; screenwriters, Gary Ross, Anne Spielberg; production designer, Santo Loquasto; costume designer, Judianna Makovsky; music, Howard Shore; supervising sound editor, Jerry Ross; choreographer, Paula Abdul; cinematographer, Barry Sonnenfeld; editor, Barry Malkin.

Tom Hanks (Josh Baskin); Elizabeth Perkins (Susan); Robert Loggia (MacMillan); John Heard (Paul); Jared Rushton (Billy); David Moscow (Young Josh); Jon Lovitz (Scott Brenner); Mercedes Ruehl (Mrs. Baskin); Josh Clark (Mr. Baskin); Kimberlee M. Davis (Cynthia Benson); Oliver Block (Freddie Benson); Erika Katz (Cynthia's Friend); Allan Wasserman (Gym Teacher); Mark Ballou (Derek); Gary Howard Klar (Ticket Taker); Alec von Sommer (First Brother); Chris Dowden (Second Brother); Rockets Redglare (Motel Clerk); Jaime Tirelli (Spanish Voice); Paul Herman (Schizo); Nancy Giles (Administrative Woman); Jordan Thaler (Administrative Clerk); Dana Kaminski (Personnel Receptionist); Harvey Miller (Personnel Director); Tracy Reiner (Test Market Researcher); James Eckhouse (Supervisor); Linda Gillin (Woman in Red Dress); Mildred R. Vandever (Receptionist); Bert Goldstein (First Executive); Kevin Meaney (Executive #2); Peter McRobbie (Executive #3); Paul J. Q. Lee (Executive #4); Debra Jo Rupp (Miss Patterson); Keith Reddin (Payroll Clerk); Lela Ivey (Bank Teller); Dolores Messina (Real Estate Agent); Gordon Press (Moving Man); George J. Manos (Limousine Driver); Vinny Capone (Photon Laser Gunfighter); Susan Wilder (Karen); John Rothman (Phil); Judd Trichter (Adam); Pasquale Pugliese (Tenor Dough Man); Tom Coviello, Richard Devia, Teddy Holiavko, Augusto Mariani, Alfredo Monti, Sergio Mosetti, Armando Penso (Singing Waiters); Edward Schick (Piano Player); F. Benjamin Stimler (Boy in Leaves); Jonathan Isaac Landau (Boy in Leaves); Samantha Larkin (Girlfriend of Cynthia); Bruce Jarchow (Photographer); Vaughn Sandman (Boy on Baseball Field).

AWAKENINGS

COLUMBIA PICTURES, 1990. COLOR, 121 MINUTES. PG-13-RATED.

Producers, Lawrence Lasker, Walter F. Parkes; associate producer, Amy Lemisch; director, Penny Marshall; book, Oliver Sacks; screenwriter, Steven Zaillian; production designer, Anton Furst; costume designer, Cynthia Flynt; original music, Randy Newman; sound/sound designer, Les Lazarowitz; cinematographer, Miroslav Ondricek; editors, Battle Davis, Gerald B. Greenberg.

Robert De Niro (Leonard Lowe); Robin Williams (Dr. Malcolm Sayer); Julie Kavner (Eleanor Costello); Ruth Nelson (Mrs. Lowe); John Heard (Dr. Kaufman); Penelope Ann Miller (Paula); Alice Drummond (Lucy); Judith Malina (Rose); Barton Heyman (Bert); George Martin (Frank); Anne Meara (Miriam); Richard Libertini (Sidney); Laura Esterman (Lolly); Dexter Gordon (Rolando); Jane Haynes (Frances); Le Clanche Du Rand (Magda); Yusef Bulos (Joseph); Gloria Harper (Dottie); Gwyllum Evans (Desmond); Mary Catherine Wright (Nurse Beth); Mary Alice (Nurse Margaret); Keith Diamond (Anthony); Steve Vinovich (Ray); Tiger Haynes (Janitor); John Christopher Jones (Dr. Sullivan); Bradley Whitford (Dr. Tyler); Max von Sydow (Dr. Peter Ingham); Harvey Miller (Hospital Director); Tanya Berezin (Psychiatrist); Peter Stormare (Neurochemist); Shane Fistell (Man in Hall); Waheedah Ahmad (Hysterical Woman); Charles Keating (Mr. Kean); Christina Huertes (Christina); Linda Burns (Fishsticks); Judy Jacksina (Hospital Receptionist); Gary Tacon (George the Security Guard); Rico Elias (Orderly #1); Mel Gorham (Nurse Sara); Chris Carolan (EEG Technician); Debra Kovner-Zaks (Cafeteria Nurse); Max Rabinowitz (Ward #5 Orderly); Gordon Joseph Weiss (Ward #5 Patient #1); Byron Utley (Ward #5 Patient #2); Anthony McGowen (Ward #5 Patient #3); Paul Montgomery (Ward #5 Patient #4); Leonard Tepper (Ward #5 Patient #5); Vinny Pastore (Ward #5 Patient #6); Howard Feller (Ward #5 Patient #7); Libby Titus (Club Singer); Michael Hyde (Bus Driver); Tomislav Novakovic (Bartender); Adam Bryant (Librarian); Anthony J. Nici (Young Leonard); Oliver Block (Leonard's Friend #1); Buck Smith (Leonard's Friend #2); John E. MacIntosh (Teacher); Steven Randazzo (Luis).

A League of Their Own

COLUMBIA PICTURES, 1992. COLOR, 117 MINUTES. PG–RATED.

Executive producer, Penny Marshall; producers, Elliot Abbott, Robert Greenhut; co-producers, Ronnie D. Clemmer, Joseph Hartwick, Bill Pace; associate producer, Amy Lemisch; director, Penny Marshall; first assistant director, Michael Haley; first assistant director: second unit, Gaetano Lisi; story, Kelly Candael, Kim Wilson; screenwriters, Lowell Ganz, Babaloo Mandel; production designer, Bill Groom; original music, Madonna (theme song: "This Used to Be My Playground"—uncredited), Hans Zimmer; supervising sound editor, Dennis Drummond; choreographer, Lou Conte; costume designer, Cynthia Flynt; cinematographer, Miroslav Ondricek; editors, Adam Bernardi, George Bowers.

Tom Hanks (Jimmy Dugan); Geena Davis (Dottie Hinson); Mark Holton (Older Stilwell); Lori Petty (Kit Keller); Madonna (Mae Mordabito); Rosie O'Donnell (Doris Murphy); Megan Cavanaugh (Marla Hooch); Tracy Reiner (Betty Horn); Bitty Schram (Evelyn Gardner); Ann Cusack (Shirley Baker); Anne Ramsay (Helen Haley); Freddie Simpson (Ellen Sue Gotlander); Renée Coleman (Alice Gaspers); Robin Knight ("Beans" Babbitt); Patti Pelton (Marbleann Wilkenson); Kelli Simpkins (Beverly Dixon); Neezer Tarleton (Neezer Dalton); Connie Pounds-Taylor (Connie Calhoun); Kathleen Marshall ("Mumbles" Brockman); Sharon Szmidt (Vivian Ernst); Pauline Brailsford (Miss Cuthbert); David Strathairn (Ira Lowenstein); Garry Marshall (Walter Harvey); Jon Lovitz (Ernie Capadino); Bill Pullman (Bob Hinson); Justin Scheller (Stilwell); Eddie Jones (Dave Hooch); Alan Wilder (Nelson); R. M. Haley (Empathetic Umpire); Don S. Davis (Racine Coach Charlie); Janet Jones (Racine Pitcher); Brenda Ferrari (Racine Catcher); Téa Leoni (Racine 1B); Laurel Cronin (Maida Gilespie); Robert Stanton (Western Union Man); Wantland L. Sandel Jr. (Doctor); Joe Krowka (Heckler); Harry Shearer (Newsreel Announcer); Blaire Baron (Margaret); Ryan Howell

(Jeffrey); Brian Boru Gleeson (Bobby); David Franks (Vacuum Salesman); Ryan Olsen (Dollbody Kid); Ellie Weingardt (Charm School Instructor); Larissa Collins (Charm School Assistant); Douglas Blakeslee (Doris' Fan #1); Joseph Slotnick (Doris' Fan #2); Brian Flannery (Autograph Kid #1); Stephen Feagley (Autograph Kid #2); Rae Allen (Ma Keller); Gregory Sporleder (Mitch Swaley); Eddie Mekka (Mae's Guy in Bar); Stephen Mailer (Kit's Date in Bar); Ray Chapman (Ticket Scalper); Joette Hodgen (Opera Singer); Lynn Cartwright (Older Dottie); Kathleen Butler (Older Kit); Eunice Anderson (Older Mae); Vera Johnson (Older Doris); Patricia Wilson (Older Marla); Barbara Erwin (Older Shirley); Betty Miller (Older Betty); Eugenia McLin (Older Ellen Sue); Barbara Pilavin (Older Helen); Marvin Einhorn (Older Ira); Shirley Burkovich (Older Alice); Dolores 'Pickles' Dries (Lady in Bleachers); Shelly Adlard, Vickie Buse, K. C. Carr, Julie Croteau, Tonya Gilles Koch, Kirsten Gretick, Stacey Gustaferro, Lisa Hand, Cheryl Jones, Shelly Niemeyer, Sally Rutherford, Lita Schmitt, Amanda Walker, Brenda Watson (Additional Players); Ray Toler (uncredited: Loudmouth from Lukash).

RENAISSANCE MAN

TOUCHSTONE PICTURES, 1994. COLOR, 129 MINUTES. PG-13-RATED.

Executive producers, Buzz Feitshans, Penny Marshall; producers, Elliot Abbott, Sara Colleton, Robert Greenhut; co-producers, Timothy M. Bourne, Amy Lemisch; director, Penny Marshall; first assistant director, Sergio Mimica-Gezzan; first assistant director: aerial unit, Cary Cordon; screenwriter, Jim Burnstein; production designer, Geoffrey Kirkland; costume designer, Betsy Heimann; original music, Hans Zimmer; additional music, Bruce Fowler, John Van Tongeren; choreographer, Donovan Henry; supervising sound editor, George H. Anderson; costume supervisor, Nick Scarano; cinematographer, Adam Greenberg; editors, George Bowers, Battle Davis.

Danny DeVito (Bill Rago); Gregory Hines (Sergeant Cass); Cliff
Robertson (Colonel James); James Remar (Captain Murdoch); Lillo Brancato
(Private Donnie Benitez); Stacey Dash (Private Miranda Myers); Kadeem
Hardison (Private Jamaal Montgomery); Richard T. Jones (Private Jackson
Leroy); Khalil Kain (Private Roosevelt Hobbs); Peter Simmons (Private Brian
Davis Jr.); Gregory Sporleder (Private Mel Melvin); Mark Wahlberg (Private
Tommy Lee Haywood); Ben Wright (Private Oswald); Ed Begley Jr. (Jack
Markin); Ann Cusack (Bill's Secretary); Jeb Brown (1st Young Executive);
Paul Abbott (2nd Young Executive); Nat Mauldin (U Love to Rent: voice);
Hakiem Greenhut (Paper Boy: voice); Roy K. Dennison (Bum); Jennifer
Lewis (Mrs. Coleman); Alanna Ubach (Emily Rago); Matthew Keeslar (Guard
Gate MP); Gary DeWitt Marshall (Traffic MP); J. Leon Pridgen II (Captain
Murdoch's Aide); J. J. Nettles (Bartender); Thomas D. Houck (Company
Commander); Robert Head, Robert Steele, Yolanda Tisdale, Julio Dominguez,
Ronald Elder, Shelia Logan (Platoon Drill Sergeants); Kenneth McKee, Jose
Ortez (MPs); Laurence Irby (Officer); Belinda Fairley (Female Private);
Christopher Baker (Laundry—1st Private); Sal Rendino (Laundry—2nd
Private); Gary T. McTague (Laundry Truck Driver); Alexander Zmijewski
(Colonel James Aide); Isabella Hofmann (Marie); Samaria Graham (Shana
Leroy); R. M. Haley (Florist); Daniel Bateman (Graduation Drill Sergeant);
Alphonsa Smith (Graduation Sergeant Major); Jim Ochs (Customs Officer);
Don Reilly (Henry V); Randy Hall (*Henry V* Lead Archer).

THE PREACHER'S WIFE

BUENA VISTA, 1996. COLOR, 124 MINUTES. PG-RATED.

Executive producers, Elliot Abbott, Robert Greenhut; producer, Samuel
Goldwyn Jr.; co-producers, Timothy M. Bourne, Debra Martin Chase, Amy
Lemisch; associate producer, Bonnie Hlinomaz; director, Penny Marshall;
assistant director, Barry K. Thomas; screenwriters, Leonardo Bercovici and

Robert E. Sherwood (of *The Bishop's Wife* script), Nat Mauldin, Allan Scott; production designer, Bill Groom; costume designer, Cynthia Flynt; original music, Mervyn Warren (songs), Hans Zimmer; gospel music production, Whitney Houston; sound, Les Lazarowitz; cinematographer, Miroslav Ondricek; editors, George Bowers, Stephen A. Rotter.

Denzel Washington (Dudley); Whitney Houston (Julia Biggs); Courtney B. Vance (Reverend Henry Biggs); Gregory Hines (Joe Hamilton); Jennifer Lewis (Margueritte Coleman); Loretta Devine (Beverly); Lionel Richie (Britsloe); Paul Bates (Saul Jeffreys); Justin Pierre Edmund (Jeremiah Biggs); Lex Monson (Osbert); Darvel Davis Jr. (Hakim); William James Stiggers Jr. (Billy Eldridge); Marcella Lowery (Anna Eldridge); Cissy Houston (Mrs. Havergal); Aaron A. McConnaughey (Teen); Shyheim Franklin (Teen); Taral Hicks (Teen); Kennan Scott (Teen); Jernard B. Burks (Pizza Man); Michael Alexander Jackson (Robber); Jaime Tirelli (Liquor Store Owner); Shari Headley (Arlene Chattan); Lizan Mitchell (Judge); Robert Colston (Bailiff); Victor Williams (Robbie); Juliehera Destefano (Receptionist); Charlotte D'Amboise (Deborah Paige); Delores Mitchell (Mary Halford); David Langston Smyrl (Hanley's Waiter); Harsh Nayyar (Christmas Tree Man); Mervyn Warren (Pianist); Roy Haynes (Drummer); George Coleman (Sax Player); Ted Dunbar (Guitar Player); Jamil Nasser (Bass Player); Helmar Augustus Cooper (Johnson Keeley); Mary Bond Davis (Bernita); Toukie Smith (Teleprompter Operator); Mozelle Hawkins Allen, Eloise Beasley, Yolanda Beasley-Prime, Cassondra M. Breedlove, Dirk Chaney, Brenda J. Childs, Anthony Dean Copeland, Hayward Cromartie, Betty Cromartie Davis, Valerie Inez Edwards, Kimberley M. Garrett, Rutha Harris, Carolyn Henry, Gary Nuckles-Holt, Teretha G. Houston, Angela L. Jones, Morris Vernon Jones, Rose Merry Jordan, Jacqueline Martin, Betty Matthews, Reverend Corey McGee, Naguanda Miller, Sharon A. Mitchell, Beverly S. Nixon, Krishna Presha, Jacqulyn V. Saunders, Constance Small, Troy L. Sneed Sr., Reverend Lawrence K. Thomas, Ulisa A. Thomas, V. Ranaldo Welcome,

Berta J. Williams, Kimberly L. Wright (St. Matthew's Choir & Band Members); Steven Brown (Drummer); Rick Carter (Bass Player); Sterling Holloman II (Lead Guitar Player); Reverend Kenneth Paden (Pianist); Dwain L. White (Organist); Aaron Jordan (Eldridge Kid); Yakin Manassah Jordan (Eldridge Kid); Joshua Jordan (Donkey—Nativity Choir); Tiffany Joseph (Shepherd—Nativity Choir); Jessica Malloy (Mary—Nativity Choir); Amia Hart (Beverly's Child); Brittany Anderson (Sheep—Nativity Choir); Christopher Malloy (Angel—Nativity Choir); Andal Fequiere (Joseph—Nativity Choir); Mark Gilbert (Wise Man—Nativity Choir); Michael Marshall (Wise Man—Nativity Choir); Shaun Purefoy (Wise Man—Nativity Choir); Tiffiny Monet Graham (Angel—Nativity Choir); Khalia Hamilton-Montoute (Angel—Nativity Choir); Marquis Bowen-Wallace (Shepherd—Nativity Choir); Lakeya Enos (Shepherd—Nativity Choir); Christine Lameisha Koon (Camel—Nativity Choir); Anthony Biggham (Lamb—Nativity Choir); Taleah Enos (Ox—Nativity Choir); Jerry Brunsin, Anthony Burnett, Kevin Mitchell, Phillip Mitchell (Painting Singers).

Note: Penny Marshall is attached to the following feature film projects as director: *Saving Grace* (in preproduction in 1998); *Wild Oats* (in preproduction in 1998); *Cinderella Man* (forthcoming). She also directed four episodes of the television series *Laverne & Shirley* (1976–83) and one episode of the television series *A League of Their Own* (1993).

(These film credits were adapted from the Internet Movie Database and other sources.)

Producer

A League of Their Own (1992)

Calendar Girl (1993)

Renaissance Man (1994)

Getting Away with Murder (1996)

With Friends Like These (1998)

Saving Grace (1998—in preproduction)

Wild Oats (1998—in preproduction)

Live from Baghdad (projected—forthcoming)

Note: Penny Marshall also produced the television series *A League of Their Own* (1993).

Actress

FEATURE FILMS

The Savage Seven (1968) Tina

How Sweet It Is! (1968) Tour Girl

The Grasshopper (1970) Plaster Caster

How Come Nobody's on Our Side? (1975) Theresa

1941 (1979) [uncredited] Miss Fitzroy

Movers and Shakers (1985) Reva

She's Having a Baby (1988) [uncredited] cameo at end

The Hard Way (1991) Angie

Hocus Pocus (1993) [uncredited] cameo

Get Shorty (1995) [uncredited] herself

The Calling (in preproduction in 1998) an archangel

Television (selected credits)

The Danny Thomas Hour (1967–68) series episodes

Then Came Bronson (1969) series episode

Love, American Style (1970) series episode

Barefoot in the Park (1970) series episode

The Feminist and the Fuzz (1971) TV movie

Getting Together (1971) series episode

Evil Roy Slade (1972) TV movie

The Bob Newhart Show (1972–73) series episodes

The Couple Takes a Wife (1972) TV movie

The Odd Couple (1972–75) series semi-regular as Myrna Turner

Banacek (1973) series episode

The Mary Tyler Moore Show (1973–76) series episodes

Paul Sand in Friends and Lovers (1974–75) series regular as
     sister-in-law

Let's Switch! (1975) TV movie

Happy Days (1975–76; 1979) series episodes as recurring
     character of Laverne DeFazio

Wives (1975) series pilot

Chico and the Man (1975) series episode

How Come Nobody's on Our Side? (1975) TV movie

Laverne & Shirley (1976–83) series regular as Laverne DeFazio

Good Heavens (1976) series episode

Blansky's Beauties (1977) series episode

Mork & Mindy (1978) series episode

More Than Friends (1978) TV movie

Bosom Buddies (1982) series episode

Taxi (1983) series episode

Love Thy Neighbor (1984) TV movie

Challenge of a Lifetime (1985) TV movie

The Simpsons (1990) series episode (voice)

The Odd Couple: Together Again (1993) TV movie

Laverne & Shirley Reunion (1995) TV special

Nash Bridges (1998) series episode

Source Notes

Epigraph

v   *"I was born with a frown."* Los Angeles Times, June 8, 1988.

Introduction

xii   A mere 9 percent . . . in 1988). *ABC Evening News,* April 12, 1998.

xvii   As she herself said . . . I'm not *that* nice.'" *Los Angeles Times,* June 8, 1988.

xvii   And a few years later . . . the studio commissary. *McCalls,* November 1992.

Chapter One: The Bronx and Beyond

22   "I hated it . . . the grocery shopping." Article #1 from the period 1976–78, available online at www.geocities.com; publication not identified.

23   "It was like . . . the cigarette went in." *Washington Post,* December 12, 1996.

23   "My mother . . . after the traumatic fact. *Premiere,* 1996.

23   And decades later . . . the world's worst child.'" *McCalls,* November 1992.

23   "I had a very high I.Q. . . . obsessed with being regular." *TV Guide,*
     April 10, 1993.

23   The Old Neighborhood . . . dubbed the "cradle of stars" *Obsession: The Life
     and Times of Calvin Klein,* by Steven Gaines and Sharon Churcher; Birch Lane
     Press, New York, 1994, p. 21.

24   "My mother wanted . . . the best husbands." Article #1 from the period
     1976–78, available online at www.geocities.com; publication not identified.

24   "I was a tomboy myself . . . Penny recalled. *Woman's Day,* July 2, 1992.

24   Of her father . . . personality of a lamppost." *Premiere,* 1996.

24   "I was the 'bad seed' . . . decades later." *People,* December 23, 1996.

24   "Her brother . . . for her to do." *Ibid.*

24   "Like many sensitive teens . . . in the late 1970s. Article #1 from the period
     1976–78, available online at www.geocities.com; publication not identified.

25   "It was Peyton Place time . . . a divorced mother. *Ibid.*

25   "The women in Hollywood . . . like an outcast." *Ibid.*

25   "When she appeared . . . was growing up. *TV Guide,* May 22, 1976.

26   "When I came out to Hollywood . . . a life or a career." An online interview
     with the journalist Rip Rense, no date.

26   "I've been accused . . . *Than Show Business.* An online interview with the
     journalist Rip Rense, no date.

29   "I'd . . . feed everybody . . . of that time. *Woman's Day,* July 2, 1992.

30   "As a tabloid-like article . . . shared kisses on the cheek.'" Article #1 from
     the period 1976–78, available online at www.geocities.com; publication not
     identified.

30   "In 1980, Carrie . . . I didn't like it." *People,* December 23, 1996.

31 "I was wild . . . what he was doing." *TV Guide,* April 10, 1993.

31 One of the workers . . . there were two rules. . . . A first-person recollection by a disinterested, non-industry figure.

32 His publicist remembers . . . according to the *High Concept* account. *High Concept: Don Simpson and the Hollywood Culture of Excess,* by Charles Fleming; Doubleday, New York, 1998, p. 164.

Chapter Two: On TV

36 The telefilm is notable . . . in the title role. *Unsold Television Pilots: 1955 through 1988,* by Lee Goldberg; McFarland and Company, 1990, Jefferson, NC, p. 187.

36 In it she played . . . their (always unseen) husbands. *Ibid,* p. 236.

The Odd Couple

37 According to her . . . he writes a sports column. Posted at the Nick at Night Web site.

37 For shy, insecure . . . for the series' stars. *Variety,* November 21, 1972.

38 "There were times . . . back into a wall." *TV Guide,* May 22, 1976.

38 When the inevitable reunion . . . came to the telefilm's "rescue." *Daily Variety,* September 24, 1993.

Laverne & Shirley

39 "I got Cindy and Penny . . . and she did it." *Daily Variety,* January 5, 1976.

39 Penny and Cindy . . . and commercializing influences. *TV Guide,* June 18, 1977.

40 "I figured . . . film to go in between." *Hollywood Reporter,* December 3, 1971.

40 Instead, the movie . . . on expository dialog." *Variety,* November 26, 1971.

40   The result was . . . relaxing mood." *Show,* April 1972.

40   In this tale . . . cutting room floor. *Ibid.*

40   They created their characters . . . own actual personalities. *New York Daily News,* 1996.

45   "The last time . . . out a lot better." *Daily Variety,* January 5, 1976.

45   (Explaining the failure . . . cast the wrong chimp.) An online interview with the journalist Rip Rense, no date.

45   Years later in 1996 . . . producers' wildest expectations. *New York Daily News,* 1996.

46   "They shot [the presentation] . . . in May 1976. *Los Angeles Times,* May 30, 1976.

50   As Garry Marshall . . . I did *Laverne & Shirley!*" An online interview with the journalist Rip Rense, no date.

50   As one fan . . . family of two women." Available online at http://english.cla.umn.edu/visiting/MJanette/Installations/amanda/main.htm

52   The "high-decibel duo . . . might just catch on." *Daily Variety,* January 27, 1976.

52   "Although it has the potential . . . too hard for laughs." *Hollywood Reporter,* January 27, 1976.

54   To explain *Laverne & Shirley* . . . it spells prole-tv." *Variety,* February 4, 1976.

54   Two years after . . . comedy in TV history . . ." *Daily Variety,* September 30, 1976.

55   "The slapstick . . . makes the show. *TV Guide,* May 12, 1979.

55   "Conventional wisdom . . . Williams was sly." *Los Angeles Times,* July 5, 1998.

55   *Laverne & Shirley* was . . . per episode to mount. *New York Times,* April 2, 1978.

59   "I had signed . . . to get unhappy." *TV Guide,* June 18, 1977.

60   "The thing was . . . she was nearly in tears." Article #1 from the period 1976–78, available online at www.geocities.com; publication not identified.

60   "The cast of *Happy Days* . . . a journalist. Classic TV, a Web site: Lori Marshall interviews her father; no date.

60   "What happened was . . . so did everyone else." *TV Guide,* August 28, 1982.

61   One of the more . . . more than adequate." *Los Angeles Herald-Examiner,* December 5, 1976.

61   "We were high . . . Next day, new messiah." *TV Guide,* April 29, 1978.

62   "We were shocked . . . go through again." *Ibid.*

62   The *Star* reported . . . number one in the ratings. *Star,* July 11, 1978.

63   "In my family . . . We'll use this someday.'" *Woman's Day,* July 21, 1992.

64   But back then . . . arguing with success. . . " *Variety,* September 7, 1978.

64   "It's slapstick . . . nothing to analyze." *Unicorn Times,* May 1978.

64   "No one else . . . wipe the floor with Phyllis." *Ibid.*

65   "My sister Penny . . . makes me happy." Classic TV, a Web site: Lori Marshall interviews her father, no date.

67   "I'm constantly asking . . . her own success. Article #2 from the period 1976–78, available online at www.geocities.com; publication not identified.

67   Maddy and Alan . . . to uncommitted lovers." ABC Press Relations, Program Information, October 4, 1978.

68   "Penny and I have . . . who's coming to dinner." ABC Press Relations, News Brief, October 10, 1978.

68   *The Story of Us* . . . Tom Hanks' wife. *Hollywood Reporter,* August 3, 1988.

68   The high price paid . . . he's sure to be humiliated. A conversation with the author, circa 1988.

69   "An unfortunate dose . . . in front of it." *Hollywood Reporter,* October 20, 1978.

69   *Daily Variety* called the telefeature . . . charmless teleplay." *Daily Variety,* October 20, 1978.

69   "Marshall, with luminous . . . with touching results." *Ibid.*

70   "Cindy was there . . . that she understood." *TV Guide,* August 28, 1982.

70   "Maybe it's good . . . will like me better." *Washington Post,*
     December 12, 1996.

71   Before *Happy Days* . . . station in New York. *TV Guide,* May 12, 1979.

71   But by the seventh season . . . no longer charming everyone. *Hollywood
     Reporter,* October 15, 1981.

72   . . . the show appeared . . . to show its age." *Daily Variety,* October 15, 1981.

72   The 1982–83 season . . . 30-percent share. *Los Angeles Times,* December 7, 1982.

72   "I did not ask . . . give it all to Penny." *TV Guide,* August 28, 1982.

74   A dozen years . . . and stuff like that." *TV Guide,* May 13, 1995.

Chapter Three: Guest Starring As . . .

77   "When I'm working . . . what day it is." *People,* December 23, 1996.

78   The project was . . . movie actually debuted. *Box Office,* May 29, 1967.

78   Now retitled *The Grasshopper* . . . Las Vegas." *Hollywood Reporter,*
     December 24, 1968.

78   They also had won . . . *The Dick Van Dyke Show. TV Favorites,* no date.

79   After the cast . . . "creative differences." Unidentified trade paper item,
     undated.

80   "Cynthia Plaster Caster" was a . . . and Savoy Brown. *Chicago Reader,*
     November 28, 1997.

81   "This time we're . . . in July 1969. *Daily Variety,* July 3, 1969.

Chapter Four: Making Movies

90   "During the 1970s . . . into a career." Classic TV, a Web site: Lori Marshall interviews her father, no date.

90   "I don't think . . . in July 1998. *Los Angeles Times,* July 5, 1998.

90   Back in 1986 . . . young female directors. Lifetime Television, June 9, 1998.

90   However, a couple of years . . . "Don't do it." *Premiere,* 1996.

90   Around the same time . . . to quit smoking. *The Rosie O'Donnell Show,* February 25, 1998.

92   Her on-camera advice . . . making a short film." Lifetime Television, June 9, 1998.

95   According to Rosie . . . know what's funny.'" *Rosie: Rosie O'Donnell's Biography,* by James Robert Parish; Carroll & Graf Publishers, New York, 1997, p. 93-94.

95   "It was a shock . . . made me crazy." *Millimeter,* May 1994.

Jumpin' Jack Flash

96   The "film's a mess . . . but a "bore." *Variety,* October 15, 1986.

96   The *Hollywood Reporter's* review . . . were judged the "main culprits." *Hollywood Reporter,* October 10, 1986.

96   In what was . . . Penny showed "promise." *Los Angeles Times,* October 10, 1986.

96   A more typical verdict . . . wallows in the predictable." *Village Voice,* October 21, 1986.

97   "If this film . . . summarized it). *Los Angeles,* November 1986.

97   "Miss Marshall directs . . . brand-new movie director. *New York Times,* October 10, 1986.

97   The type of criticism . . . Penny Marshall's direction." Unidentified home-video trade publication; video-release review, August 1987.

98   And as veteran actor . . . can make a picture." *Newsweek,* July 19, 1993.

98   *Jumpin' Jack Flash* . . . directly into his brain. The URL of the complete list is www.nww.com/netfilms.

99   But theatrical revenues . . . video-rental revenues. *Whoopi Goldberg: Her Journey from Poverty to Mega-stardom,* by James Robert Parish; Birch Lane Press, 1997, p. 148.

100   Perhaps it could . . . was jettisoned anyway. *Newsweek,* December 30, 1985.

100   Three weeks . . . staff were fired. *Newsday,* October 10, 1986.

100   Zieff explained . . . about the script." *Hollywood Reporter,* November 22, 1985.

100   However, Penny was . . . the screen project. Parish (*Whoopi*) op. cit., p. 146.

100   "I called my brother . . . you've done good." *Time Out,* March 13, 1991.

101   In her 1996 *Premiere* . . . hint of what really may have happened. *Premiere,* 1996.

101   "Don't ask," . . . We're evolving." *Newsweek,* December 30, 1985.

101   Years later, . . . she wanted to see." Parish (*Whoopi*) op. cit., p. 146.

Big

102   "Who would have . . . sprightly and sure-handed?" *Wall Street Journal,* June 2, 1988.

106   "A formula fantasy movie . . . from start to finish." *The New Yorker,* June 27, 1988.

106   "She has a gracious touch," *New York* magazine, June 13, 1988.

106   "directed . . . with some communicated enjoyment." *New Republic,* July 4, 1988.

106   "Miss Marshall minimizes . . . mercifully sweet." *New York Times,* June 3, 1988.

106   *Daily Variety*, which . . . smoothly on screen." *Daily Variety,* May 31, 1988.

106   While the . . . "'Big' is a triumph." *Dallas Morning News,* June 3, 1988.

106   For the delicacy . . . career to date. *Los Angeles Herald-Examiner,* July 12, 1988.

106   Robert De Niro . . . to take the part). *Ibid.*

107   According to the . . . F. A. O. Schwartz on Fifth Avenue. *Hollywood Reporter,* June 28, 1988.

107   "I whine, then I sulk . . . Pepsi mixed with milk." *Life,* July 1988.

108   To complement the film's . . . steak sandwiches." *Los Angeles Times,* June 2, 1988.

108   The post-premiere party . . . edge of a nervous breakdown." *Ibid.*

Awakenings

111   As Janet Maslin . . . reality was bizarre." *New York Times,* December 20, 1990.

112   Responding to the widespread . . . fit everything in." *Time Out,* March 13, 1991.

113   "None of Sayer's patients . . . conditioning exercises." *Los Angeles Times,* January 28, 1991.

113   "[Marshall's] talent is . . . blandness ring true.)" *The New Yorker,* February 11, 1991.

114   The producers sent . . . read the Oliver Sacks book. *Ibid.*

114   Though by the time . . . 1991 issue. *Ibid.*

114   There was one . . . "sort of vegetative state." *Premiere,* January 1991.

115   In addition to . . . Leonard's mother's house. *Awakenings* production notes.

115   Exactly four months . . . the awakened patients. *Los Angeles Times,* December 30, 1990.

115   The studio's marketing . . . in New York. *Screen International,* March 22, 1991.

116   Though attended by Penny . . . brother Garry Marshall." *Los Angeles Times,* December 14, 1990.

116   "One of the most . . . said the *L.A. Weekly. L.A. Weekly,*
      December 21–27, 1990.

116   "This film is full . . . agreed *Screen International. Screen International,*
      December 21, 1990.

116   "Daniel Day-Lewis . . . pointed out. *Los Angeles Daily News,* December 20, 1990.

116   "Any movie about . . . the man he is playing." *Time,* December 24, 1990.

117   For the *Hollywood Reporter* . . . the holiday season." *Hollywood Reporter,*
      December 13, 1990.

117   And so it did . . . in video-store rentals. Internet Movie Database business
      information.

117   Penny Marshall got almost . . . lets them carry the ball." *Hollywood Reporter,*
      December 13, 1990.

118   "You know [why] she talks . . . exactly what she wants." *TV Guide,*
      April 10, 1993.

118   During one take . . . yelling out, "Oh, No!" *Premiere,* January 1991.

118   "Everyone heard it . . . a person on set. Item, undated and unidentified.

118   Marshall recalled, "I'm going . . . so we just shot." *Premiere,* January 1991.

118   The actor was rushed . . . able to return. *Hollywood Reporter,* December 8, 1989.

119   "My reservations are . . . I walked off the set." *Los Angeles Times,*
      December 23, 1990.

119   While the film . . . Bronx Psychiatric Center. *Newsweek,* February 11, 1991.

A League of Their Own

120   During the AAGPBL's heyday . . . per admission). *Los Angeles Times,*
      June 28, 1992 (1 of 2 articles).

121   "It seemed the story . . . on the completed film. *Ibid.*

121   "We got on a plane . . . Clemmer recalled. *Hollywood Reporter,* August 21, 1992.

121   There she learned . . . we said yes." *Hollywood Reporter,* August 24, 1992.

122   "Basically, they tend . . . very different arena." *Ibid.*

123   Twentieth Century-Fox . . . on the baseball script. *Los Angeles Times,* June 28, 1992 (2 of 2 articles).

123   Fox's *A League of Their Own* . . . a budget of $18 million. *Variety,* September 30, 1992.

125   Then in post-production . . . forced to deny. *Los Angeles Times,* June 10, 1992.

125   "She'd never played baseball . . . She's amazing." *People,* June 29, 1992.

125   "I knew there was . . . end of the bat, OK?'" Parish (*Rosie*), op cit., p. 84.

126   With her customary . . . it's play baseball." *Ibid,* p. 85.

126   Her skill with a bat . . . the rave notices. *Ibid.*

126   "It was a little tough . . . testy at the same time." *US,* August 1992.

127   That party's bill of faire . . . cookies galore." *Hollywood Reporter,* June 30, 1992.

127   (Given Madonna's prominence . . . recording artist.) *Long Beach Press-Telegram,* July 27, 1992.

127   In New York . . . "into a free-for-all." *US,* August 1992.

127   In Evansville . . . were, of course, elsewhere." *Wall Street Journal,* July 8, 1992.

127   The disappointed Indianians . . . the Evansville economy. *Ibid.*

127   Right before *A League* . . . film with no balls." *Variety,* June 20, 1992.

127   At the same time . . . unfavorable test screenings. *People,* June 8, 1992.

128   Then a newspaper . . . money for the studio." *New York Times,* June 25, 1992.

128   In addition to such factors . . . [received] $2 million anyway." *Ibid.*

129   In a chatty colloquy . . . somebody else gets the credit." *Premiere,* 1996.

130   Without ever specifying . . . amiable and ingratiating." *Time,* July 6, 1992.

130   Asked why he'd taken . . . baseball spa for the summer." *Los Angeles Times,* June 24, 1992.

131   Of the actress . . . words in the same way." *Los Angeles Times,* July 5, 1992.

131   Abbott was also . . . process on the series." *Daily Variety,* January 18, 1993.

132   "The Monkey's Curse . . . And she goes, 'Okay.'" *People,* April 19, 1993.

132   A profile by . . . catching like, well, *girls. TV Guide,* April 10, 1993.

132   Marshall's only refuge . . . how she likes to live." *Ibid.*

Renaissance Man

133   At first, she was . . . an Oscar Levant for our times. *Los Angeles Times,* June 8, 1988.

134   "'I could just sleep . . . in mid-1988. *Ibid.*

134   The same reporter . . . a limp hand in the air." *Ibid.*

134   "I never aspired . . . as far back as *Laverne & Shirley. Time Out,* March 13, 1991.

135   This time, though . . . was now against illiteracy. *San Francisco Chronicle,* January 6, 1995.

135   As for Danny DeVito . . . manipulative military atmosphere." *Ibid.*

136   "In *Renaissance Man* . . . I use a lot of that stuff." *Millimeter,* May 1994.

136   "Shakespeare always scared me . . . relates to our everyday lives." *Ibid.*

137   The movie reduces . . . of Marshall's mawkishness." *Washington Post,* June 3, 1994.

137   "A labored, unconvincing comedy . . . dismissive critical view. *Chicago Sun-Times,* June 3, 1994.

137   Just before Penny Marshall . . . about both gays and Madonna. *Don't Call Me Marky Mark,* by Frank Sanello; Renaissance Books, 1999.

137   "'I just wanted to meet . . . Wahlberg said." Sanello, *Ibid.*

138   "By the time I . . . That faith was everything." Sanello, *Ibid.*

138   "Wahlberg was subjected . . . rap on screen." Sanello, *Ibid.*

138   "I literally owe Penny . . . major butt-smooching." Sanello, *Ibid.*

139   Later, she told . . . before a picture's opening. *Los Angeles Times,* August 7, 1994.

139   She cited . . . frantic post-production period. *Los Angeles Times, Ibid.*

The Preacher's Wife

140   When *Daily Variety's* senior . . . It's a great loss, personally." *Daily Variety,* October 9, 1996.

140   And in a gracious . . . people lending support." *People,* December 30, 1996.

140   Two months later . . . were white sneakers. *Washington Post,* December 12, 1996.

141   "Penny was the absolute . . . I could trust her 100 percent." World African Network on the Web, no date.

141   In the same story . . . organic to the film." *Ibid.*

142   There was even . . . directing a film called *Dear God* (1996). *USA Today,* October 29, 1997.

142   The Hollywood religious-movie . . . in their own lives." *Ibid.*

143   "I went with Whitney . . . just quite exciting." Mr. Showbiz, a Web site: an interview, 1997.

143   When Penny made . . . It was quite thrilling." *Washington Post,* December 12, 1996.

143   "We were in Yonkers . . . action with the ladders." *Premiere,* 1996.

145   "The story is so predictable . . . of the "engaging" cast. *San Francisco Chronicle,* December 13, 1996.

145   Calling the plot . . . force-fed treacle." *Time,* December 16, 1996.

145   "Penny Marshall . . . may not be . . . their steadfast old-fashionedness." *USA Today,* July 10, 1998.

145   *Boxoffice* magazine . . . it's the thought that counts." *Boxoffice,* December 1996.

Chapter Five: Carrying On

Rosie, Kmart, and Victoria's Secret

157   "People tend not . . . Lego, or a CD player." *Detroit News,* November 10, 1995.

157   According to the Kmart . . . savvy qualities." *Ibid.*

157   "Rosie and I are people . . . We're regular people." Mr. Showbiz, a Web site: an interview, 1997.

157   The customer . . . if they're a bit older." *Detroit News,* November 10, 1995.

157   There was Penny . . . and "The War Room." *People,* December 23, 1996.

158   Two years after . . . didn't quite say it all. *USA Today,* November 3, 1997.

158   When Penny appeared . . . and lots more." Parish (*Rosie*), op. cit., p. 220.

158   And, as it turned out . . . not celebrities." *USA Today,* November 3, 1997.

159   Six months later . . . several items." Kmart Corporation press release, April 8, 1998.

160   Back in the summer . . . *A League of Their Own. Daily Variety,* June 16, 1992.

160   In another example of . . . a three-dollar rebate. *Daily Variety,* December 15, 1992.

161   "All of a sudden . . . free toys for my grandson." Mr. Showbiz, a Web site: an interview, 1997.

161 The spot featured . . . to the actors' performance." Victoria's Secret press release, August 22, 1997.

On the Road to 2000

162 For example, after his success . . . a map to paradise." *Daily Variety,* July 13, 1998.

162 Penny and Cindy think . . . in the mid-1990s. *People,* June 6, 1995.

162 A few years later . . . or blowing things up." *Los Angeles Times,* July 5, 1998.

163 Asked who might play . . . *The Slums of Beverly Hills*). *Ibid.*

164 And still, after almost . . . "Penny 'Laverne DeFazio' Marshall." *Los Angeles Times Magazine,* September 20, 1998.

164 Twirling down the runway . . . work with puppets." *Entertainment Weekly,* August 15, 1997.

166 In 1995, for example . . . prosecution team. *People,* November 6, 1995.

166 "He said, 'I crashed.' . . . he'd steal anything." *Premiere,* 1996.

167 When comic actor Phil Hartman . . . his least-successful movie. MSNBC news report, June 9, 1998.

167 (In typical tabloid fashion . . . he narrowly escaped.") *Globe,* June 30, 1998.

168 The occasion of the . . . for the big party. *St. Paul Pioneer Press,* June 16, 1997.

168 Some of the favored 300 . . . to comply with basic requests." *Ibid.*

168 Ringleader of the rebels . . . of the partying celebs." *Ibid.*

169 Per the Associated Press . . . she delayed the ship's departure." *Associated Press,* August 31, 1998.

169 After the Chicago Bulls' . . . in Penny's lap!" *National Enquirer,* June 30, 1998.

170 So with those rules . . . She prays for best pal Penny Marshall." *National Enquirer,* September 22, 1998.

171   In the aftermath . . . "praying" for Penny Marshall. *Ibid.*

173   According to a *Reuters* . . . with the filmmaker. *Reuters,* February 26, 1998.

174   Penny, again, who . . . along to 'Miss You.'" E! Online, February 16, 1998.

175   As if on cue . . . for Universal. Mr. Showbiz, a Web site: Wednesday, June 18, 1997.

175   The writer, a former musician . . . a long-ago love affair. *Hollywood Reporter,* June 17, 1998.

176   Both *Grace* and *Life* . . . preproduction fast track." *Variety,* August 12, 1998.

177   "The feds say . . . one newspaper article. *New York Daily News,* February 15, 1998.

177   "One script I want . . . with the Braddock family." *Los Angeles Times,* July 5, 1998.

178   When the *National* . . . *still,* Penny Marshall. *National Enquirer,* March 28, 1998.

178   Budgeted at only five . . . to bear God's child." *Hollywood Reporter,* June 17, 1998.

179   It is "blessed with . . . *Daily Variety* review. *Daily Variety,* March 20, 1998.

179   *With Friends Like These* . . . to defer their salaries." *Los Angeles Daily News,* April 20, 1998.

179   "All the showbiz . . . when friends are involved." *Daily Variety,* March 20, 1998.

181   "I have no social life . . . in 1992. *Woman's Day,* July 21, 1992.

Index